TACTICS OF HOPE IN LATINX CHILDREN'S
AND YOUNG ADULT LITERATURE

JESUS MONTAÑO AND
REGAN POSTMA-MONTAÑO

Tactics of Hope in Latinx Children's and Young Adult Literature

University of New Mexico Press • Albuquerque

© 2022 by University of New Mexico Press
All rights reserved. Published 2022
Printed in the United States of America

First paperback printing 2024

ISBN 978-0-8263-6383-1 (cloth)
ISBN 978-0-8263-6632-0 (paper)
ISBN 978-0-8263-6384-8 (electronic)

Library of Congress Control Number: 2021952519

Founded in 1889, the University of New Mexico sits on the traditional homelands of the Pueblo of Sandia. The original peoples of New Mexico—Pueblo, Navajo, and Apache—since time immemorial have deep connections to the land and have made significant contributions to the broader community statewide. We honor the land itself and those who remain stewards of this land throughout the generations and also acknowledge our committed relationship to Indigenous peoples. We gratefully recognize our history.

COVER ILLUSTRATION *Libertad* © Ester Hernandez. Statue of Liberty National Monument New Jersey New York, ca. 1976.
DESIGNED BY Mindy Basinger Hill
COMPOSED IN Warnock Pro

TO THE NEXT GENERATION OF READERS AND ACTIVISTS,

Grace, Pearl, Robin, and Amelia (Arco) Iris

Contents

Acknowledgments	ix
Introduction	1

CHAPTER ONE — 23
Reading for Conocimiento Mirrors in Farmworker Kid Lit: Roots of Transformation and Activism

CHAPTER TWO — 52
Border Kids in the Land of Nepantla

CHAPTER THREE — 77
The Cultural Wealth of Diasporic Youth

CHAPTER FOUR — 104
Kids' Agency and Empowerment in an Era of Family Deportation

CHAPTER FIVE — 135
The Role of the Border Artista

Afterword	161
Notes	163
Works Cited	169
Index	179

Acknowledgments

Shortly after an election that promised to build a wall along the US/Mexico border, and thus a wall in every community across this nation where Latinx people live, we stared with blank shell-shocked eyes at our friends, our family, and our colleagues. *What could be done?* we wondered aloud. Better yet, what could we, as scholars and teachers, best do? Those moments of bewilderment eventually led to resolve, not only that something must be done but also that it must be done for all. In these moments, we also realized that if something was to be done, it would be done with the help of many people. To build a better community is to build it with the help of community. In this acknowledgment, we trace how our communities beckoned us, supported us, and encouraged us when we desperately needed it.

We begin by thanking Phillip Serrato for his invaluable help in this project. Tough love is a mixture of tough and love, and yet it invariably veers toward the love side of the equation. His copious comments told us of his engagement with the book project; his generous sharing of his time and his knowledge told us that he believed in this project. His encouragement holds a special place in our hearts.

We remain especially indebted to our editor, Elise McHugh. From our first meeting, in between sessions at the Southwest Popular/American Culture Association (SWPACA) Conference, to the last iterations of our chapters, she remained steadfast in her support. The best way to explain how much she meant is to tell a story of the before and after. In the before-COVID times, we met at a Starbucks in downtown Albuquerque. At the meeting she reified how important our project was to her and to the press. This came at a time when we were wading deeply, at time feeling as though we were over our heads with revisions and reorganizations. The meeting also was memorable because it was the last in-person meeting we had for the year. COVID-19 protocols shut down our nation a few weeks thereafter. A few months later, we met via Zoom. As we noted, we are deeply indebted to her for the trust she had in us and in our project.

We also would like to thank our vibrant and dynamic colleagues at Hope College. Where would we be without Deborah Van Duinen, for example? Her uncanny ability to place people in positions to thrive has not gone unnoticed. Allowing us to present our work at the NEA Big Read Lakeshore and Michigan Humanities Little Read events were instrumental as we developed and redeveloped our arguments on the importance of literature to young and not-so-young readers of children's and young adult literature. Thanks also go out to Christiana Salah, who kept pushing us to consider the interconnectedness of diversity and inclusion movements. Ernest Cole ensured we would have proper resources for our work; he also centered our work in the curriculum, allowing us to see how interwoven scholarship and teaching truly are. Lastly, thank you, Natalie Dykstra, for believing in us.

This book has been made possible by funding and resources from Hope College, the Office of the Provost, the Dean of Arts and Humanities, the Department of English, the Department of World Languages and Cultures, and the services at Van Wylen Library. Support from the Nyenhuis Collaborative Faculty Grant and the Andrew J. Mellon Grand Challenges Initiatives were instrumental in the completion of this book project. Special thanks to the grant readers and grant administrators of these programs.

A shout-out to our community, Holland, Michigan. We thank the librarians at Herrick District Library and the teachers in the greater Holland area. To our pastors who daily remind us of the importance of keeping hope, we love you. To coffee shops (Lemonjello's and 205) who kept us awake and allowed us to use your services for hours at a time, we thank you. To the breweries in the area, I hope you know how much you mean to us. Please, to all, keep doing what you do best.

To our families, thank you for your patience. When the birthday cards came in a few weeks late or we answered your text a few days later because we were busily doing our research and writing, thank you. You posted funny things on our social media pages, you sent us jokes and told us stories—this is to say that you understood how precious laughter is. To our sisters and brothers, Dalia, Lynda, Blake, Lance, and Pierce, please know that not a day went by when we did not yearn to hold you in our arms and hear your stories face to face. To Charlene Montaño Nolan, our hearts beat in unison, of this I know.

Grateful acknowledgment is made to the following publishers and rights holders for use of text and images:

Illustrations by Zeke Peña, copyright © 2019 by Zeke Peña, and excerpts from *My Papi Has a Motorcycle* by Isabel Quintero, text copyright © 2019 by Isabel Quintero. Used with permission of Kokila, an imprint of Penguin Young Readers, a division of Penguin Random House LLC. All rights reserved. UK and Commonwealth rights courtesy of Zeke Peña and Isabel Quintero, used with permission of Fletcher & Co., New York.

Side by Side / Lado a lado: The Story of Dolores Huerta and Cesar Chavez / La historia de Dolores Huerta y César Chávez by Monica Brown and illustrated by Joe Cepeda. Copyright © Joe Cepeda.

Illustration by Raúl Colón, copyright © 1997 by Raúl Colón; and excerpts from *Tomás and the Library Lady* by Pat Mora, text copyright © 1997 by Pat Mora. Used by permission of Alfred A. Knopf, an imprint of Random House Children's Books, a division of Penguin Random House LLC. All rights reserved.

Border-Lines: Journal of the Latin Research Center for use of selections from "Creative Words, Creative Acts: Tactics of the Artist-Activist in Tomás Rivera's *...y no se lo tragó la tierra* and Helena María Viramontes' *Under the Feet of Jesus*," vol. X, 2016, pp. 69–90, by Regan Postma-Montaño.

Zeke Peña, Cover image of *They Call Me Güero: A Border Kid's Poems* by David Bowles. Cover illustration by Zeke Peña (zpvisual.com).

From North to South / Del norte al sur by René Colato Laínez and illustrated by Joe Cepeda. Permission arranged with Children's Book Press, an imprint of Lee & Low Books, Inc., New York, NY 10016. All rights not specifically granted herein are reserved.

Aida Salazar, Betita's picture poems. *Land of the Cranes* by Aida Salazar. Reprinted by permission of Scholastic Inc.

Zeke Peña, Gabi's zine cover and page of female anatomy. *Gabi, A Girl in Pieces* by Isabel Quintero. Illustration by Zeke Peña with Isabel Quintero (Cinco Puntos Press, 2014).

TACTICS OF HOPE IN LATINX CHILDREN'S
AND YOUNG ADULT LITERATURE

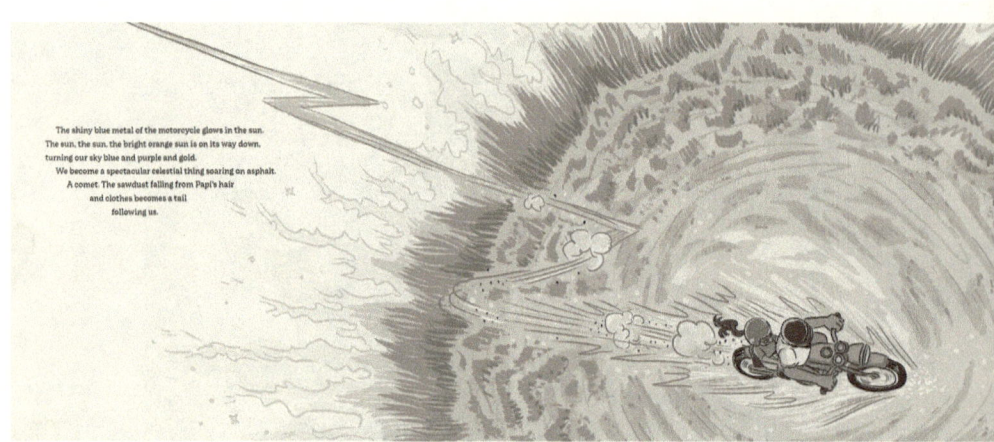

FIGURE I.1 Zeke Peña, Daisy and her Papi soar together on the motorcycle. Illustrations by Zeke Peña, copyright © 2019 by Zeke Peña. Used with permission of Kokila, an imprint of Penguin Young Readers, a division of Penguin Random House LLC. All rights reserved. UK and Commonwealth rights courtesy of Zeke Peña, used with permission of Fletcher & Co., New York.

Introduction

> Books saved my sanity, knowledge opened the locked places in me and taught me first how to survive and then how to soar.
>
> GLORIA ANZALDÚA / *Borderlands / La Frontera*

"My papi has a motorcycle," Daisy Ramona tells us in a Latinx children's picture book that bears the same title as her exclamation. Motorcycles, perhaps even more than automobiles, gesture at mobility and freedom, at the adventure garnered with the wind in one's face. Her simple declaration that her father has a motorcycle therefore positions us to anticipate what journey will unfold from the seat of a motorcycle. We soon find out, as her father's truck pulls into their driveway. Though he is exhausted from his work building homes, he "always has time for me," Daisy tells us as she tears out of the house with both of their helmets in hand. With an "¡Agárrate! / Hold on!," they take off on their ride around town. As Daisy relates, "we become a spectacular celestial thing soaring on asphalt. A comet" (Quintero, *My Papi*).

We are drawn to *My Papi Has a Motorcycle* (2019), written by Isabel Quintero and illustrated by Zeke Peña, for the way it allows us to join in this motorcycle journey as Daisy and her dad wind their way through their hometown. On their ride, for example, they pass Abuelita's church and Tortillería la Estrella. When Daisy spots her librarian, Mr. García, coming out of Joy's Market, she gives him a Latinx upnod (a form of greeting) that he reciprocates. This deep dive into the inner intricacies of Latinx culture is further highlighted in the illustrations, which show that Latinx children laugh in English (*ha ha*) and in Spanish (*ja ja*). Even the animals translanguage in Daisy's community as the cats mix *meow* with *miau* and dogs combine *woof* with *guau*, showing off their code-switching dexterity. This merging of languages and cultures is further made evident in the geography of the place: the post office is next to "la panadería where Papi buys conchas on Sunday mornings," and the bright colors of the houses "blend into one another redbluegreenorangepink." As they continue their journey, Daisy and her papi pass by the various murals that tell of the city's origins as "the lemon capital of world" and showcase the immigrants who worked in the citrus groves. They also cruise by Abuelito and Abuelita's yellow house, "the one with the lemon tree that grew from the seeds of the lemons Abuelito used to pick not far from here." Their eventual aim is to visit the new homes that Papi is building, though they also plan to stop at Don Rudy's Raspados for a shaved-ice treat.

In this journey through Daisy's town, *My Papi Has a Motorcycle* allows us to see the world, specifically Daisy's Latinx world, through her eyes. Away from the white gaze that often envisions Latinx neighborhoods as dangerous, Daisy presents her hometown as a loving place where English and Spanish are spoken, where businesses that cater to a Latinx clientele sit side by side with government offices and churches, and where a child and her dad can ride their motorcycle around town, in this way emphasizing their mobility and freedom. Through Daisy's eyes, we witness how seemingly disparate languages and cultures, as well as geographical places, blend together. Instead of assimilation that insists on English-only and virulent forms of nationalism that privilege white American culture above others, Daisy presents her world as a natural composite of various linguistic and cultural elements woven together. What a joyous journey indeed!

Inspired by Daisy, we begin our book by imagining what the world would look like if we saw it through the eyes of a Latinx child or young adult. If we take *My Papi Has a Motorcycle* as a guide for our adventures, we find that, like Daisy, many of the characters in the picture books and young adult novels chosen for our study live in *nepantla*, Gloria Anzaldúa's term for the interstitial place between seemingly disparate elements. Anzaldúa's term evokes the in-between spaces. As she explains in *This Bridge We Call Home*, "Bridges span liminal (threshold) spaces between worlds, spaces I call nepantla, a Nahuatl word meaning tierra entre medio. Transformations occur in this in-between space, an unstable, unpredictable, precarious, always-in-transition space lacking clear boundaries" (1), and these kinds of spaces can offer amazing insights, new ways of seeing and being and doing. Like Daisy, Güero in *They Call Me Güero* (2018) by David Bowles and Lupita in *Under the Mesquite* (2011) by Guadalupe García McCall, for example, the young characters in our study navigate the nepantla spaces and, through this journey, transform themselves and their contexts to reflect their lived experiences and the shared dreams of their communities. That is to say, in these spaces where cultural hybridity and translanguaging are everyday realities, children and young adults, as presented in the works we analyze, offer keys to transform the world. They offer this transmuted world for us to see. Entailed in this gesture is that we, too, will be transformed in the ways we see. Our project thus follows the directive of Aurora Levins Morales, who urges that "as adults, we need to listen to children more than we talk to them. We must back the initiative of children themselves, secure resources and share skills, respect their right and ability to lead themselves, and learn to let them lead us" (108). Our intention in this book is to listen to children and young adults and, in this, to let them lead us.

Children of Conocimiento

As we listen to children, let us consider specifically how children experience intersecting facets of identity—race, ethnicity, gender, sexuality, and others—and, from this lens, how children engage with issues of exclusion, discrimination, and other injustices. While some critics and readers, notably those invested in the idea of childhood innocence that is free of discourse on controversial topics,[1] may disparage our insistence that children and young adults be consulted on such matters, as Julia Mickenberg and Philip Nel remind us, "Neither children nor literature for them can be extricated from politics. By choice or by default, children often get drawn into the 'adult' worlds of politics, violence, and power struggles" (445). Children are fully aware of politics and of the injustices that affect them directly, such as those related to deportation in our examination of *Efrén Divided* (2020) by Ernesto Cisneros in chapter 4. Because of his age, however, Efrén is not invited into discussions on, nor is he allowed to engage with, issues of deportability that affect his family and his community. Yet, when his amá is deported, what Efrén showcases, as he translates his newfound awareness of deportation into activism, is that children and youth, as well as the literature written for them, can, as Levins Morales posits, address problems that stymie our nation and world: "Children have far less tolerance for overt injustice than do adults. From Soweto to Managua we have seen young people take to the streets, propelling mass movements forward into open rebellion almost faster than adults could build organizations behind them" (107). Further, Marilisa Jiménez García asserts that foregrounding such youth involved in revolutionary practices allows readers to imagine the possibilities for young people:

> In young adult literature, a medium known for its propensity toward problem resolution, what problems do Latinx writers

for youth seek to resolve? Latinx young adult literature (YA) demonstrates that the promise of a young person transitioning into, though never reaching, adulthood forms part of how Latinx writers imagine the work of recovering from racial and colonial violence. Whereas earlier generations emphasized stories of migration and assimilation, recent Latinx YA serves as a window into how authors narrate the promises and failures of cultural nationalism of past generations and how they imagine youth participating in revolutionary practices today, including accessing alternative forms of literature and education beyond and apart from established academia. (231)

Following the trajectory of Jiménez García's argument, children and youth in Latinx children's and young adult literature propose in their imaginings revolutionary ways to recover from racial and colonial violence. What Jiménez García and Levins Morales track in their discussions is that children and youth create in their imaginings new realities and, from these epistemological shifts, they propel movements and participate in revolutionary practices that bring about societal transformations. Our argument is that healing from the violence of racism, sexism, binarism, and other forms of exclusions and oppressions can be found in the voices, the stories, and the activisms of children and young adults, especially as these are presented in literature for young readers.

Our critical approach for illustrating the need of children to lead us in questions of exclusions and injustices is powered by Gloria Anzaldúa's theorizations of *conocimiento*. Conocimiento, from the Spanish word for "knowledge," is redefined by Anzaldúa to incorporate, as AnaLouise Keating describes, "self-reflection, imagination, intuition, sensory experiences, rational thought, outward-directed action, and social-justice concerns" ("From Borderlands" 10). Much like her theories of mestiza consciousness and *la facultad*, conocimiento is transformative in nature. Conocimiento, much like her earlier theories, begins in oppressive contexts and moves toward transformative healing via the deepening of perception. In her theories of conocimiento, Anzaldúa further "underscores and develops the imaginal, spiritual-activist, and political dimensions implicit in her previous theories" ("From Borderlands" 10). In this way, conocimiento can be seen as a nonlinear journey from inner works to public acts. It begins with an *arrebato*, or a *susto* that fractures the self. Seemingly floundering in chaos, the next stage is nepantla, the interstitial, liminal space where one is torn between different perspectives. Though the processes may zigzag, the next few stages involve the Coatlique state, where the cost of knowing is exacted; a call to action, the crossing over to conocimiento; and then putting the pieces of Coyolxauhqui back together through personal and collective stories. The possibilities and potentials are revealed in the final two stages, a clash of realities, as new imaginings contest older forms of knowing, and finally a shift in reality that set in motion the acting out of the vision in forms of activism (Anzaldúa, "Now Let Us Shift" 546–74).

Anzaldúa arrived at these processes of conocimiento shortly after 9/11, when she experienced an arrebato at seeing the towers in New York City fall. In her *testimonio*[2] given shortly after, Anzaldúa speaks to the physical and psychological fragmentation caused by the attack:

> The day the towers fell, me sentí como Coyolxauhqui, la luna. Algo me agarró y me sacudió, frightening la sombra (soul) out of my body. I fell in pieces into that pitch-black brooding place. Each violent image of the towers collapsing, transmitted live all over the world then repeated a thousand times on TV, sucked the breath out of me, each image etched on my mind's eye. Wounded, I fell into shock, cold and clammy. The moment fragmented me, dissociating me from myself. (*Light / Luz* 9)

With seer-like vision, Anzaldúa notes that in the aftermath of the towers falling Americans would be faced with two paths. One path, the one of *desconocimiento*, would lead into ignorance, fear, and hatred; this easier path "uses force and violence to socially construct our nation" (*Light / Luz* 19). The other path, the more difficult one of conocimiento, "leads to awakening, insights, understandings, realizations, and courage, and the motivation to engage in concrete ways that have the potential to bring us into compassionate interactions" (19). As we came to find out, the United States would choose the path of desconocimiento. The attacks, although they had nothing to do with Mexicans, Mexican Americans, or immigrants from Latin America, radically altered migration policies and increased prejudice toward Latinx people and other Brown people. As Francisco Alba underscores, "the US approach to managing Mexican migration changed radically after the attacks on US soil on September 11, 2001. Before the attacks, expectations were high, particularly among Mexican political leaders, that a long-term, mutually agreed-upon strategy could finally be implemented to manage the flows of Mexican migrants to the United States" (17). The attacks resulted in a reconfigured understanding of migration as a US national security issue, including the criminalization of undocumented migration (Romo 3). Further, the fear of future attacks and subsequent policies fueled xenophobia; it was not long before "terms like 'illegal alien' and 'illegal immigrants'—sometimes shortened to 'illegals'—predominate[d] in the contemporary discourse about immigration" (Anguiano 93). In other words, alienization, racialization, and criminalization, as Anzaldúa foretold, would become the dominant features of a twenty-first century America.

In the midst of a fearful nation that became hostile and violent toward Latinx people, Anzaldúa provides balm and wisdom: "We must use creativity to jolt us into awareness of our spiritual/political problems and other major global tragedies so that we can repair *el daño*" (*Light / Luz* 19). With conocimiento, she tells us, we can recognize and repair *el daño*, the damage that is caused not only by the terrorist attacks but also by racisms and exclusions resultant from, as we came to find out, America's path toward desconocimiento. For our purposes, we utilize Anzaldúa's theorizations of conocimiento to examine the way children and youth, as represented in literary works for young readers, engage with conocimiento to counter forms of desconocimiento. This includes fighting the deportation regime, as we will discuss in chapter 4. Conocimiento, we posit, permits Efrén in *Efrén Divided*, Betita in *Land of the Cranes* (2020) by Aida Salazar, and José in *From North to South / Del norte al sur* (2013) by René Colato Laínez and illustrated by Joe Cepeda to recognize the oppressions in their lives and provides them the understanding and awareness to challenge and transform them. In another example, from chapter 5, Julia in *I Am Not Your Perfect Mexican Daughter* (2017) by Erika L. Sánchez and Gabi in *Gabi, a Girl in Pieces* (2014) by Isabel Quintero use *autohistorias* to reveal their complex inner lives, specifically the struggles in negotiating Latinx identity and challenging gender norms imposed on them by parents and society, and from these counter-stories and self-inscriptions they disrupt the seemingly neat separation between cultures and create a *mestizada*, a new cultural mix, through creative acts (*Light / Luz* 49). In this way, conocimiento narratives, as Sonia Rodríguez notes, "highlight how knowing is a healing process captured within the stories and exemplified through the characters. Conocimiento is an opportunity to recognize the oppressions that direct the characters' existence and provide a means to challenge and transform them" (10). Rodríguez also underscores that creative acts "serve as catalysts that allow them [Latinx youth] to develop their identity while disrupting and challenging various systems of oppression. Their creativity is born out of trauma and oppression and therefore functions as more than self-expression; instead, the young Latinas' creativity forges a path toward healing that impacts them and their communities" (9). In utilizing Anzaldúa's notions on conocimiento, specifically calling attention to the function of creative acts, such as "writing, art-making, dancing, healing, teaching, meditation, and spiritual activism—both mental and somatic (the body, too, is a form as well as site of creativity)" ("Now Let Us Shift" 542), Rodríguez posits that creative acts "offer both an opportunity to challenge and transform existing epistemologies and the possibility to create new, more liberating ones" (11).

In *Tactics of Hope in Latinx Children's and Young Adult Literature*, we are interested in the way that conocimiento fosters hope in dealing with oppressions and forges "a path towards healing that impacts them and their communities" (Rodríguez 9). Put another way, we are attentive to the forms of *resistance* that conocimiento fosters and look for the ways that conocimiento forges personal and societal *transformations* in and by Latinx children and youth. Resistance, as we discuss above, includes creative acts to destabilize and contest the deportation regime or the writing of autohistorias to challenge easy notions of cultural identity. As for how conocimiento forges personal and societal transformations, Cristina Rhodes notes that for Latinx children and youth "who affect change on the individual level within themselves, become outwardly-oriented, able to activate change and transformation in the world" ("Processes of Transformation"). As Rhodes further describes, "transformation not only signals that social change is propelled by individual reconfiguration, but also supplies a unique framework to understand the symbiotic relationship between change and activism in children's literature" ("Processes of Transformation"). These transformations serve "as an avenue to explore activism, change, and amelioration in Latinx youth literatures—and, perhaps, *all* minoritized youth literatures" ("Processes of Transformation"). Conocimiento, in this sense, braids the personal with collective; it emphasizes a nonlinear, zigzagging at times, trajectory from personal transformation to societal transformations.

This symbiotic relationship between inner works and public acts, to use Anzaldúa's terms, is the basis for our understanding of societal change and social justice activism in children's and young adult literature. By exploring these transformations, such as the way that Betita in *Land of the Cranes* uses her picture poems to make visible the plight of children in Immigration and Customs Enforcement (ICE) *hieleras* and thus create change in those who read them, our goal in this book is to highlight the ingenious, creative ways in which young people propel transformations of self and society.

Aspects of transformation, personal as well as collective, in the literary works under analysis in our study allow us to see the wisdom in Levins Morales's directive that we learn to let the children lead us. What we find, via the works analyzed, is that children and young adults utilize conocimiento to resist injustices and by their resistance transform our world. These transformations of how we see and understand the world, we believe, can be as simple and yet as beautiful and powerful as a child and her father riding a motorcycle through their hometown. This is to say that if we, as adults, could experience the world through Daisy, as she hears languages blending and sees cultures merging, we would be transformed.

Tactics of Hope

The title of our book, *Tactics of Hope in Latinx Children's and Young Adult Literature*, captures our focus on both the forms of resistance and the transformations conocimiento propels as well as the importance of books for young readers by Latinx authors and artists in this endeavor. Latinx books, we posit, are instrumental in the creation of a more just and equitable world. We must, therefore, recognize the role of authors and illustrators in this work. If we return to the opening two-page spread of *My Papi Has a Motorcycle*, we will see this emphasis on Latinx books foregrounded by the illustrator. The image features Daisy reading while she waits for her father in the motorcycle shed. Daisy, as we can tell in the illustration, reads a selection from the Lowrider series by Cathy Camper and Raúl the Third. This artful upnod from one illustrator, Zeke Peña, to another, Raúl the Third, clues us into the way that Daisy, beyond loving motorcycle rides with her father, also is a reader of Latinx literature for children. For us, it is as important that she is a good reader as it is that she is a good reader of Latinx literature for children and young adults. That she is both is not surprising.

One of the ways that Latinx literature for young readers, such as *My*

Papi Has a Motorcycle, can create a more just and equitable world is through foregrounding and thereby affirming lived experiences of Latinx peoples. Isabel Quintero writes in the author's note to *My Papi Has a Motorcycle* that the book is a love letter "to my father, who showed me different ways of experiencing home, and to Corona, California—a city that will always be a part of me" (*My Papi*). The picture book is, in scope, a recovery project as Quintero recounts "one of my fondest memories from when I was a little girl" when she "learned words like carburetor and cariño, drill and dedication" from her father (*My Papi*). In this way, *My Papi Has a Motorcycle* casts a light on working-class experiences in Latinx culture to foreground how these seemingly disparate elements, carburetors and *cariño*, go together. At play in the picture book is that her father works hard all day, noted in Daisy's emphasis that her father is "covered in sawdust and smells like a hard day at work" (Quintero, *My Papi*). Adding to our sensory perceptions, she also tells us that his hands "are rough from building homes every day" (Quintero, *My Papi*). Simply put, her father should be too tired to take Daisy on a motorcycle ride. And yet, as the picture book shows, carburetors and cariño go together, and as such daughter and father "comet" to their destination: "He's going to show me the new houses he's working on" (Quintero, *My Papi*). Seeing the world through Daisy's eyes allows us a glimpse of a loving relationship between father and daughter; it also makes us take notice of the people who build houses like her father and the painters, drywallers, and floor layers who greet Daisy and Papi when they arrive at the work site. As Quintero notes, we should be mindful of who "are the people who get streets named after them, and who are the people who lay the asphalt" (*My Papi*). In this way, Quintero clues us into the way her picture book shines a spotlight on Latinx people and places made invisible in the everyday workings of our country.

In the course of our study, one recurring theme has been the conviction with which Latinx authors and artists center the lives and experiences of Latinx people. As Frederick Luis Aldama notes about the Latinx writers and artists he interviewed for *Latino/a Children's and Young Adult Writers on the Art of Storytelling*, they "talk about the deliberate choice to create through their literature social mirrors that would reflect positive images of Latino youth, to create a literature that would affirm young Latinos and that would propel them forward toward engaging with and then transforming the larger world" (14). It is not by accident, therefore, that Latinx authors and artists such as Isabel Quintero and Zeke Peña

FIGURE I.2 Zeke Peña, Daisy learns about lowriders and motorcycles. Illustrations by Zeke Peña, copyright © 2019 by Zeke Peña. Used with permission of Kokila, an imprint of Penguin Young Readers, a division of Penguin Random House LLC. All rights reserved. UK and Commonwealth rights courtesy of Zeke Peña, used with permission of Fletcher & Co., New York.

make the shift toward representing the people who lay the asphalt or who build the house in their works. We find the same "deliberate choice" made by Guadalupe García McCall in her transfiguration of Homer's *Odyssey* into a Latinx mythological realist novel that features *lechuzas*, a chupacabra, and other figures from Latinx culture in *Summer of the Mariposas* (2012), analyzed in chapter 3. As García McCall notes, "we have myths and legends and monsters and heroes and ancient deities who are just as interesting as the ones in the original text" ("Teacher's Guide" 2). Author Aida Salazar, in another example analyzed in our chapter 4, positions deportations and the separation of families at the center of her novel. Salazar highlights the injustice at the heart of these national policies by underscoring the notion that people should not be deported from and their mobility should not be impeded within the confines of their mythical homeland. As the title references, *Land of the Cranes* is set in Aztlán, the mythical homeland of the Aztecs, which legends say is in the American Southwest. In this way, Betita and her family do not emigrate to the United States as much as they are returning to their homeland. Salazar's "deliberate choice" allows young Latinx readers to reimagine themselves, not as intruders to the nation but as the natural heirs to this place.

We find Aldama's term "deliberate choice" vital to our understanding of the way that Latinx authors and artists purposefully center Latinx lived experiences and intentionally construct worlds from Latinx cultural repertoires. In *Tactics of Hope*, we consider this deliberate choice a kind of tactic, or to use a Chicana feminist term, a *movida*, which retains hope.[3] As María Eugenia Cotera, Dionne Espinoza, and Maylei Blackwell inform in *Chicana Movidas: New Narratives of Activism and Feminism in the Movement Era*, movida "often carries with it connotations of not only the strategic and tactical but also the undercover, the dissident, the illicit—that which is not part of approved and publicly acknowledged political strategies, histories, and economic and social relations" (Cotera et al. 2). In this way, movida "destabilizes normative practices and ideologies insofar as these practices and ideologies enact relations of subordination, inequality, or invisibilization" (Cotera et al. 3). Seeing these movidas, or tactics as we will call them in our book, as forms of resistance allows us to trace how Latinx authors and artists of children and young adult literature destabilize unjust and inequitable practices and ideologies by presenting characters and stories that are more equitable and that make visible Latinx culture. In *My Papi Has a*

Motorcycle, for example, the placement of "Papi," a term of endearment a young person would call their father, in the title showcases the way these tactics are revolutionary in nature as the title of the book moves dexterously between English and Spanish. Understanding how tactics "map a field of resistance, innovation, and transformation" (Cotera et al. 12) allows us, in the words of Tomás Ybarra-Frausto, to "retain hope" (86). Put another way, we retain hope that the tactics utilized by Latinx authors and illustrators, such as the translanguaging deployed in the title of *My Papi Has a Motorcycle* as well as the picture book's positive representation of working-class Latinx experiences, offer young Latinx readers the mirrors necessary for them to see themselves and by which to make themselves.

Daisy in the aforementioned illustration of *My Papi Has a Motorcycle* fortunately finds such a mirror and thus validation as she reads a Latinx graphic novel. The "deliberate choice," to use Aldama's terminology, of Isabel Quintero and Zeke Peña to center the lives and experiences of Latinx people, we believe, allows young Latinx readers the necessary literary mirrors vital for propelling them toward "engaging with and then transforming the larger world" (Aldama 14). As Cristina Rhodes shows in her study of Matt de la Peña's *Mexican Whiteboy*, Danny's struggles with his identity, which at times in the case of Danny lead to self-harm, can be traced to the lack of literary mirrors in his reading that would have allowed him to accept his hybrid identity. As she notes, "Danny's struggle for identity parallels the difficulties Latinx readers face in seeking mirrors in books" ("'Seemingly on the Inside'" 12). While literary mirrors that reflect how "the rich and multifaceted realities of minoritized children and adolescents is vital to their ability to realize their identities and to interact with the world around them," the reality is that "textual mirrors to support identity formation for Latinx child readers are scarce" (1). Rhodes goes on to notes that mirrors in books are becoming even more important as "the political zeitgeist furthers the divide between privileged and minoritized populations" and yet at the same time "data still indicate that Latinxs have a long, uphill battle in rough terrain to gain a foothold in children's literature" (12).

Thus, even as we find hope that Latinx children's and young adult literature confronts overt injustices as well as the daily threat of assimilationist narratives that privilege normative whiteness, we pause to look at this time at the "long, uphill battle in rough terrain" that Latinx authors and artists face. As we find in the data, literary mirrors in which young

Latinx readers find themselves are scarce. In fact, we look at them with dismay. In 2019, the publication date of *My Papi Has a Motorcycle*, the Cooperative Children's Book Center (CCBC), a library of the School of Education at the University of Wisconsin–Madison "committed to identifying excellent literature for children and adolescents and bringing this literature to the attention of those adults who have an academic, professional, or career interest in connecting young readers with books" received 4,035 children's and young adult books, from both small and large presses (the large majority of those published that year) ("About," *Cooperative*; "Books by"). Of those 4,035 books, only 243 were written or illustrated by Latinx authors and artists. As dismal as these numbers are, they in fact have been climbing. In 2016 there were only 60 books by Latinx writers and authors, compared with 118 in 2017 and 207 in 2018 ("Books by").[4]

Social media initiatives may have something to do with the small uptick. The website We Need Diverse Books began as a Twitter exchange by Ellen Oh and Malindo Lo to express their frustration with the lack of diversity in children's and young adult literature. From its social media platform, it now has grown into "non-profit and a grassroots organization of children's book lovers that advocates essential changes in the publishing industry to produce and promote literature that reflects and honors the lives of all young people" ("About Us," *We Need*). The guiding mission of their program is "to create a world in which all children can see themselves in the pages of a book" ("About Us"). While We Need Diverse Books brings attention to the importance of diverse creators and diverse books, we also highlight the work of #DignidadLiteraria and #LatinxPitch in their endeavors to bring better and more accurate, as well as more nuanced, representations of Latinx culture and people. Formed shortly after the *American Dirt* debacle, in which author Jeanine Cummins (who self-identified as white and then changed her identification to Latinx when promoting her book) misrepresented the lives and experiences of Mexican migrants, #DignidadLiteraria is committed "to combat the invisibility of Latinx authors, editors, and executives in the U.S. publishing industry" (*DignidadLiteraria*). David Bowles, author of *They Call Me Güero* (examined in chapter 2), is one of the cofounders. At the heart of their initiative is a belief "in the social and political power of wholly authentic Latinx voices and that it is the duty of the publishing industry and literati to use their full power and privilege to elevate these voices" (*DignidadLiteraria*). #LatinxPitch likewise seeks to "raise up Latinx voices and representation in children's literature" (*Latinx Pitch for Kid Lit*). Their project includes an annual Twitter pitch party in which Latinx creators (writers and artists) are asked to submit stories that "showcase these talents and promote Latinx expertise and skills to a wider community" (*Latinx Pitch for Kid Lit*). Their goal in this is to increase representation of Latinx voices in publishing by showcasing untapped talent to prospective publishing editors. Importantly, they also host mentorship meetings for Latinx creators. We believe both of these initiatives, #DignidadLiteraria and #LatinxPitch, are instrumental toward ameliorating the dismally small number of Latinx creators.

We call attention to the vital work of Latinx authors and artists in creating stories that mirror young Latinx readers, thereby affirming their identities in the face of assimilationist narratives that privilege normative whiteness. These literary and cultural interventions, we argue, should be seen as subversive tactics and forms of dissidence. After all, naturalizing Latinx spaces and normalizing Latinx ways of being and doing confronts national and societal policies and practices that wish to eradicate them, either by exclusion in the form of deportations or by erasure in the form of assimilation. For this reason, we situate the work of Latinx authors and illustrators of children's and young adult literature within critical theories of movidas, that is, within revolutionary tactics that recover and rework the invisible and submerged worlds of Latinx people. Through such tactics, we argue, young readers are provided mirrors in which to see themselves and by which to make themselves. While we cannot emphasize enough the importance of these literary mirrors and windows to young readers, we also note the dearth of Latinx literature on the shelves of US libraries and bookstores. As such, even as we laud books that feature characters and stories that more accurately portray the lived experiences of Latinx children and young adults, we also lament the challenges that Latinx creators face in publishing their works. The hope we retain can be found in current initiatives that seek better representation and equity to the publishing industry. As we highlighted, Latinx authors and artists in our study are deeply engaged in practices that contest and challenge the publishing industry that marginalizes their work. Tactics for retaining hope, in this sense, mean breaking down the gates that keep Latinx works out. For these books offer much to young readers, as our epigraph from Gloria Anzaldúa reads: "Books saved me knowledge opened the locked places in me and taught me first how to survive and then how to soar" (*Borderlands / La Frontera* 19). We believe that such books as the ones analyzed in this study will help kids to survive and teach them how to soar.

Chapter Capsules

In a recent interview, Isabel Quintero, author of *My Papi Has a Motorcycle* and *Gabi, a Girl in Pieces*, notes that the reason she writes is to exist, given the "negation of our existence, and the omitting of our stories and histories" ("'My Writing'"). This gives her pause because, as she states, we "cannot escape our past; our past determines what choices we make for the future. It determines how we act, how we see ourselves ... how past traumas—our parents', our ancestors'—affect our lives and the lives of our descendants" ("'My Writing'"). To exist, Quintero posits, is to know your stories and histories, which are under threat by "oppression by omission," her term for America's erasure of Latinx stories and histories.

Quintero's observations open a space for us to reflect on the nature of our book, which centers conocimiento as a guiding force for the resistance against erasures by omission and for the transformations resultant from the knowledge and awareness of how past and current traumas affect Latinx lives. Determining how to heal el daño caused by these traumas, in our view, is the endpoint of conocimiento, that is, as young Latinx people who read works such as *Gabi, a Girl in Pieces* transform themselves in order to then transform the world. Conocimiento, we believe, counters the negation of our existence and the omitting of our stories and histories by insisting that knowledge and awareness of Latinx creative and cultural output is necessary for inner works to become public acts, for activism to unfold from the transformations inherent in conocimiento.

Centering Gloria Anzaldúa's critical concepts allows us to dwell on pivotal sites of contestation, where children and youth lead the way in countering oppressive policies and practices that would negate their existence. Our project admittedly is concentrated along the southern borderlands of the US Southwest. This choice is intentional. The southern border is a hot zone for injustices perpetrated against Latinx people, both US citizens and migrants who use the area as a corridor for entrance into the United States. The southern border, in this regard, desperately needs Latinx children's and young adult literature. As we discuss in our book, authors of Latinx children's and young adult literature have risen to the challenge, providing counter-stories and counter-histories to contest racist practices and policies in the region. Moreover, these books deliberately place children and youth at the center of the struggle to bring conocimiento to an area of widespread desconocimiento. The children and young adults in the books chosen for our study beckon young, and not so young, readers to see the world, as well as the new realities they imagine, through their eyes. In this way, they lead us into new worlds.

In the following chapter capsules we briefly describe how these children and youth open their worlds for us to see. From this lens, one way to read *Tactics of Hope in Latinx Children's and Young Adult Literature* is by imagining the movement from book cover to book cover as a motorcycle ride across Latinx children's and young adult literature. The destination is not as important as the journey, and, as such, the journey will zigzag between topics and themes, though always within the purview of conocimiento, germane to Latinx people. Given the nonlinearity (which we adamantly pursued), in the following chapter capsules we briefly describe the books selected for study and the critical focus at play in each chapter. Our hope is that this motorcycle ride, which is informed by Daisy and Papi making their way around their hometown, illuminates the ways that Anzaldúa's theoretical formulations on conocimiento can be deployed to further our understanding of resistance and transformation in Latinx children's and young adult literature.

CHAPTER 1 / READING FOR CONOCIMIENTO MIRRORS IN FARMWORKER KID LIT: ROOTS OF TRANSFORMATION AND ACTIVISM

The power of Quintero's assessment that the past determines "how we act" and "how we see ourselves" in the present frames our first chapter. We delve into the past, specifically as it is related to farmworker justice, by looking at picture books *Side by Side / Lado a lado: The Story of Dolores Huerta and Cesar Chavez / La historia de Dolores Huerta y César Chávez* (2010) by Monica Brown and illustrated by Joe Cepeda and *Tomás and the Library Lady* (1997) by Pat Mora and illustrated by Raúl Colón. These books present the long history of hardship in the fields and the hard-won successes of historical figures such as Dolores Huerta, César Chávez, and Tomás Rivera, respectively. We propose that understanding the travails experienced and tactics deployed by these historical figures provides young readers with conocimiento mirrors in which they can see themselves, their histories, and their present realities reflected and from which they can project futures in which they are activist leaders. Following this analysis of the picture books, we consider young adult novel *Under the Feet of Jesus* (1995) by Helena María Viramontes, highlighting the way the novel situates the struggle, *la lucha*, in a more present reality. Given the gravity of the situation, where children and youth struggle daily with hazardous work conditions as well as impediments to their educational goals, Estrella's activism offers a conocimiento mirror in which young readers can see themselves contesting the oppressions that affect them. It is our position that these books, in enacting moments of critical self-knowledge and the ways that awareness "pushes us into engaging the spirit in confronting our social sickness with new tools and practices whose goal is to affect a shift" (Anzaldúa, *Light / Luz* 19), allow young readers to witness conocimiento transformations even as they begin their own transformations. In this way, we see these books as conocimiento mirrors in which young Latinx readers can see themselves and their lived reality in the texts and then begin the process "whose goal is to affect a shift" in themselves and in the world around them.

CHAPTER 2 / BORDER KIDS IN THE LAND OF NEPANTLA

In this chapter, we highlight the way nepantla, the interstitial place "where at once we are detached (separated) and attached (connected) to each of our several cultures" (*Light / Luz* 56), funds conocimiento in border kids who reside along the US/Mexico border. At play in our invocation of nepantla is an acknowledgment that while nepantla is a place of bewilderment, nepantla also is the site of resistance and of transformation for bicultural and translingual border kids. Inherent in Anzaldúa's theories on the borderlands is the notion that the US/Mexico border is *una herida abierta*, an open wound, where "lifeblood of two worlds merg[es] to form a third country—a border culture" (*Borderlands / La Frontera* 25). The protagonists in the two novels analyzed in this chapter, Lupita in Guadalupe García McCall's young adult verse novel *Under the Mesquite* (2011) and Güero in David Bowles's young adult poetry collection *They Call Me Güero: A Border Kid's Poems* (2018), utilize conocimiento to create a sense of belonging that bridges the cultural and national divides. Even as American assimilationist policies and practices seek to separate them from their lived experiences, Lupita and Güero deploy conocimiento to learn about their cultures and histories and to utilize this knowledge for creating a bicultural and translingual sense of self. Inhabiting nepantla, we argue, allows Lupita and Güero to fund forms of resistance against assimilation and single narrative models and, by accepting the paradoxes of this liminal space, to transform themselves and the world around them.

CHAPTER 3 / THE CULTURAL WEALTH OF DIASPORIC YOUTH

In this chapter we investigate the processes at play when diasporic youth engage with their cultural wealth. We posit that young adult novels *Maximilian and the Mystery of the Guardian Angel: A Bilingual Lucha Libre Thriller* (2011) by Xavier Garza and *Summer of the Mariposas* (2012) by Guadalupe García McCall draw on cultural wealth from their real and imagined homeland as a resource to challenge deficit thinking and to reveal, for their young readers, the possibilities entailed in being holders and creators of valuable cultural knowledge. In the process of establishing these transnational ties between and across nation spaces, we argue, these novels put forward a reparative theory that accounts for the way diasporic peoples can heal by rewriting "the stories of loss and recovery, exile and homecoming, disinheritance and recuperation, stories that lead out of passivity and into agency, out of devalued into valued lives" (Anzaldúa, *Light / Luz* 143). In our reading of *Maximilian and the Mystery of the Guardian Angel* and *Summer of the Mariposas*, we point to the movement from loss and disinheritance, in other words, deficit thinking, to forms of agency and cultural wealth. That is, these novels demonstrate how artfully assembling pieces gathered from many places, from over there as well as from here, reflect and project a lived experience that is necessarily intertwined in at least two nations. Further, they highlight the reparative value in knowing that one possesses great cultural wealth.

CHAPTER 4 / KIDS' AGENCY AND EMPOWERMENT
IN AN ERA OF FAMILY DEPORTATION

With Anzaldúa's call to "rise up in testimony" in mind, this chapter concerns bearing witness to what it means and feels like to be deported and/or to have a loved one deported, from the perspectives of Latinx children and young adults. We position deportation at the center of our discussion, first to recognize and acknowledge trauma and, second, to bring light to a healing process for these *heridas* currently devastating Latinx children and families in the United States. In this, we believe that the young adult novels *Efrén Divided* (2020) by Ernesto Cisneros and *Land of the Cranes* (2020) by Aida Salazar, and the picture book *From North to South / Del norte al sur* (2013) by René Colato Laínez and illustrated by Joe Cepeda, provide testimonies that bear witness to the systemic, officially sanctioned, and nationally funded racism at the root of the deportations of Latinx people in the United States. Our argument is that these testimonies, beyond acknowledging the heridas, also serve as LatCrit counter-stories that intentionally foreground reparative tactics that challenge the dominant discourse on race and belonging. LatCrit counter-storytelling, in this sense, becomes a form of healing. As Levins Morales reminds us, "when the stories of the abused are transformed and push their way into public space, their power to undermine the dominant narrative and shake up how people perceive reality can be tremendous" (58). Our aim is to focus our critical attention on stories of deportation and to push them into the public space, in this way undermining racist understandings of Latinx peoples. These reparative processes construct new realities on foundations of belonging and equity.

CHAPTER 5 / THE ROLE OF THE BORDER ARTISTA

An autohistoria, Anzaldúa explains, "goes beyond the traditional self-portrait or autobiography; in telling the writer/artist's personal story, it also includes the artist's cultural history—indeed, it's a kind of making history, of inventing our history from our experience and perspective through our art" (*Light / Luz* 62). In this chapter we argue that protagonists Julia, in *I Am Not Your Perfect Mexican Daughter* (2017) by Erika L. Sánchez, and Gabi, in *Gabi, a Girl in Pieces* (2014) by Isabel Quintero, are border *artistas* who utilize creative acts to share their autohistorias in these young adult novels. These autohistorias, for Julia and Gabi, reveal their complex inner lives, specifically the struggles in negotiating Latinx identity and challenging gender norms imposed on them by parents and society. *I Am Not Your Perfect Mexican Daughter* and *Gabi, a Girl in Pieces* underscore the transformations inherent in inner work that lead to public acts that are at the center of conocimiento. In this way, the novels function as studios in narrative form in which the young Latinx characters can artfully fashion themselves. For Julia and Gabi, to be border artistas involves making knowledge through self-inscription, placing and blending together the pieces of identity in new ways, showcasing the power of Latinx in its artful creation of the self to social revolutionary and transformative ends.

So You Know Us

We end this introduction with a note about ourselves. In many ways we are Anzaldúa's children. We find comfort in interstitial places, whether in our daily lives or in our academic ones. Nepantla, in this way, has become home, as we move easily through languages and cultures. Regan is a natural Spanish speaker, even as her first language was English. The inverse is true of Jesus. While Jesus grew up as a transnational kid, it is Regan who maintains connections with communities in Central America and regularly travels with college students there. The list keeps going, as do the ways that our figurative mother has taught us well. She told us, for example, of the importance of books and then she imparted the critical concepts necessary to illuminate how resistance and transformation transfigure the world. In this, she taught us that our roles in society and in academics would be reparative in nature. Reflected in this book are the possibilities engendered by her guidance and her generosity to us, as well as to all her children.

Regan: A few years ago, I sat in a classroom watching from across the room as one of my college student mentors read with her sixth-grade mentee after finishing up some math homework. The mentee had chosen Carmen Lomas Garza's *In My Family / En mi familia*, and they gazed together at the bright images of a Mexican American community in Texas. I could tell that the sixth-grade student felt proud, sharing with her mentor about her family traditions she saw illustrated in the book. In a new space for her, in the frigid Michigan winter, this book saved her, for she was mirrored in it, and it allowed her to feel pride, to soar. In many ways it is through my experience as director of the Step Up mentoring program, a sister program to the TRIO Upward Bound program at Hope College, that I realized the need for and power of Latinx books for young readers. My hope is that the books in this study will make it into kids' hands and that the analyses we provide bolster librarians, teachers, and others invested in kids and literacy.

In another way, I come to this project having grown up as a white child with little access to books about people that did not look like me, even though I lived in a community with a sizable Latinx population. It was not until high school, as an exchange student in Bolivia, that I began to read Latin American and Latinx authors and to know the power of books as window into the experiences of others. For non-Latinx readers of our book, I am eager for the ways that our analyses may offer new ways of seeing and understanding the rich offering of Latinx literary and cultural production for young readers to our world.

Jesus: I loved *lucha libre* when I was a child. El Blue Demon was my favorite, although I came to admire el Santo as time went along. They were my earliest heroes. And, to be honest, I needed them. Like Betita in *Land of the Cranes*, I was an undocumented child. Needless to say, as a child the stress and anxiety of being deported or having a loved one deported, both of which happened, were unbearable. Reading saved me, even if it was reading magazines and *fotonovelas* about my heroes. Then, as my imagination roared to life in envisioning my life intertwined with theirs, I came to believe that the world and everything in it was open to me. I was a child living at the fringes of an empire still unfolding: assimilationism would change my name, would try to cure me of my diasporic imagination, and would have me believe that certain literary expressions were better than others. And yet I had my heroes.

My interest in Latinx children's and young adult literature as such comes from the understanding that others, like me once, are desperately in need of the worlds that erupt from books. My hope is that such books will allow them to examine and engage with their struggles as they come to better understand themselves. In this way, I believe that I grew up to be the *luchador* I dreamed of becoming.

A Note on Terms, or Why We Choose *Latinx*

"Latinx" is the term most commonly used in our field of study. It is the standard in academic work, and creative pieces are marketed under the term. Many of the authors and artists in our study use "Latinx" to self-identify themselves and their work, though in most cases, they also use further cultural descriptors. We strongly believe that "Latinx" as a cultural signifier does not supersede or negate other identifiers of people from the Latin American or Caribbean diasporas living in the United States.[5] Indeed, as Roy Pérez, in a scholarly exchange on the term "Latinx," notes, the term supplements rather than replaces other ethnic terms:

> Latinx can exist alongside Puerto Rican, Mexican, Cuban, and Chicana/o/x, as a tool in the discursive box. I tell my students that when we're talking about Latinx populations in general terms, it's perfectly alright [sic] to stumble through a chain of slippery signifiers, and I regularly drop some version of "Chicanx/Rican/Latina/o/x" when I'm speaking in class, refusing to impose and stick to a particular label unless specificity calls for one. Language offers that fluidity and we should take advantage of it. (deOnís 83)

From this vantage point, "Latinx" functions as a boon in an already rich repertoire of cultural signifiers. It serves the purpose of bringing together diverse groups with a more inclusive label, and this can be used toward social or political ends.

In our eyes, "Latinx" also is a self-identifying way of aligning cultural interests with social justice imperatives, namely, issues of gender and sexuality but also issues of national and transnational belonging. By moving beyond the gendered "a/o" in Latino and Latina, for example, "Latinx" problematizes easy notions of gender and sexuality whereby one is coded as either male or female (with no option for nonbinary gender identification). As Nicole Guidotti-Hernández explains, "Latinx" "provides a window to imagine something other than gender normativity and repression" (157). It also moves beyond the structure of Spanish language in its use of a nonstandard word ending ("x"), thereby complicating notions of linguistic as well as national identity. Sandra Soto-Santiago posits that "the use of the 'x' goes beyond the issue of gender because it attempts to be inclusive of all those who identify as part of the super diverse Latinx population and to embrace our uniqueness within the Latinx community. This includes gender, sexual preferences, and transnationality, among many others" (deOnís 85). The term invites complexity and difference, propelling in this way notions of interconnectivity. We use "Latinx" in this book to underscore the importance of inclusion in these matters of cultural belonging.

CHAPTER ONE

Reading for Conocimiento Mirrors in Farmworker Kid Lit
Roots of Transformation and Activism

> Roots represent ancestral/racial origins and biological attributes; branches and leaves represent the characteristics, communities, and cultures that surround us, that we've adopted, and that we're in intimate conversation with . . . Luckily, the roots of my tree are deep enough in la cultura mexicana and strong enough to support a widespread branch system. Las raíces that sustain and nourish me are implanted in the landscape of my youth, my grandmother's stories of la Llorona, my father's quiet strength, the persevering energy de la gente who work in the fields.
>
> GLORIA ANZALDÚA / *Light in the Dark / Luz en lo oscuro*

We live in a country where Latinx children and adolescents work long hours, and usually under dangerous conditions in agricultural fields. The 2011 documentary film *La Cosecha / The Harvest*, directed by U. Roberto Romano, for example, calls our attention to the 400,000 children and adolescents in the United States who labor as migrant farmworkers—often suffering long hours, pesticide exposure, extreme heat, dangerous working conditions, racial discrimination, and interrupted schooling. Under the administration of US president Donald Trump (2017–21), these issues became more pressing due to increased immigration enforcement and moves toward pesticide deregulation.[1] Even as advocacy groups such as the United Farm Workers of America and Farmworker

Justice[2] continue in their work to maintain and increase basic protections for children and adult migrant and seasonal laborers, one of the most pressing issues for the children of migrant and seasonal farmworkers, aside from basic needs such as access to water, food, and housing, is their longer-term educational aspirations.

Thus, while potential is equally distributed across our national community, opportunity is not. One of the most onerous opportunity gaps is found in education, principally in how our national community does or does not equitably prepare all children for foundational and future educational success. In this, inequality to access, racisms, and disproportionate economics have ensured that large segments of our community are not afforded the same opportunities by which to realize their rich and varied potentials.

Books, we believe, can help build bridges over opportunity gaps in education, especially books that center reading and activism for young readers. The books chosen for our study, *Side by Side / Lado a lado: The Story of Dolores Huerta and Cesar Chavez / La historia de Dolores Huerta y César Chávez* (2010) by Monica Brown and illustrated by Joe Cepeda, *Tomás and the Library Lady* (1997) by Pat Mora and illustrated by Raúl Colón, and *Under the Feet of Jesus* (1995) by Helena María Viramontes, trace the long history of hardship in the fields, ranging from the 1950s of a young Tomás Rivera and the 1960s of Chávez and Huerta, to more contemporary times in Viramontes's novel. These books emphasize knowing the history of injustice in the fields and the long legacy of leaders who fought for justice and envisioned a better future. The picture book *Side by Side / Lado a lado*, based on the lives of the farmworker movement leaders Dolores Huerta and César Chávez, offers a window into how these historical figures used their activism to make change. Of such books that engage the past, Aurora Levins Morales notes that "history is the story we tell ourselves about how the past explains our present, and the ways we tell it are shaped by contemporary needs" (71). In this way, *Side by Side / Lado a lado* highlights the capacity of books to tell of past injustices and the heroes who fought for justice while also being attentive to resistance in the present. In other words, history "is a powerful resource with which to explain and justify the present and create agendas for the future" (Levins Morales 59).

If *Side by Side / Lado a lado* tracks the lives of important civil rights leaders, *Tomás and the Library Lady* illustrates how books build bridges across societal divides. Based on the life of Tomás Rivera, foundational author in Chicanx literature and lauded educator who grew up in a migrant farmworker family, the picture book, on the surface, offers a lesson on friendship based on common interests found in reading and learning. The friendship between Tomás and the library lady, in our reading, however, is built not only on common interests but also on conocimiento. As we will show, *Tomás and the Library Lady* contests easy binaries between oral traditions and literacy-based education. It further challenges monolingualism and highlights how young people like Tomás have knowledge to offer those, like the library lady, in positions of power. Tomás, we argue, has as much to teach the library lady as she does him. In this sense, the picture book widens the scope of interconnectivity underscored in *Side by Side / Lado a lado*. In choosing to discuss *Tomás and the Library Lady* we specifically are interested in the educational accomplishments and writing legacy of Tomás Rivera.

The same holds true if we see *Under the Feet of Jesus* as a *künstlerroman* in which a young Estrella becomes the writer Helena María Viramontes. The young adult novel highlights the development of the artist, drawing on the künstlerroman form, to showcase farmworker and artist-activist Estrella's[3] use of creative thought, words, and action to aid her farmworker community. Hazardous working conditions, exposure to pesticides, and adverse housing issues are endemic problems for many Latinx children and young adults who work the fields. Estrella models ways to combat these problems by utilizing conocimiento to gain insights as to the nature of these problems and then by acting in ways that challenge these oppressions. In this way, we argue, Estrella provides a literary mirror in which young Latinx readers can see themselves as activists.

As these brief descriptions show, all three books feature young protagonists who develop into strong activist leaders. It is our argument that these books function as "conocimiento mirrors" (our term) for young Latinx readers who see can themselves, their histories, and their present realities reflected, and further find their potential futures mirrored as they begin to imagine the possibilities of activist leadership for their generation. While it would please us to believe that these books will magically provide a path that young readers can follow from the fields to academic success, this is hazardous at best.[4] Instead, our argument is that these books mediate the transition between the desconocimiento—the path of ignorance, fear, and hatred present in many US policies and practices, including the educational system—and conocimiento. As Sonia Rodríguez in "Conocimiento Narratives" has persuasively argued, "reading these children's texts as conocimiento narratives suggests that the conclusions of the texts are not guarantees of a better future but instead offer Latinx children the possibility to imagine new realities" (27). The books in our study, if we follow Rodríguez's line of thought, illustrate the transformational possibilities inherent in conocimiento, the ability to envision new realities. From this lens, these books, in enacting moments of critical self-knowledge and the ways that awareness "pushes us into engaging the spirit in confronting our social sickness with new tools and practices whose goal is to affect a shift" (Anzaldúa, *Light / Luz* 19), allow young readers to witness conocimiento transformations even as they begin their own transformations. In this way, we see books as "conocimiento mirrors" in which young Latinx readers can see themselves and their lived reality in the texts and then begin the process "whose goal is to affect a shift" in themselves and in the world around them.

As conocimiento mirrors, books offer much to young readers. In her preface to *Borderlands / La Frontera*, Anzaldúa states that "books saved my sanity, knowledge opened the locked places in me and taught me first how to survive and then how to soar" (19). We find reassuring hope in the words of Anzaldúa. Books, we believe, have the power to save new generations of Latinx children and young adults, for they allow young Latinx readers to explore ways in which knowledge opens up locked places, thus allowing them to first survive and then soar. It is our argument that the books considered in this chapter, as well as other books that call attention to the plight of and the possibilities for Latinx children in the fields, offer much for readers. If, on one hand, these books point to and challenge current and past conditions in the agricultural fields, on the other hand they recognize, as Anzaldúa notes, that "the purpose of education is not only to fight against oppression but to heal the wounds that oppression inflicts and to cultivate individual and collective growth—laying the foundation for justice and balance" (*Light / Luz* 181). Conocimiento, in this sense, functions as a model of education in which both hands work in unison: one breaks down injustices while the other hand heals the wounds inflicted by those injustices.

In the following sections, we discuss how *Side by Side / Lado a lado*, *Tomás and the Library Lady*, and *Under the Feet of Jesus* lay "the foundation for justice and balance." Our goal is to show how these books offer a way forward to long-standing and current injustices in the agricultural fields. As we discuss the books in this study, it will become evident, if it has not already, that farmworker kids face grave injustices right now.

Conocimiento, we believe, provides a necessary path forward by theorizing healing as a critical tool in the search for social justice. In this way, conocimiento pushes us to engage with the reparative qualities of reading, with the transformational possibilities entailed in imagining new realities.[5]

Side by Side / Lado a lado

Side by Side / Lado a lado highlights the historical struggles and successes of Dolores Huerta (1930–) and César Chávez (1927–1993),[6] cofounders of the National Farm Workers Association (NFWA), which later became the United Farm Workers of America (UFW). The narrative arc of the story brackets the childhoods of Dolores and César with their activism as adults. The picture book thus begins with each activist, Dolores and César, as children in their respective home states. In New Mexico, Dolores talks so much that her grandfather exclaims, "Dolores, you must have seven tongues!" Meanwhile in Arizona, we meet a young César, who is described as a "very good listener" when he attends to his mother as she cries at the loss of the family's home. The picture book follows this pattern of presenting Dolores on the left panel and César on the right panel with each page chronicling the ways conocimiento informed their childhood, youth, and their early adult years. Dolores, for example, joins the Girl Scouts, and raises money for soldiers fighting in World War II. Later, as a young schoolteacher, she notices that the farmworker children "come to school cold and barefoot, too hungry to learn as well as they could." César, in the corresponding pages, has to drop out of school and work in the fields to help his family. In the fields, César, his friends, and family are "hurt by dangerous tools and had mean bosses who sprayed the plants with poisons that made the farmworkers sick."

The picture book continues moving through different yet seminal moments in the lives of Chávez and Huerta until "something special happened, Dolores and Cesar met." Recognizing that César's "dreams would bring hope to thousands of farmworkers" and that Dolores "had great courage," they begin their activist journey, side by side. From this point forward, the picture book illustrations present Dolores and César together on two-page spreads, doubly emphasizing their connection and work side by side, while the narrative describes Dolores and César on their journey together as they invite farmworkers to join La Causa from the backs of flatbed trucks along the side of the fields. The picture book also showcases how Dolores and César organize a grape boycott in response to pesticide misuse and, of course, it shows them as they lead a 340-mile march to Sacramento to demand better wages. Near the end of *Side by Side / Lado a lado*, the narrative shows that "Dolores and César had many victories, because they knew that, *together*, all things were possible" (emphasis ours).

Our argument is that by portraying the arc of Huerta and Chávez's lives from childhood into their later years, moving from individual acts to collective solidarity, *Side by Side / Lado a lado* offers young readers a modeling device by which they can trace out their lives and their struggles for justice. *Side by Side / Lado a lado*, in this way, functions as a conocimiento mirror in which young readers see themselves in the text, imagine themselves participating in the transformations of Dolores and César from creative, thoughtful children to successful leaders, and witness, in the process, their evolving inner growth. Moreover, as the title of the picture book and the merging of the Dolores and César's lives suggests, leaders succeed largely because they work side by side with others.

¡Sí, Se Puede! An Empathetic Community of Leaders

UFW's motto, *¡Sí, Se Puede!*, can be translated from its Spanish into English as either "Yes, It Can Be Done!" (a more literal translation) or "Yes, We Can!" (a more robust translation and one which President Barack Obama used to great success). The latter translation, for our purposes, signals the importance of the "we" in the social justice movement. In this, the picture book envisions a new reality in which radical interconnectedness, the "we," is the key to success, both personal and social. This is not just the "we" of César and Dolores, however, but of a greater sense of interconnectedness and solidarity among farmworkers and allies as they show empathy and act for justice.

This kind of empathy as part and parcel to solidarity comes to the forefront in Anzaldúa's notions of interconnectedness. Speaking to Anzaldúa's notions, AnaLouise Keating posits that if we are to arrive at this place where alliances are forged not on uniformity but on unity, it will be crucial to enact empathy in this (new) relational form of thinking:

> Exploring the differences between us, I seek commonalities between your experiences and mine. Empathy—the willingness to

FIGURE 1.1 Joe Cepeda, Dolores and César invite farmworkers to join *La Causa*. *Side by Side / Lado a lado: The Story of Dolores Huerta and Cesar Chavez / La historia de Dolores Huerta y César Chávez* by Monica Brown and illustrated by Joe Cepeda. Copyright © Joe Cepeda.

imaginatively enter your life through reading, through conversation, through storytelling—is crucial to this search. When "I" empathize with "you," I enact a relational form of thinking, a back-and-forth movement. Immersing myself in your stories, I listen without judging, I listen with open heart and open mind. I travel into your emotions, desires, and experiences, then return to my own. But in the return, I am changed by my encounter with you, and I begin recognizing the commonalities we share. ("Forging" 522–23)

Side by Side / Lado a lado illustrates the importance of empathy clearly in its narrative and illustrations. Early in the picture book, for example, readers take note of the ways young César and Dolores witness the pain of those around them: the lack of water in the fields, the horrible and cramped housing for itinerant workers, the hunger of children, and the prevalence of dangerous tools and noxious pesticides. As for young readers who have been shown what César and Dolores witnessed, Suzanne Keen observes that empathy can be "provoked by witnessing another's emotional state, by hearing about another's condition, or even by reading" (62). Reading *Side by Side / Lado a lado*, if we follow Keen's theoretical angle, allows young readers to empathize with the workers. While research in the field of cognitive psychology suggests that the act of reading, especially fiction, can improve readers' emotional abilities, on a visual level, for young readers in particular, Maria Nikolajeva, in "Picturebooks and Emotional Literacy," points out that the visual images alongside text makes picture books the "perfect training fields for young people's theory of mind [the capacity to understand how other individuals think] and empathy" (354). Thus, by engaging with the models of Dolores and César via the picture book, much like Dolores who watched her mother and "learned to think of others," children develop their ability to care. Questions posed in the picture book, such as when César asks Dolores over a meal with their families, "If we don't help the farmworkers . . . who will?," serve to provoke empathy in readers who may find themselves echoing these questions in their lives.

Side by Side / Lado a lado showcases how empathy is foundational, on one level, for making the boundaries between self and others more permeable, and, on another level, how empathy leads to radical notions of interconnectivity, which we argue, is the catalyst for social justice. It is important to note that the modeling of empathy in *Side by Side / Lado a lado* impacts young Latinx readers from farmworker communities as well as other young readers with less contact with this particular community. In her article on reading stories and empathy Andreea Deciu Ritivoi suggests that "narratives can foster such understanding of not just characters who are or seem to be like us but also, and more importantly, of those who do not resemble us at all. Empathy can emerge from a better understanding of experiences, rather than from relating to a familiar character, or a character in a familiar situation" (55). *Side by Side / Lado a lado* engages with all readers and welcomes everyone to join in the struggle. The ability of the picture book to engage with a variety of readers and develop empathy creates a greater effect.

Thus, when young readers interact with *Side by Side / Lado a lado*, they find themselves invited to share in the emotions of others, to identify problems, and to work together, side by side, to change society and in the process to bring forth a new reality. By positioning the notion of "side by side" at the center of Dolores and César's successes, in fundamental ways, the picture book showcases how best to understand the "we" in "Yes, We Can!" As the picture book informs us, "all things are possible" if we, as in "yes, *we* can," work together, side by side. *Side by Side / Lado a lado*, we posit, offers young readers a way to use their creativity and imagination to develop different epistemologies that reframe their successes, away from simple personal gain and into better models that at their core "embed your experiences in a larger frame of reference, connecting your personal struggles with those of other beings on the planet, with the struggles of the Earth itself" (Anzaldúa, *Light / Luz* 119). In this way, *Side by Side / Lado a lado*, as a conocimiento mirror, leads young readers into an unfolding transformation in which their goals will be to open opportunities for others, in much the same way Dolores and César did for them.

"Dolores Still Works and Marches for Justice"

Side by Side / Lado a lado proposes a new reality in which collaboration and communal support are the hallmarks. As we move toward the end of the picture book, for example, the illustrations seem to merge with the narrative and rhetorical arc of the story. Whereas few people appear on each page when Dolores and César work individually at the beginning of the picture book, the number of people rises exponentially when the two leaders come together, and the strength of their solidarity is further emphasized by the movement to illustrations on two-page spreads. Therefore, as the picture book progresses, more and more people will join the cause, culminating in the multitude that marches in honor of César when he died in 1993. In this penultimate scene, the illustration asserts the power of collaboration—of relying on the strengths of others in the movement for justice—by showing different facets of society coming together. There are children as well as older adults. A few people have backpacks, thus representing high school and college-age students. Two matachines are in the image, as well as a man with long hair and a beard, perhaps denoting a hip professor. All these people uniting reinforces the importance of collaboration in social justice activism. In this illustration, young readers *see* the result of Dolores and César's work mentioned on the preceding pages, "For thirty years, Dolores and Cesar worked and listened and talked and marched—side by side." Through Dolores and César's engagement with the community and invitation to others to join the struggle, the picture book informs the reader that the activists have created a new reality in which the power of inclusion, of interconnectivity founded on unity as posited by Keating, is the foundational reason for their social justice successes.

By situating the importance of "side by side," the picture book, we argue, also displaces the masculine hero story that for many years has positioned César Chávez at the front of a movement and places in its stead a radical new way of seeing the world. *Side by Side / Lado a lado*, by rewriting the important role of Dolores Huerta in the farmworker movement and by grounding success in collaboration and community, provides young readers a vision of what that new reality looks like:

> Then something special happened. Dolores and Cesar met.
>
> Dolores saw that Cesar had great faith. His dreams would bring hope to thousands of farmworkers.
>
> Cesar saw that Dolores had great courage. She would stand up and fight for what was right.
>
> Side by side, Dolores and Cesar began their journey.

In this way, *Side by Side / Lado a lado* rewrites one of the more powerful (male-dominated) narratives of Chicanx history. By foregrounding the work of Dolores Huerta and placing her at equal level with César Chávez, the book esteems her accomplishments and suggests to young female readers their ability to make significant change like Dolores. A

FIGURE 1.2 Joe Cepeda, Farmworkers march in honor of César Chávez. *Side by Side / Lado a lado: The Story of Dolores Huerta and Cesar Chavez / La historia de Dolores Huerta y César Chávez* by Monica Brown and illustrated by Joe Cepeda. Copyright © Joe Cepeda.

brief review of scholarly as well as popular work indeed demonstrates the lack of recognition given to Huerta. Put simply, in the history books Huerta is not side by side with Chávez. By presenting them side by side, the picture book undoes the binary of male/female, leader/follower. Yet it does not simply invert the binary but places the two activists as collaborative companions on a journey. Even at the end of the book when Dolores seems to be leading marches alone after César's death, we learn "Dolores still works and marches for justice for the poor."

Side by Side / Lado a lado, by rewriting the important role of Dolores Huerta in the farmworker movement and by grounding success in collaboration and community, provides young readers with conocimiento mirrors for their burgeoning activism. In describing the source of her power to fight injustices, Anzaldúa notes that "las raíces that sustain and nourish me are implanted in the landscape of my youth, my grandmother's stories of la Llorona, my father's quiet strength, the persevering energy de la gente who work in the fields" (*Light / Luz* 67). It is our belief that books on historical and cultural figures matter, namely, because of the importance of knowledge about the past to current young readers, specifically to young seasonal and migrant farmworkers. The vital difference between injustices in the past and injustices now is that we have books on farmworker justice and activism to challenge current injustices and embolden young activists. *Side by Side / Lado a lado*, in this sense, is crucial in this endeavor to right present injustices by centering a long history of resistance at the core of the Latinx experience for young readers. Knowing about "las raíces" makes new realities possible. In this regard, rewriting the role Dolores Huerta in the movement creates, for readers, a new root that will sustain and nourish them. As Anzaldúa notes, such *raíces* become "your spiritual ground of being, your connection to your inner self, which is your greatest strength" (*Light / Luz* 68). The past, in this model proposed by *Side by Side / Lado a lado*, is a source of great strength and as such a source of great cultural wealth.

Tomás and the Library Lady: Conocimiento Storytelling

The picture book *Tomás and the Library Lady* is based on the experiences of Tomás Rivera (1935–1984), a migrant farmworker from Texas who became a distinguished author of Chicanx literature, founder of the Chicano literary movement, professor, and university administrator.⁷ *Tomás and the Library Lady* centers on one particular, significant experience in the life of young Tomás: his encounter with books. Rivera's great accomplishments, the picture book highlights, begin in an Iowa library where he develops a friendship with a local librarian. In this way, the picture book positions Rivera's later achievements as emanating from the monumental moment when Tomás finds what worlds can open and what joy can be found in such explorations by the simple task of reading.

The picture book begins with Tomás—tired, hot, and longing for "his own bed, in his own house in Texas"—as he travels in the family's old rusty car to Iowa for corn-picking season. While the parents work the fields, Tomás plays ball with little brother Enrique and brings buckets of water to his parents; he also listens to the stories of Papá Grande (his beloved grandfather), "the best storyteller of the family." In one such instance, Papá Grande, under the shade of a tree, tells a legend of a man in the forest: "'*En un tiempo pasado*,' Papá Grande began. 'Once upon a time . . . on a windy night a man was riding a horse through a forest. The wind was howling, *whooooooooo*, and the leaves were blowing, *whish, whish* . . .'" Tomás loves the stories. However, because he knows the ending to all of Papá Grande's stories, his grandfather urges him to visit the library: "There are many more [stories] in the library. You are big enough to go by yourself. Then you can teach us new stories." Tomás heeds his grandfather's request and visits the library the next day.

As the narrative transitions between life in the fields and the library we notice that it further moves from the oral tradition exemplified by the grandfather to textual communities, which will be exemplified in the person of the library lady. And yet it would be a fallacy, we argue, to see the temporal arc of the narrative, as it traces Tomás's journey from his grandfather's stories to books in the library, as a linear model of progress in which textual literacy is a more advanced and thus a better form of art or meaning making than oral storytelling. For one, the picture book is clear that the impetus for the library visit comes from Papá Grande. In fact, it is Papá Grande who understands that Tomás's growth, if it is to continue, will take place at the library.

Breaking down this false dichotomy between orality and literacy, we posit, places Tomás on the path toward conocimiento, for as Anzaldúa tells us, "storytelling and reading and listening to stories is not only how we make sense of ourselves, our lives, and our place in the world, and how we make the Self. Storytelling is healing when it expands the

FIGURE 1.3 Raúl Colón, Papá Grande tells a story beneath a tree.
Illustration by Raúl Colón, copyright © 1997 by Raúl Colón.
Used by permission of Alfred A. Knopf, an imprint of Random
House Children's Books, a division of Penguin Random House LLC.
All rights reserved.

autohistorias (self-narratives) of the tellers and the listeners, when it broadens the person that we are" (*Light / Luz* 177). Disrupting a linear model of education that insists on seeing textual literacy as superior in turn allows us to see orality and literacy as complementary modes of learning wherein the true objective is making sense of the world, our place in it, and, what is more, our sense of self. As Anzaldúa explains, healing comes as conocimiento expands our horizons, of self and of others. In the picture book, Tomás is pointed toward the library so that the stories he reads will continue his growth and, importantly, so that, as his grandfather tells him, "Then you can teach us new stories." At stake, therefore, is the continued personal growth of Tomás and the communal growth that correspondingly will develop as Tomás tells his migrant community the new stories he discovers.

Tomás's journey, it would seem, is circuitous as it winds its way from under the shade of a tree to the library and back again. Thus, while Tomás first finds joy in his grandfather's stories, his visit to the library offers him the possibility of bringing that critical knowledge back to this family and community. Further, as the picture book reveals, the two modes of storytelling inflect each other in young Tomás's experience. Later in the narrative, after Tomás has visited and has checked out books from the library, for example, Papá Grande asks Tomás to read aloud from the library book: "'Read to me in English,' said Papá Grande. Tomás read about tiger eyes shining brightly in the jungle at night. He roared like a huge tiger. Papá, Mamá, and Enrique laughed. They came and sat near him to hear his story." In reading from the library books aloud, Tomás draws his family into the story. He combines the content of a picture book (a literary text) with traditional oral storytelling techniques—words, gestures, and sounds that engross the audience. The corresponding illustration reinforces this fusion of the text with the performative voice; Tomás reads from the book with Papá Grande looking intently at him and the family huddled around. In this regard, by reading the library book in the style of his storytelling grandfather, Tomás widens his family's world by exposing them to new narratives. Not only does he bridge orality and textual literacy, he likewise increases the family's bond as an interpretive community, to draw on theorist Stanley Fish's term, in their shared understanding of these stories (484). Given the challenges the family faces, due to discrimination in the United States based on race, ethnicity, language, occupation, and socioeconomic status, this sense of community offers much in the way of surviving and thriving.

FIGURE 1.4 Raúl Colón, Tomás reads to his family. Illustration by Raúl Colón, copyright © 1997 by Raúl Colón. Used by permission of Alfred A. Knopf, an imprint of Random House Children's Books, a division of Penguin Random House LLC. All rights reserved.

Tomás and the Library Lady's understanding of orality and literacy likewise positions young Latinx readers to seek value in the full composite of their lives. Since literacy is associated with US mainstream culture and orality with traditional Latinx cultures, *Tomás and the Library Lady*'s presentation of these modes as a kind of continuum proves striking. This is especially true given the historical and contemporary tensions over orality and literacy in the western world. Walter Ong in *Orality and Literacy* reminds that understanding the relationship between orality and literacy and the implications of this relationship "calls for wide, even vast, learning, painstaking thought and careful statement. Not only are the issues deep and complex, but they also engage our own biases" (2). These biases can take on racial/ethnic overtones, as folklore scholar David Shuldiner points out in his article on the debate over orality versus literacy in public education. For many traditional cultures, including that of Tomás's family, orality serves as a primary mode of learning, in contrast to US mainstream schools where textual literacy is champion (Shuldiner 194). Oral storytelling also serves as a way of transmitting culture and, as Shari Stone-Mediatore underscores, of resisting oppression by maintaining control of one's self-representation (23). By presenting orality and literacy as two parallel "vehicles for learning" (Shuldiner 198), *Tomás and the Library Lady* invites readers to value both modes. When readers witness the joy of Tomás as he listens to his grandfather and as he finds book "treasures" at the town dump, they learn the value of both. *Tomás and the Library Lady* thus dismisses the idea that learning can only occur in one particular place—either in the oral history of the culture of origin or in US mainstream educational establishments. Papá Grande's request for Tomás to find new stories at the library thus encourages a view of learning, and by extension identity, that is inclusive of both.

Understanding orality and literacy as complementary modes of learning, as opposed to a hierarchy of value, and seeing the circular route of learning espoused by Papá Grande further clarifies the dynamic between Tomás and his grandfather. If, as we suggest, Tomás is on the path toward conocimiento, that is, of awareness and healing, he is placed on this path by his grandfather. It is our argument that Papá Grande's oral storytelling, and the tradition from which it unfolds, present Tomás with vital and enriching possibilities for nurturing his awareness of the world, of his community, and of himself. Once on this path, Tomás is better able to see his interconnectedness with his family and his community.

Further, we believe that his growing conocimiento also allows him to see his interconnectedness with others, who may be outside of his family and community. In this way, conocimiento is vital for its generative possibilities. As Anzaldúa notes, "to be in conocimiento with another person or group is to share knowledge, pool resources, meet each other, compare liberation struggles and social movements' histories, share how we confront institutional power, and process and heal wounds" (*Light / Luz* 91). This plays out in the picture book with the other titular character, the library lady.

Enacting Conocimiento

In many ways, Tomás, a young, Mexican American migrant boy, and the library lady, a tall, educated, Iowan, adult female, could not be more different; and yet books as well as Tomás's burgeoning conocimiento bring them together. Tomás and the library lady first meet at the library, where, during his first visit, she asks Tomás about his reading interests, which are tigers and dinosaurs. The library lady then offers to check out library books in her name so Tomás can take them with him to share the books with his family. Their relationship continues to grow with each trip Tomás takes to the library. As their relationship grows, we also see the beginnings of conocimiento between Tomás and the library lady, specifically in the way they "share knowledge, pool resources" as they confront the boundaries that divide them in order to "process and heal wounds" (*Light / Luz* 91).

One of these divisions, a wound between them, it would seem, is Spanish language. As Gloria Anzaldúa reminds us in *Borderlands / La Frontera*, "So, if you want to really hurt me, talk badly about my language. Ethnic identity is twin skin to linguistic identity—I am my language. Until I can take pride in my language, I cannot take pride in myself" (81). Yet in the face of English-only movements and state laws that ban or otherwise discourage bilingual education,[8] *Tomás and the Library Lady* conceives of literacy broadly in its inclusion of English and Spanish in the text. Designed for readers in early elementary school, the text is written primarily in English with select phrases in Spanish. This inclusion of Spanish in the text and the celebration of Tomás's Spanish-language ability affirms the value of the Spanish language and bilingualism. The picture book also takes an important step forward by having Tomás teach the library lady Spanish:

Tomás would smile. He liked being the teacher. The library lady pointed to a book. "Books is *libro*," said Tomás.
"*Libro*," said the library lady.
"*Pájaro*," said Tomás, flapping his arms.
The library lady laughed. "Bird," she said.

By asking Tomás to teach her key words in Spanish, the library lady draws on Tomás's expertise and affirms Tomás by shifting him from the role of student to teacher. He indeed becomes the expert of the Spanish language in this particular moment. Tomás widens the path of conocimiento by inviting, via his Spanish instruction, the library lady to join him and his family in newfound forms of awareness and understanding. Near the end of the picture book, as Tomás and Papá Grande visit the library to say goodbye and thank the library lady with a small package of pan dulce from Tomás's mom, the library lady does her best to speak Spanish with Papá Grande: "*Buenas Tardes, señor*" and "*Gracias.*" With these courteous words, the library lady proves Tomás's ability as a teacher and extends her kindness to Papá Grande. In this way, the use of Spanish alongside English by characters in the text models the possibility of using multiple languages as an asset; it validates diversity in language and culture for young Latinx readers.

We end our examination of *Tomás and the Library Lady* with an anecdote. Asked to describe what she would take from the picture book, one young reader at an elementary school that author Pat Mora visited in Des Moines, Iowa, commented, "Friendships can develop between two people with a common interest. It was like that in the story because they had a common interest in reading and they became friends" (Des Moines). This young reader wisely notes that readers are leaders namely because they can bridge differences and build communities.

Books—a shared interest of Tomás and the library lady—create magic, imagining worlds while also allowing others into those imagined worlds. The last stanza of the poem "Library Magic," penned by Mora in honor of summer reading and dedicated to Tomás Rivera, underscores what comes from reading:

"¡Vamos! Let's all go to the library!"
Join the fun, a treasure house that's free.
Bring your friends and family.
Stories, computers, maps and more,

facts, fun. Enter the magic door.
Like Tomás, open books and soar.
Be a reader. Explore galore.

Reading, as the poem suggests, allows for the broadening of one's world. Literacy allows for explorations through fiction, nonfiction, technology, and maps. Here, readers become explorers who chart new territories. This poem, like the picture book *Tomás and the Library Lady*, points to literacy as a powerful tactic. It encourages children and youth to grow through reading, and to invite others along for the journey, to "bring your friends and family." It is not surprising that *Tomás and the Library Lady* ends with Tomás in the back seat of the family's car reading "a shiny new book," a gift from the library lady, as the family heads back to Texas. In that moment, "Papá Grande smiled and said, 'More stories for the new storyteller.'" With these words his grandfather affirms Tomás in his role. Tomás is learner and reader at the library and in school, and he is a storyteller for his family. He brings back good stories to refresh, unite, and sustain them, and to carry them into new worlds.

The Development of an Artist-Activist in *Under the Feet of Jesus*

In "The Truth Our Bodies Tell" Aurora Levins Morales tell us that the neoliberal imperative "to turn every possible gift life offers into private money and extract from our bodies and our planet, our cultures and our ordinary needs, every single penny's worth of profit, no matter what the cost" (48) is the reason that her mother "died of a blood cancer linked to one of the pesticides marketed and often imposed on farmers in Puerto Rico and around the world, by companies repurposing World War II nerve gasses and expertise to kill insects while promising better living for all" (47). This essay in *Medicine Stories* is her histerimonia, "because 'testimonio' comes from the custom of Roman men swearing on their testicles, which I don't have, and because the idea of hysteria has been used for many centuries to dismiss and silence those who are considered unreliable witnesses, especially women" (48). Levins Morales's histerimonia, an embodied and creative act of truth-telling, allows her not simply to write about suppressed knowledge and oppressed peoples; she writes from within them, as one of them.

For our purposes, Levins Morales, one of the essayists in *This Bridge*

Called My Back, along with Gloria Anzaldúa, Cherríe Moraga, and others, artfully positions us to see the financial depravity at the core of injustices in the agricultural fields as well as ways to challenge, via her counter-storytelling form, the histerimonia, "the ruling definitions of human worth, the nature of work, of ability, of aliveness, what it means to produce, what we should value" (49). The reason is simple: *Under the Feet of Jesus* engages such questions of injustices in the field and how they impact the most vulnerable—the young, impoverished, and/or undocumented. Like Levins Morales's essay, *Under the Feet of Jesus* challenges "the ruling definitions of human worth" through the creative acts of young female protagonist Estrella who resists and advocates for her struggling farmworker community. Estrella's thoughts, words, and actions draw attention to the injustices and offer hope for resistance.

With the term "artist-activist" we hope to articulate a kind of creative visionary who takes time and energy, utilizing imaginative thoughts, words, and actions as maneuvers for justice.[9] Estrella, in this way, is an artist in formation whose creative work cannot be separated from her activism. Her creative work in the novel recalls Chela Sandoval and Guisela Latorre's term "artivist": "a hybrid neologism that signifies work created by individuals who see an organic relationship between art and activism" (82). For the scholars, this melding of art and activism "advances the expression of a mode of liberatory consciousness," specifically Anzaldúa's *la conciencia mestiza*, which allows for a breaking down of all kinds of borders and finding the convergences in "creative expression, social activism, and self-empowerment" (82).

Under the Feet of Jesus establishes this association with artists by following the conventions of the künstlerroman or artist's development novel genre,[10] as Dan Latimer points out in his analysis of the novel (342). While Estrella is not a typical artist, she possesses qualities of artists—the ability to see and express truths of their lives and their surroundings in inspired ways. Further, she goes beyond the prototypical künstlerroman quest of finding her place within society; indeed, the novel explores the "crucial effects particular to ethnic contexts and patterns of economic deprivation," to use the words of Annie Eysturoy in her analysis of künstlerroman embodiments in the Chicana novel (134). Put another way, the abuses Estrella witnesses in her community emboldens her to respond, and she becomes an artist-activist in her use of creative tactics on the quest for justice. Anzaldúa highlights this connection between conocimiento and creative response: "A heightened consciousness or awareness that I call 'conocimiento' and some call 'love' (which may be the same thing) stirs the artist to take action, propels her toward the act of making. This conocimiento initiates the relationship between self-knowledge and creative work" (*Light / Luz* 40). Through her knowledge of self and community, Estrella is propelled "toward the act of making."

Words to Comfort, Words to Fight

Estrella's family in *Under the Feet of Jesus* is desperately poor. They move from job to job in California's Central Valley and, like many real-life migrant workers and families, must endure terrible working conditions and grueling work for little pay. Mere survival, that is, keeping food on the table and staying healthy, is a clear objective for Estrella and her family. Given these dire circumstances, *Under the Feet of Jesus* poignantly and artfully highlights the need for artist-activists who utilize words and stories to build and maintain community, to see deeper realities, and to speak and act for those who cannot do so for themselves. Put another way, artist-activists use words and stories toward reparative and restorative ends, for themselves as well as for their community.

Estrella first learns of the power of words from Perfecto Flores, her mother's companion. While the actual lesson revolves around the names of tools and their use, such as claw hammer, screwdriver, crescent wrench, hacksaw, sledgehammer, pry bar, chisel, and axe, she soon learns that the names "gave meaning to the tools. Tools to build, bury, tear down, rearrange, and repair" (26). While the scene begins with Estrella exasperated because the "curves and tails of the tools made no sense and the shapes were as foreign and meaningless to her as chalky lines on the blackboard" (25), she realizes that words, like tools, can "build, bury, tear down, rearrange and repair" (26). The clarity given by this moment of conocimiento allows her to remember how a teacher once asked her why her mother never gave her a bath. As Estrella gains awareness of the power of words, she realizes, for the first time, that "words could become as excruciating as rusted nails piercing the heels of her bare feet" (25). Estrella, as her conocimiento awareness grows, comes "to understand how essential it was to know these things" (26). It was then that "she began to read" (26). In our interpretation, reading means more to Estrella that simply understanding the chalky lines on the blackboard. Reading, in this sense, also entails understanding the structures and systems that oppress, like rusted nails on bare feet, and which via conocimiento need to be torn down and rearranged. Words, in this sense, become tools that stir an artist-activist "to take action, [that] propels her toward the act of making" (Anzaldúa, *Light / Luz* 40).

Estrella builds and maintains community in many ways with her words, drawing on words differently according to what each person needs. For example, she entertains her younger siblings with song and dance, allowing them to release their tension from being shut up in the house all day: "Estrella had carried the fussing twins in the hoop of her arms, and sat them in front of an overturned zinc bucket and handed them wooden spoons" (18). Although this angers her mother Petra, the children enjoy their time and Estrella, too, in her dance "like a loca," finds an outlet from her frustration and grows her bond with her siblings (19). Estrella also intellectually engages her friend and fellow fieldhand Alejo, who aspires to be a geologist, by discussing the nearby La Brea tar pits with him. While the two lay under the old Ford, escaping from the heat, Alejo shares how oil is made. Estrella asks him, "You like to talk, don't you?"—making it apparent that Alejo has few people with whom to share his passion in the farmworker community (87). In her relationship with Maxine Devridge, the novel underscores her ability to build community with someone considered dangerous and an outsider in the migrant community. The Devridge family is infamous in the migrant community for violence and for uncleanliness, causing the other migrants to pitch their tents far away from the family (28–29). Estrella comes to overlook these issues, at first because Maxine shares books and magazines, and later she attempts to become the girl's friend.

Estrella builds this community most poignantly by thanking Perfecto, and thus she emphasizes the power of words as the building blocks of community. Near the end of the novel, just after Perfecto has driven Alejo to the hospital Estrella turns to him and says, "Thank you, Perfecto Flores" (155). The experience deeply impacts him, as no one has thanked him before:

> Perfecto sat behind the steering wheel, the warm hum of the engine under his feet. He had given this country his all, and in this land that used his bones for kindling, in this land that never once in the thirty years he lived and worked, never once said thank you, this young woman who could be his granddaughter had said the words with such honest gratitude, he was struck by how deeply these words touched him. (155)

As this example shows, Estrella uses language as a tactical tool of affirmation. She knows that words could become weapons to inflict pain; however, she chooses instead to use the words to comfort Perfecto.

While *Under the Feet of Jesus* illustrates how Estrella builds community by listening attentively to others and by reassuring them with words that build rather than tear down, the novel also showcases Estrella's conocimiento awareness of the deep structures and systems at play in their lives. For example, in the conversation between Estrella and Alejo, as they lay under the Ford to escape the heat and discuss the nearby La Brea tar pits and the origin of oil, Estrella's ability to understand the physical reality at another level becomes apparent:

> —You know where oil comes from? He asked in a whisper . . .
> —Probably a leak from the motor.
> —I don't mean that.
> —Why are you asking me?
> —If we don't have oil, we don't have gasoline.
> —Good. We'd stay put then.
> —Stuck, more like it. Stuck.
> —Aren't we now? (86)

Alejo then explains how bones, rocks, leaves and other debris fell into the sea millions of years ago and eventually became tar oil. While Alejo looks at the tar pits from a geological perspective, Estrella, as an artist-activist, understands this process as a metaphor for the abuse of her people. Estrella's thoughts return to the tar pits when the white suburban nurse charges them excessively for minimal services:

> She remembered the tar pits. Energy money, the fossilized bones of energy matter. How bones made oil and oil made gasoline. The oil was made from their bones, and it was their bones that kept the nurse's car from not halting on some highway, kept her on her way to Daisyfield to pick up her boys at six. It was their bones that kept the air conditioning in the cars humming, that kept them moving on the long dotted line on the map. Their bones. Why couldn't the nurse see that? (148)

In making this leap from a physical to a metaphoric level, Estrella does the work of the artist by seeing beyond a physical reality.[11] Her weary community, busy in the fields and at home, does not often have the time or energy to see beyond the immediate reality, thus Estrella sees beyond for them. As Latimer signals, "The petroleum becomes in her mind, the correlative, the estranged value, of the labor of her underpaid, under-appreciated people" (335). This ability to see deeper realities leads Estrella to speak and act out for justice.

Under the Feet of Jesus further highlights the artist-activist role of speaking for those who cannot speak for themselves in the central action of the novel. When the family is at the clinic with Alejo, attempting to get help for his illness, Estrella becomes the literal and figurative voice for her people. Due to his illness from the pesticides, Alejo physically cannot speak and Perfecto and Petra are unable to communicate in English (126). When nurse explains that the family must take Alejo to the hospital and charges them for the visit, Estrella becomes angry. She tries to convince the nurse to let Perfecto fix the leaky toilet or do other work around the clinic in exchange for medical services. However, the nurse refuses the offer and takes their last $9.07, claiming that she is making them a deal as the original bill was $15.00. After the family returns to the car, knowing that they have no money for fuel to go to the hospital or to pay at the hospital, Estrella decides to take action. She returns to the clinic with Perfecto's crowbar in hand, and demands the nurse return the money:

—Give us back our money.
—Excuse me?
. . .
—I'll smash these windows first, then all these glass jars if you don't give us back our money.
—You listen here!
Estrella slammed the crowbar down on the desk, shattering the school pictures of the nurse's children, sending the pencils flying to the floor, and breaking the porcelain cat with a nurse's cap into pieces. (149)

This scene elucidates Estrella's work with both words and action on behalf of her people. Curiously, she combines words (a metaphoric tool) with a literal tool, the crowbar. She later explains the need for this violent act, rooted in oppression: "They make you that way, she sighed with resignation. She tried to understand what happened herself. You talk and talk and talk to them and they ignore you. But you pick up a crowbar and break the pictures of their children, and all of a sudden they listen real fast" (151). Her violent words, which threaten the nurse and her office, recall Judith Butler's insistence in *Excitable Speech* that "oppressive language is not a substitute for the experience of violence. It enacts its own kind of violence" (9). However, in this case, the threat is not enough to get the money back and Estrella also must act to save Alejo. Mary Louise Pratt in "Harm's Way: Language and The Contemporary Arts of War" suggests that this scene in the novel "enacts the commonsense relation between language and violence . . . : Violence erupts when language fails, violence is called forth by the failure of language" (1526–27). In this way, the novel takes an assertive step in its insistence on the use of thought, word, *and* action. The artist-activist is one who must move against injustice consistently with words and with actions, too.

Summoning All Who Strayed

The title of the novel comes from the fact that Estrella's mother Petra entrusts her life and her family's well-being to Jesus, literally placing their precious documents under the feet of a small plaster statue of Jesucristo. When the statue falls and breaks, Petra and the family are distraught, given this symbolic beheading.[12] In the final scenes of the novel, shortly after Petra decides that she cannot repair the statue, she heads outside. Before she does, she licks her fingers and sizzles out the wicks on the candles. Outside, Perfecto is deep in thought about their future. As she makes her way toward him, she is clutching the head of the statue of Jesucristo in her hand. If anyone can fix it, she now understands, it is Perfecto.

While this scene is unfolding, in another part of the house, the smoke from the extinguished candles bothers Estrella. Seeking fresh air, she climbs out of the window and walks toward the barn. The novel ends with Estrella climbing up the rafters of the barn and standing on the termite-softened shakes that remind her of the snake under the feet of Jesus in the statue: "Estrella remained as immobile as an angel standing on the verge of faith. Like the chiming bells of the great cathedrals, she believed her heart powerful enough to summon home all those who strayed" (176). Ellen McCracken asserts that in this scene, "Estrella herself symbolically replaces the image [of Jesus] as she stands tall atop the barn" (183). Put another way, Estrella now is fully cognizant of her role as an artist-activist who aids her community.

Thus, while the novel begins with Estrella learning about the power of words, it ends with an artist-activist ready to change the world. Estrella's words of comfort for Perfecto, her attentive listening of Alejo's stories, and her understanding of the structures and systems that oppress her and her family reveal that Estrella will be the change the world desperately needs. Estrella, in other words, utilizes conocimiento to imagine new realities. This moment, as she stands like an angel summoning all who stray, evokes Anzaldúa's concept of *ensueño* in which dreams and hopes trend toward new realities:

> I use the word "ensueño" in several guises: as illusion and fantasy; as un sueño que se hace realidad, a dream that becomes a reality; as a way to bridge the reality of the dream with the reality of the nondream . . . A type of creative fantasy, ensueños are simply another reality. The reasoning mind's reality is not higher than the imagination's. I am interested in the place/space (nepantla) where realities interact and imaginative shifts happen. (*Light / Luz* 35)

It is our understanding that Estrella, as an artist-activist, demonstrates the ability to see beyond the daily struggles of farmwork to the injustice embedded in it. As she stands on the barn roof, furthermore, we believe that she utilizes ensueño as a way to *dream* the new reality into being. This is to say that she imagines an ensueño as simply another reality that will interact with other realities. In these imaginative shifts, new epistemologies and new worlds come into being.

Ensueños, in this sense, become a powerful component of conocimiento mirrors. Like Estrella, Latinx youth in the agricultural fields often are narrowly defined by their poverty, by their work which is seen as menial, and by deleterious racist notions. By seeing themselves through Estrella's conocimiento-fueled activism, young Latinx readers can begin the process of understanding words as tools and the way those tools can be used to tear down systems of oppression. In this way, *Under the Feet of Jesus* invites young Latinx readers to become artist-activists—"authors" and "actors" with their words and actions on behalf of their communities. Before new realities can be created, Anzaldúa reminds us, they first must exist as a dream, un ensueño. Our hope in this is that young Latinx readers of *Under the Feet of Jesus*, especially those in the agricultural fields, see in this conocimiento mirror the way they, too, can utilize their ensueños to create new realities.

Conclusion

The role of conocimiento mirrors is perhaps best evidenced in the biographical note on Tomás Rivera in *Tomás and the Library Lady*. Accompanying the note, a black and white photograph shows Rivera smiling in a library with a document in his hand. The text below the photograph shares biographical details about Rivera's life, including his experiences as a migrant worker and later as a writer, professor, administrator, and national education leader. Readers further learn that "the campus library [at University of California at Riverside] now bears the name of the boy who was encouraged by a librarian in Iowa." Young readers, in this way, are invited to envision themselves, like Tomás Rivera, moving from the roles of migrant farmworkers to positions of leadership that are made possible through reading and education. Much like the young Tomás who found a new world in the library, the biographical note suggests to young readers that they, too, will be able to withstand difficult circumstances, grow their communities, and ultimately thrive in their professional lives.

Similar to *Tomás and the Library Lady*, *Side by Side / Lado a lado* shows young readers how important historical figures, in this case Dolores Huerta and César Chávez, nurtured conocimiento notions as children and young adults and then utilized vital aspects of conocimiento in activist work. For both picture books, as Aurora Levins Morales reminds us, history "is a powerful resource with which to explain and justify the present and create agendas for the future" (59).

Under the Feet of Jesus brings our critical eye into the present by showcasing how Estrella learns of the power of words and knowledge, that is, how she gains conocimiento. Words are tools, the novel tells, that can be used, like the crowbar, to fight injustices. Moreover, the novel ends with Estrella having an ensueño in which she believes she can summon all who have strayed, or put another way, those who like her family are lost to the world's reckoning. In this way, the novel is future laden, as Estrella's ensueño signals an agenda for the future. Conocimiento mirrors, in this sense, not only allow young readers to see themselves actively changing the world of the present, but also they can allow for the imagining of new realities in the future.

Side by Side / Lado a lado, Tomás and the Library Lady, and *Under the Feet of Jesus* enact moments of critical self-knowledge and awareness that push us into "confronting our social sickness with new tools and practices whose goal is to affect a shift" (Anzaldúa, *Light / Luz* 19). All three books, we believe, provide conocimiento mirrors in which young Latinx readers can see themselves, their histories, and their present realities reflected, and further find their potential futures mirrored as they begin to imagine the possibilities of activist leadership for their generation. In this way, conocimiento pushes us into engaging with the reparative qualities of reading, with the transformational possibilities entailed in imagining new realities.

CHAPTER TWO

Border Kids in the Land of Nepantla

En este lugar entre medio, nepantla, two or more forces clash and are held teetering on the verge of chaos, a state of entreguerras. These tensions between extremes create cracks or tears in the membrane surrounding, protecting, and containing the different cultures and their perspectives. Nepantla is the place where at once we are detached (separated) and attached (connected) to each of our several cultures.
GLORIA ANZALDÚA / *Light in the Dark / Luz en el oscuro*

In the poem that opens the first chapter of *Borderlands / La Frontera*, Gloria Anzaldúa describes the border as a "1,950 miles-long open wound / dividing a *pueblo*, a culture" (24). Anzaldúa goes on to state that this *"herida abierta"* (24) remains in a constant state of transition, as the "lifeblood of two worlds merging to form a third country—a border culture" (25). This border culture is the subject of this chapter. At play in our study is an examination of how border kids, that is, children and young adults who live in this land of nepantla or in-betweenness, become *"un puente tendido"* (25), a bridge between the United States and Mexico. As Anzaldúa describes in her poem, children play, moving across the border line freely, connecting the spaces: "Beneath the iron sky / Mexican children kick their soccer ball across, / run after it, entering the U.S." (24). Our argument is that border kids through the processes of conocimiento challenge and contest the divisions that seemingly attempt to "distinguish *us* from *them*" (25, italics in original) and from them construct new worlds where languages merge, where one cultural imaginary unites both sides of the border, and, as such, where nepantla, the in-between space/interstitial place, becomes home.

This chapter considers two books for young readers, Guadalupe García McCall's young adult verse novel *Under the Mesquite* (2011) and David Bowles's young adult poetry collection *They Call Me Güero: A Border Kid's Poems* (2018). Set in the US/Mexico borderlands, both books foreground the brokenness caused by the geopolitical and physical border between the United States and Mexico. At the same time, the books highlight the continual processes of awareness, interconnectivity, and healing in the midst of fragmented border spaces. *Under the Mesquite* and *They Call Me Güero*, we argue, seek to heal this trauma through a "labor of re-visioning and re-membering" (Anzaldúa, *Light / Luz* 124), that is, through counter-storytelling in which "la búsqueda de conocimiento, of seeking experiences that'll give you purpose, give your life meaning, give you a sense of belonging" is a "quest story of ordeal and distress, cyclical life stages, and identity transformations" with a return, "bringing new knowledge to share with others in your communities" (143). Conocimiento, in this way, involves a resolute desire to "rewrite the stories of loss and recovery, exile and homecoming, disinheritance and recuperation, stories that lead out of passivity and into agency, out of devalued into valued lives" (143). Thus, while the border is a broken place and the United States has followed the path of desconocimiento—allowing ignorance, fear, and hatred to fuel misguided views of who belongs in the national imaginary—these books serve as critical tools for Latinx young readers to counter this desconocimiento. Through their stories, *Under the Mesquite* and *They Call Me Güero* ask readers to learn from and to participate in the ongoing and continual process of "re-visioning and re-membering" (Anzaldúa, *Light / Luz* 124), of "unmaking and making" (Anzaldúa, "Let Us Be" 312), the US/Mexico border region. In this way, the books sow the seeds of conocimiento with the prospect that these seeds will come to fruition in the lives of young readers. Our objective in this chapter is to propose such a way forward, a path funded by our belief that conocimiento—offered to readers via books—yields fruit hundreds of times the size of the seed. Books plant the seeds of conocimiento in readers, young and old. Reading, in this way, is transformative.

Under the Mesquite

THE TRANSPLANTING OF LUPITA

Under the Mesquite, a künstlerroman verse novel, traces the story of Lupita through her high school years in Eagle Pass, Texas, a border town in the "Valley" (the Rio Grande Valley of Southeast Texas) that nestles itself next to Piedras Negras, Coahuila on the other side of the border. Lupita and her family are not originally from El Águila, The Eagle (as they playfully call their town): "When I was six years old, / our family left our beloved Mexico / and moved to *los Estados Unidos*" (10). Once in the United States, the family begins the process of setting down roots, as evidenced in the literal plantings in the family's yard: a tall mulberry tree and a garden of "rosebushes, / rows and rows of them, / all the way down to the street" (10).

As is common for people who live in the borderlands, Lupita and her family move seamlessly between two worlds, in geography and language:

> Growing up *en los Estados Unidos*,
> every weekend we were
> more than eager to escape
> the suburban world of *El Águila*
> to indulge in the simple pleasures
> of Papi's rural hometown
> across the border, where we
> were true Mexicans, for a day. (142)

Therefore, even as Lupita and her family adjust to life in the United States, they refuse to live solely on one side of the border, in one world. Instead they flow back and forth across the borderline each weekend as part of their family routine. The following passage adds to our understanding of what this means:

> The chain-link fence on the bridge
> was like a harp, and our fingers
> would play a joyful tune upon
> its rib cage as we traipsed along,
> looking down at the laughing
> waters of the Rio Grande
> until we reached that other world,
> the one we missed so much. (40)

In this, the border fence becomes a musical instrument that the family plays as they make their way across the international bridge. These kinds of complex dual allegiances become increasingly significant after Lupita's mother has been diagnosed with cancer. The summer of her chemo treatments, as they watch "Mami come and go / back and forth from the hospital / in a nauseated haze" (56), the family crosses "the border to meet / Abuela Inez at her church, / Nuestra Señora de Guadalupe"

(56–57). At church they light candles and pray for their mother: "Our only requests are / that the chemo treatments / ravaging her body / do not weaken her spirit" (57). The poem ends with the family eating elotes, toasted ears of corn sold by street vendors, in the plaza. Careful readers will pick up the spiritual ways in which the family finds solace in Mexico, and further, how this spiritual comfort is found in culturally resonant practices.

This brings us to a relevant question: What would happen if Lupita and her family followed the national script for assimilation in the United States? In other words, what if there were a *wall* inside this novel rather than fluid movement across the US/Mexico border each weekend for the family outing? Let us pretend, if you will, that *Under the Mesquite* was written specifically to prove the kinds of racist assimilation policies and practices we find common in the United States. This novel would feature an immigrant who, like Lupita, entered through official channels into the United States. Although the protagonist initially struggles to fit in due to differences in language and food customs, as illustrated in Lupita's poem "En Los Estados Unidos,"[1] immigrant literature often speaks of these obstacles as preludes to assimilation. This linear process of assimilation, based primarily on European immigration to the United States, conceives a slow thinning of ethnic identity with every subsequent year and every subsequent generation (Portes 149). For Lupita this would mean immigrating to the United States legally, encountering linguistic and cultural obstacles, and moving away from Mexico and the borderlands under the proper tutelage of American social and cultural practices. This narrative of assimilation provides a figurative road map for a journey that begins at the border and proceeds in linear fashion to a future where ethnic identity is but a soft glow.

And yet, as laughable as that kind of reading of *Under the Mesquite* seems, we also know that borders by their nature mean to divide and that the pressures for assimilation are strong. This brings us to another relevant question: What happens when people refuse to be divided? In other words, what do we make of Lupita and her family living in one world and traveling to the that other world, the one they missed so much?[2] With one foot planted on one side and one foot planted on the other, figurately and botanically speaking, *Under the Mesquite* asks young readers[3] to experience such resistances and from these imaginings position themselves to challenge *walls* that mean to divide, whether physical walls or figurative ones that seem to be sprouting up in schools and neighborhoods. In this, it is our argument that *Under the Mesquite* can be read as a resistance novel that proposes a composite of both sides of the border.

Instead of a wall in the text, *Under the Mesquite* imagines a new reality. In this, the novel, as a künstlerroman, utilizes a mesquite tree and what transpires "under the mesquite," namely, writing, to illustrate what living in two worlds means. While the title of the novel implies that there is one mesquite, in actuality we know that there are two mesquites in question. First, there is the mesquite in Mami's garden at their home in Texas that refuses to go away, of which Lupita says, "the mesquite is my confidant. / I lean back against its sturdy trunk / and read aloud every word / imprinted *en mi corazón*" (123). Then, the second mesquite grows in Mexico, at her grandmother's house, where Lupita convalesces following her mother's death:

> Later I find a tall mesquite
> to sit under;
> and with my pen in hand,
> I open my journal
> to a blank page and begin
> writing a whole new batch of poems,
> poems filled with memories
> and hope, because that's
> what Mami would've wanted. (195–96)

Two mesquites: one in the United States and one in Mexico. Space, in this regard is transformed, and the mesquites, much like her two homes in Mexico and the United States, become one. Lupita finds herself at home under the mesquite on both sides of the geopolitical border.

THE MAKING OF A NEPANTLERA-ROMAN

While *Under the Mesquite* can be classified generically as a künstlerroman,[4] a portrait of the artist as a young person, it should likewise, we suggest, be considered a *nepantlera-roman* (our term), a portrait of a nepantlera as a young resistance fighter. Our reading of *Under the Mesquite* posits that Lupita actively chooses to become a *nepantlera*, which as Anzaldúa notes, "To become *nepantleras*, we must choose to occupy intermediary spaces between worlds, choose to move between worlds like the ancient *chamanas* who choose to build bridges between worlds" (*Light / Luz* 93).

To become a nepantlera, however, is not an easy task. As Lupita finds out, it can be lonely and risky to position oneself between worlds. In the poem "Drama," for example, Lupita is instructed on ways to lose her accent. Her drama teacher, Mr. Cortés, gives the class candy Blow Pops and then instructs them and Lupita specifically to "'put these in, one on each side / of your mouth, *como ardilla listada*.' / He puffs out his cheeks with air / to demonstrate, making a chipmunk face" (66). He continues, "If you're serious about acting— / and I think you are—then you need to / lose your accent" (67). The poem ends with a surprised Lupita saying, "I have an accent?" (67).

What begins as a ubiquitous scene in which students in a drama class receive voice lessons turns quickly into one fraught with the politics of linguistic assimilation. Much like the use of marbles by Henry Higgins to rid Eliza Doolittle of her Cockney accent in *My Fair Lady*, the Blow Pops in this scene in *Under the Mesquite* have the disquieting intention of eliminating Lupita's accent, in this case the Mexican-ness in her speech. These "voice lessons" in short time become a divisive point for Lupita and her friends. In the poem entitled "To Be or Not to Be Mexican" (an allusion to Hamlet's soliloquy and with the same grave undertones), Lupita's friends mock her newfound ways of speaking:

"Anyone want my enchi-lady?"
Sarita says, picking up an enchilada
with her fork and showing it to
a group of our friends
who are sitting with us in the cafeteria.

I shake my head
and take a bite of my burrito.
When I look up again,
everyone around me is laughing,
but I don't get the joke. (78)

The jokes continue, this time with "tacos" as the word of choice: "Sarita glances at me sideways, / holds up a taco, and says, / 'How about a tay-co? / Anyone want a tay-co?'" (79). When Lupita stands up for herself, saying "I don't talk like that" (80), her friends point out:

"Yes, you do," Mireya jumps in.
"You talk like you're one of *them*."

> She spits out the word in disgust
> and looks down at her lunch tray,
> like she can't stand the sight of me.
>
> "One of *them*?" I ask.
>
> "Let me translate for you,"
> Sarita sneers. "You talk like
> you wanna be white." (80)

Like Lupita, readers are made to shudder at the insistence by Sarita to "translate" the subject of the conversation. The next gesture is just as cutting and hence as important:

> "What," Sarita asks, "you think you're
> Anglo now 'cause you're in Drama?
> You think you're better than us?"
>
> "No—"
>
> "Then stop trying to act like
> them," Mireya says accusingly.
> "You're Mexican, just like the rest of us.
> Look around you. Ninety-nine percent
> of this school is Mexican.
> Stop trying to be something you're not!" (81)

Again, readers may wince at the double entendre in this conversation on the words "act" and "drama," and how these two words combine to move beyond the limits of a simple lunchroom spat between friends. We can gather from Mireya's admonishment that people have choices as to how to act and perform their cultural identity. Lupita, to Mireya, is playing her role wrongly.

This scene posits a simple voice lesson—one in which the "voice" is normalized as white. Lupita's friends pick up on the nuance of ethnic identity long before she does. And, the episode ends with an appeal by Lupita for a more holistic view of her ethnic identity: "Being Mexican / means more than that. / It means being there for each other. / It's togetherness, like a *familia*. / We should be helping one another, / cheering our friends on, not trying / to bring them down" (83). Lupita's appeal does little to assuage her friends, and the last lines of the poem are more for her self-assurance than a convincing persuasion: *"I'm not acting white! I want to shout / after my so-called friends"* (83).

Lupita's words remind us that being Latinx should be more than language or any other arbitrary signifiers. Linguistic options as well as other identifiable Latinx traits should be a matter of choice; yet, there is a long history of language, specifically English, being used as cudgel to divide and marginalize, as Dina Gavrilos explains:

> studies point to the function of whiteness as silent "strategic rhetoric," constituting an invisible, universal, and normative racial position in everyday practices. This scholarship (from rhetorical scholars) helps explain the unspoken, taken-for-granted symbolic link between English and national identity that enacts hierarchical ethnic and racial divisions. English functions so powerfully as a culturally unifying symbol of national identity in mainstream national culture that its white, Anglo-specific roots seem invisible. (116)

The "voice lessons" thus are not simply about being "serious about acting"; they become silent, invisible agents of a cultural assimilation project whose goal is to link the English language and American national identity with whiteness and create divides along racial and ethnic lines. The "normalization" of voice in this scene seeks to pit those who oppose these instruments of discrimination and those, like Lupita, who lose their accents. The scene ends with Lupita and her friends, Sarita and Mireya, at loggerheads over the issue of linguistic assimilation. In this, readers are asked to witness the ways in which American cultural politics asks young Latinx people to choose between the tribes of "American" and "Mexican."

In this, it is imperative to underscore how easy it would be to misread *Under the Mesquite*. All that is required is to side with Lupita and dismiss Sarita and Mireya. All that is necessary is to point to a stellar student (Lupita) and suggest from her success in drama class (and later in University Interscholastic League [UIL] school tournaments) that she is a model for cultural and linguistic assimilation. We hear again the old "keys to success" story that is built around the idea of performing whiteness via the English language.[5] In effect, all that is required to misread *Under the Mesquite* is to build a *wall* in the text, positing the benefits of this linear process of assimilation that requires first that English is acquired and second that it is practiced in daily life, a movement toward Americanness that is code for whiteness. Thankfully, the text resists such a reading. On a linguistic level, the text includes many Spanish words and idioms, affirming those like Lupita who move easily between languages and thus for whom translanguaging is a part of daily life. This linguistic intermixing of vernacular English and Spanish shows ways of belonging that are indeed bilingual and bicultural.

While it may seem to some that no resolution has been found for Lupita in her drama class, it is precisely this lack of resolution that positions readers in the liminal spaces between cultures and nations, refusing, in this case, to choose either alternative. Instead, the text offers the possibility of a third space—straddling both alternatives. In this, *Under the Mesquite* positions young readers to consider the in-betweenness of Latinx identity, by holding them between worlds, asking them to dwell in the liminality where answers do not come easily and are always in the process of negotiation. In asking readers to suspend judgment, *Under the Mesquite* undercuts notions of Americanness as a by-product of English language choice. The poem "To Be or Not to Be" ends, but its lack of resolution means it will tenaciously hold on to both sides of the argument as if both sides of the border were held together as well, because what the scene presents cannot be resolved, for like Hamlet there is no answer when it comes to be or not to be (in this case) Mexican.

All this, of course, if readers allow the scenario in *Under the Mesquite* to unsettle, to make uncomfortable and as such to negotiate the cracks between worlds. As Anzaldúa highlights, this living in these intersections, the cracks between worlds, offers much: "This perspective from the cracks enables us to reconfigure ourselves as subjects outside the us / them binary. Dwelling in liminalities, in-between states or nepantlas, las nepantleras cannot be forced to stay in one place, locked into one perspective or perception of things or one picture of reality" (Anzaldúa, *Light / Luz* 82). Thus, instead of trying to choose between Lupita on one side and Sarita and Mireya on the other, readers might act on what this nepantlera-roman has been trying to tell us all along: to embrace both sides, that is, to become *nos/otras*.

THE NEPANTLERA RETURNS TO WRITE

Under the Mesquite is a novel about writing, as künstlerromans and nepantlera-romans anticipate that the young protagonist will grow up to write the text being read. In "Poems from Under the Mesquite," we find that after Mami's death Lupita struggles emotionally with this new reality. Fearing that his daughter is "going to fall / when he's not there to catch me, / afraid I'm going to hit the ground / hard and keep rolling" (178), Papi decides to send Lupita to his mother, Abuela Hortensia:

> He wants me to go back
> and talk to my childhood friends,
> be close to the people
> and things I grew up with,
> spend time in nature,
> go out at night
> just to watch the fireflies
> create their own daylight in the dark
> the way I used to
> when I was young. (186)

In the next poem, "At Abuelita's House," we are shown how the comforts of her grandmother's home and the presence of people who care for her allow Lupita time to think and to dream. As she confesses to her childhood friend,

> I used to imagine myself
> moving to New York
> to be in a Broadway show,
> or becoming a photojournalist
> and backpacking through Europe. (190)

Still grieving from her mother's death, however, Lupita finds herself unsure about her future. It is only when her grandmother tells her, "sometimes it's best to take things down / and start all over again. / It's the way of the world, Lupita. / No use fighting it" (193–94) that Lupita begins the changes necessary to fulfill her dreams of going to college and beyond. She does this explicitly by turning to her writing:

> Later I find a tall mesquite
> to sit under;
> and with my pen in hand,
> I open my journal
> to a blank page and begin
> writing a whole new batch of poems,

> poems filled with memories
> and hope, because that's
> what Mami would've wanted. (195–96)

As this scene in which Lupita returns to writing elucidates, *Under the Mesquite* as a Latinx künstlerroman foregrounds the process of self-discovery and the negotiation of ethnic identity. In this way, the text serves as a testament to the connections between ethnic identity and autobiographical writing. It provides a creative matrix under which the act of writing becomes synonymous with the constitutive parts of ethnic identity formation, and this act of writing can provide hope to young readers. Lupita's taking up the pen evidences the beginning of the künstlerroman circle since the end of every künstlerroman is the beginning of a wider arc. What Lupita learns about self-transformation also holds the promise of transformation for her community.

The power of nepantlera-romans is that they reveal the processes of transformation, how self-agency leads to envisioning and creating new realities, and then the importance of returning to plant the seeds of conocimiento for future readers. As Cristina Rhodes has astutely noted:

> These processes of transformation create a sort of ouroboros, wherein individual transformation is tied to recognizing systemic oppression and confronting it within oneself then undoing system oppression which cannot occur until individual transformation has taken effect and the more the young character becomes familiar with system inequality, the more they realize the internal and external changes that need to be made. The interconnection of individual and external change implies that transformation is ever evolving, always changing, and perpetually reflective. ("Processes of Transformation")

For *Under the Mesquite*, the narrative ends with Lupita moving to Alpine, Texas, to attend college, which she says feels like a "welcomed uprooting / for me. I am transplanting myself / to a whole new place, / with a new kind of language to learn" (206). Though her years in college are left unstated, we are assured by the künstlerroman form of Lupita's success in the wider world. Many years thence Lupita will return in much the same way as Tomás Rivera, Sandra Cisneros, and Francisco Jiménez returned to write . . . *y no se lo tragó la tierra / . . . And the Earth Did Not*

Devour Him, *The House on Mango Street*, and *The Circuit*, respectively. Lupita echoes this sentiment, noting that much like the loose pieces of papers swirling in the parking lot, she too knows the yearning to be lifted by the wind, and like those pages "someday my words will / take flight and claim the sky" (207).

They Call Me Güero

BORDER KIDS

To be a border kid, the opening poem of *They Call Me Güero* tells us, means to "wake up early Saturdays / and cross the bridge to Mexico" along with your dad (9). The Mexican town where you are headed is "like a mirror twin of our own, / with Spanish spoken everywhere just the same / but English mostly missing till it pops up / like grains of sugar on a chili pepper" (9). Put differently, other than increased use of English on the US side of an otherwise Spanish-speaking borderlands, the speaker of the poem, young Güero, notes that there are few cultural differences between the twin borderland cities. Güero and his dad indeed move fluidly between and within spaces, languages, and cultures. After breakfast at their "favorite restorán," he and his dad "walk down uneven sidewalks, chatting / with strangers and friends in both languages" (9). They then load their car with "Mexican cokes and Joya / avocados and cheese, tasty reminders of our roots" (9) and head back to their US mirror twin city. This, then, is why it is "fun to be a border kid" (9), that is, to move physically, culturally, and linguistically between the two worlds. As Güero's father instructs him, "You're a border kid, a foot on either bank. / Your ancestors crossed this river a thousand times. / No wall, no matter how tall, can stop your heritage / from flowing forever, like the Río Grande itself" (9).

And yet, as Gloria Anzaldúa reminds us, growing up "between two cultures, the Mexican (with a heavy Indian influence) and the Anglo (as a member of a colonized people in our own territory) . . . [is] not a comfortable territory to live in, this place of contradictions" (*Borderlands / La Frontera* 19). Sure enough, on their way back to their US town, Güero's "smile fades" as he looks at how the "border fence stands tall and ugly, invading / the carrizo at the river's edge" (9). This awareness of the geopolitical and physical border and how it divides becomes even more present in the poem "Checkpoint." On their way from the Texas Rio

Grande Valley to San Antonio in central Texas at a border checkpoint station, Güero's entire family is subjected to the harrowing everyday reality for Latinx people living in the borderlands: proving they belong. As Güero tells us, "we're innocent, sure, but our hearts beat fast" (11). Even as they are allowed to pass through, the children in the back seat are having a hard time understanding "why we have to prove every time / that we belong in our own country" (12).

As we open our examination of *They Call Me Güero*, we call attention to the everyday realities of life for border kids. On the one hand, as described above, border kids move readily, culturally and linguistically as well as physically, between the United States and Mexico. And yet, on the other hand, as "Checkpoint" shows, the border feels like a "quarantine zone between white and brown" (11) where Brown people have to prove they belong. From this we argue that *They Call Me Güero* draws attention to the "fun" parts of being a border kid while also revealing the nefarious parts, such as how border kids must prove they belong in the United States. In this, we take our cue from Güero's father, who instructs the distraught and angry children in the back seat that, first, they will have a good time in San Antonio, even going to eat at Tito's, and, second, what changes come will be up to them: "It's up to us to make the change, / especially los jóvenes, you and your friends. / Eyes peeled. Stay frosty. Learn and teach the truth" (12). He then slides a CD into the car stereo that features Los Tigres del Norte belting out "La Puerta Negra." The song's refrain, "pero ni la puerta ni cien candados / van a poder detenerme," makes clear that no door nor a hundred locks will keep stop the kids from learning and teaching the truth, specifically as the truth involves revealing and reveling in border culture.

In the following sections of our analysis of *They Call Me Güero*, we trace this transformation as border kids, undeterred by walls or doors or locks, utilize education (learning and teaching), along with other forms of counter-storytelling, to create a new reality that bridges rather than divides. Border kids do so, we argue, by listening to the wisdom of their elders—the way that Güero listened to his father's advice concerning the border wall and checkpoint, for example. We then focus on educators who utilize border conocimiento in their pedagogies. These pedagogies activate burgeoning awareness in border kids, thus encouraging them to form their particular modes of conocimiento. Finally, we discuss how Güero uses creative acts, in the form of poetry, to understand and articulate his complex, intersectional cultural identity.

TO LEARN *CASA ADENTRO* IS TO LEARN FROM THE ELDERS

Family lore, Güero tells us, can keep you safe from the "dangers / of this crazy, mixed-up place" (17). "There are monsters lurking," and, therefore, "like lots of border kids, / my first song was a lullaby / that my abuela sang / to warn me and to mystify" (17). Following this first experience with his grandmother's tales as a baby, storytelling only continues in Güero's life as he grows older. While these stories are entertaining, they also are educational. In one instance, for example, when Güero is caught stealing cookies from other people's plates, rather than spank him or raise her voice, Abuela Mimi tells him a story about la Mano Pachona, "a hairy claw that crawls through the dark" (43). As the story goes, the hand originally belonged to a Mayan wizard who held fast to his people's gods but who was dismembered—all of his limbs cut off—by the Spanish Inquisition. Unbeknownst to the Spanish, the wizard had cast a spell on his left hand and now "it seeks its revenge, waiting / for naughty boys with Spanish blood" (43). Abuela wraps up her story by connecting what happened to one victim, a light-skinned *güerito* who liked to steal cookies. In this rendering, the Mano Pachona grabs the cookie thief when he goes to the restroom. Not looking before he sits, the Mano "reached up and grabbed him / and pulled him into the sewer!" (44). Understanding that the güerito in the story looks and acts a lot like him, Güero "trembled, / snot bubbling in my nose" (45) as his grandmother told him to stop stealing cookies, which as he says, "I did. Forever" (45).

We feature Abuela Mimi's stories in this chapter because they highlight the role of storytelling for cultivating a sense of belonging in the present from connections established with ancestral knowledge and philosophies. In this way, learning from elders, what Catherine Walsh and Edizon León in their study on Afro-Andean thought and philosophies, term ancestrality, "implies a learning of and from what preceded me, to be allied or united with those who came before me" (215). Ancestrality, to Walsh and León, encompasses more than knowing traditions and customs; it is an existence-based construction that is deployed in the struggle for equitable societal and political transformations (216). Ancestrality, in this sense, helps the recuperation and reconstruction of existence and liberty in the present through a rich attachment to collective memory, philosophies, and knowledges inherited from ancestors (Mignolo and Walsh 43). As Walsh and León posit, ancestrality can be understood not simply as an inheritance but as a living bond with the past that affirms cultural identity in the present, where learning from elders who resisted in the past sows a sense of belonging to combat struggles for existence and freedom today (Mignolo and Walsh 43). Learning from this decolonial pedagogy, in turn, awakens *casa adentro* (in-house) processes of identity consolidation, which in Walsh and León's work on Afro-Andean cultures entails "a strategy that works toward a reinforcing and strengthening of 'lo propio,' one's own" (224).

For our purposes, we underscore the continuities between Afro-Andean cultural productions, with their decolonial turn toward diasporic, ancestral knowledge and philosophies, and Latinx cultural practices that likewise ground cultural identity as resultant from recreative dialogues between the past and the present. We deploy ancestrality for the way it enlists storytelling as a component for recuperating cultural knowledge that may be occluded or misvalued in educational sites, such as schools, and for awakening a sense of self that is affirmed by these deep historical and cultural ties.

Through her lullabies and stories Abuela Mimi offers a way of understanding the world through Latinx collective history and communal memory. In the case of the purloined cookies, for example, she emphasizes that la Mano Pachona originates from an act of rebellion by the Mayan wizard, first by refusing to denounce his Mayan gods and then by placing a curse on his left hand, a curse that will plague those with Spanish blood from thence forward. As Abuela Mimi continues her story, she draws a parallel between the Spanish, who want to dispossess the Mayan wizard of his culture and belief systems, and the cookie thief. In other words, the cookie thief behaves like the Spanish during the Conquest. This decolonial turn in her story reinforces for Güero the importance of not stealing "sweets / that didn't belong to him" (44)—or, like the Spanish, he will be haunted by those he stole from. Interestingly, many years after the cookie theft incident, Güero still cannot help but wonder "if one day I'll sit down / to meet my destiny at last" (45). Because Abuela Mimi tells the story of la Mano Pachona in the place of spanking or yelling, we are left to infer that Abuela Mimi, in scaring Güero, also enacts her revenge. Like the Mayan wizard and his malevolent hand, Abuela's story, in this regard, continues to haunt Güero for stealing the cookies.

While Abuela Mimi begins Güero's ancestrality-based education by singing lullabies that warn and mystify, and by telling stories that inculcate Latinx history and memory, she is not the only elder who encourages Güero to cultivate a strong sense of casa adentro. In the poem "Uncle

Joe's History Lesson," for example, Güero learns about occluded or misvalued history from Uncle Joe, who is "the family chronicler, / a cowboy philosopher, / and our local expert in / Mexican American history" (55). In one instance, Uncle Joe tells Güero that when he (Joe) was a child, instructors at his school did not "teach us / about our gente" (55). If they did teach something, such as the Treaty of Guadalupe Hidalgo, they made it "sound like a blow struck for democracy / instead of the violent land-grab it was" (55). To go along with the erasure or whitewashing of Mexican American history, Uncle Joe also informs us that his name was changed from José to Joseph and then to Joe. And, if he spoke Spanish in school, "¡PAS! You got smacked" (55). Hearing this, Güero is "spellbound and angry," not understanding how a person as smart as Uncle Joe could be treated so badly by the educational system. Joe continues by stating that he tried hard to not let the macro- and microaggressions get to him. However, in high school he

> Turned in a paper
> for world history about the Conquista.
> I worked so hard on it, did research,
> revised and edited, todo ese jale.
> Know what I got? An F. I'm not kidding.
> Teacher said it was too good.
> Obviously plagiarized. After that, pos,
> I gave up. Gatekeepers weren't letting
> this Chicano through. (56)

Walsh and León state that the role of the elder, such as Uncle Joe for our purposes, is "to keep alive the memory of this ancestral belonging, that is to say, to continue with its construction. It is to maintain a bond with the past, putting into effect this past today through the cultivation of a sense of belonging" (217). Uncle Joe's testimonio on the deleterious effects of racist policies and practices common in the educational system of his childhood both informs Güero of what came before him and also, as Walsh and León argue, helps Güero understand these inheritances of oppression and resistance as a tie between past and present. To be allied or united in this way, ancestrality posits not only a sense of belonging between ancestors and present-day people, but also it advances the idea that from such strength will come cultural and societal reconstructions. With this in mind, the poem "Uncle Joe's History Lesson" ends with a mandate for Güero:

Don't you let them stop you, chamaco.
Push right through them gates.
It's your right. You deserve a place
at that table. But when you take your seat,
don't let it change you. Represent us, m'ijo,
all the ones they kept down. You are us.
We are you. (56)

Casa adentro is reliant on listening to and learning from elders (Mignolo and Walsh 43). We find ancestrality and casa adentro important critical concepts for understanding the role of storytelling in Latinx communities with its emphasis on elders, such as abuelita philosophers and family historians. The stories told and the history retold are not solely for the acquisition of knowledge or information. Instead, the crux of ancestrality and casa adentro appears to be activist in nature. As Uncle Joe reminds Güero, it is up to those instructed by the elders to "represent us" at the table, specifically "all the ones they kept down" (56). From this lens, therefore, it is our argument that storytellers in *They Call Me Güero* strategically strengthen a sense of belonging, what Joe calls "you are us / We are you" (56), and also propose a way forward in which young readers push through the gates and take their rightful place at the table.

BORDER EDUCATORS AND THEIR CONOCIMIENTO

In Zeke Peña's illustration in the front cover of *They Call Me Güero*, our redheaded, freckled poet/protagonist runs in the desert, closely followed by his dog, Puchi, all the while sporting a mask featuring the Aztec trickster, the Feathered Coyote. The Huehuecoyotl mask was made out of papier-mâché by Güero for a "thematic unit" in Mr. Gil's classroom, as part of an innovative pedagogical assignment that has the students learn about masks from around the world, focusing primarily on Mexico and Korea. Along with writing and reflecting on ancient rituals and newer traditions surrounding masks, Mr. Gil, together with Ms. Wong, who teaches English, invite Celeste de Maíz, an expert mask maker, to show the students how to create their own papier-mâché masks. Güero's mask, based on the Aztec god of music and mischief, as well as wisdom and storytelling, is "all decked out / with orange and gold feathers" (36). The hardest part of the assignment for Güero is deciding whether his mask hides or reveals his true identity. With a mask, he notes, you "can pretend to be something else . . . or you can show your true self" (35). The mask assignment is such a hit with the students that the following weekend, they "walk out to the desert at the city's edge . . . strap on our masks / and run through the chaparral / chasing lizards and spiders, / playing out our secret selves / to earth and sky" (36).

Teachers like Mr. Gil and Ms. Wong, in our estimation, are "border educators" who deploy "border conocimiento" as part of their pedagogical repertoire. In *Border Thinking: Latinx Youth Decolonizing Citizenship*, Andrea Dyrness and Enrique Sepúlveda note that these "insurgent educators [act] from an episteme that emerges from everyday life in the borderlands—of border-crossing, transnational lives in which migrant subjects learn to maneuver, make do, create new ways of being, and improvise complex cultural negotiations of oppressive, racialized bordered spaces embedded in multiple, contrasting linguistic systems and spaces" (36). To Dyrness and Sepúlveda, border educators "illustrate Anzaldúa's notion of praxis as self-transformation and self-reintegration toward a 'coherent whole'" (67), that is, they showcase conocimiento, in pedagogical form. Like the teachers and educators that form Dyrness and Sepúlveda's ethnographic study, Mr. Gil and Ms. Wong, we argue, fill the voids of official curricula by asking border kids to reflect "on their relationships to multiple communities and to facilitate the expression of complex, fluid, multiple identities" (Dyrness and Sepúlveda 26). The Aztec mask that Güero constructs allows him to nurture a burgeoning awareness of his complex, fluid multiple identities. Since Güero is a border kid with a foot on each bank of the Rio Grande, the mask promotes Güero's growing conocimiento by allowing him to understand more fully how border kids, as a result of their relationships to multiple communities, can maneuver, make do, and create new ways of being.

In contrast to Güero, Uncle Joe is never afforded the opportunity to realize his full academic potential. As he explains, the "gatekeepers weren't letting / this Chicano through" (56). To Dyrness and Sepúlveda, the opposite of border educators who deploy conocimiento pedagogy are teachers who "were conscripted into reproducing old colonial arrangements that called for brown, black, and cultural Others to be integrated into the margins of school life, producing a marginality predicated on the sacrifice and dispossession of their languages, cultural practices, and ways of being in the world" (47). As one of Dyrness and Sepúlveda's interlocutors, an ESL teacher states that "part of the problem is culture,

FIGURE 2.1 Zeke Peña, Cover image of *They Call Me Güero: A Border Kid's Poems* by David Bowles. Cover illustration by Zeke Peña (zpvisual.com).

95 percent of it is. It's all about assimilation time. Some kids need more time to assimilate. They need to speed up the process of assimilation. They need to be integrated more" (45). For our purposes, the gatekeepers, who would not let Uncle Joe through the gate because of their adherence to colonial arrangements premised on the dispossessing, violently if needed, Latinx children and young adults of their language, cultural practices, and ways of being, provide a strong contrast to educators like Mr. Gil and Ms. Wong who tap "into a deeper *conocimiento* about cultural liminality, border existence, and what it means to be in community" (63). As Sepúlveda says of his own experiences as a border educator, "it was our borderlands imaginary that compelled us to act, to depart, to rebel against authorized pedagogies and *acompañar* youths in a dialogical and poetic interrogation of migration through oppressive structures and social realities" (63).

As a case in point, Ms. Wong has her English class interrogate Aztec, Mayan, Chinese, and Korean cosmologies in relation to the rabbit on the moon. In her lesson plan, Ms. Wong plays songs from her childhood, such as "Bandal," which describes the moon gliding across the night sky as *"a little white boat carries a bunny and a tree"* (32). She also has the class read a poem by Miguel León-Portillo that he wrote in Nahuatl, the language of the Aztecs: *"I could contemplate the night birds / and the rabbit in the moon at last"* (33). As Güero tells us, "my mind is totally blown" (32). He continues by emphasizing the power of border educators who nurture conocimiento in their young charges: "Ms. Wong becomes a hero to me" (34). Not only does Güero begin to realize his potential as a reader of poetry, understanding "how Frost's snow-filled woods symbolize death / or why Soto drops an orange, glowing like fire, / into the hands of a love-struck boy my age" (34), but also, as he tells us, "one day it just happens: / I put pen to paper, and my soul / comes rushing out in line after line" (34).

We see this emphasis on border education echoed in Bowles's work as a middle-school teacher as well. In one particular instance, Bowles found himself working with a group of boys who were flailing with their readings. Instead of sticking to the official curriculum, he utilized conocimiento pedagogies that nurtured in the students an awareness of themselves as border kids. As Bowles explains, "I brought in 'Oranges' by Gary Soto, a poem in which they could see themselves reflected, adjacent to their own cultural experience as Mexican American kids. It was hugely successful. They identified with the boy in the poem. I was able to get them to try writing about their own lives, to find the 'orange' in their own personal stories" (Salvadore).

Bowles's *They Call Me Güero* pays tribute to the work of border educators—such as Mr. Gil and Ms. Wong—who deploy conocimiento in their pedagogy. What Mr. Gil and Ms. Wong in the poems, and Bowles in his writing and life, illustrate is that students thrive under insurgent border pedagogies that emerge from everyday life in the borderlands. What is more, as Güero says of Ms. Wong, border educators can open up a whole new world (32).

LOS DERDS

As to the power of books, Anzaldúa notes that "books saved my sanity, knowledge opened the locked places in me and taught me first how to survive and then how to soar" (*Borderlands / La Frontera* 19). She continues her discussion on the power of reading in "Memoir—My Calling; or, Notes for 'How Prieta Came to Write'" by stating, in third person, that Prieta, a younger version of Anzaldúa, always had her head in a book: "The encyclopedias, *Aesop's Fables, The Call of the Wild*—which she read thirteen times. She read *Jane Eyre* and *Meditations* of Marcus Aurelius thirteen times too. *Don Quixote*, pocket westerns—anything she could lay her hands on" (235). In all, "Prieta tenía un amor al conocimiento, a love of knowledge" (235). Books, as Anzaldúa describes, "called to her" (236). Then it happened; books "later called her to writing" and she had to choose. Prieta, as we know, eventually chose to write and, because of her choice, "she experienced numerous visions and changes in the configuration of her identity" (237). Writing, in this sense, is transformative.

Güero, likewise, began his journey with a love of conocimiento, a quest for knowledge that would allow him to transform himself as well as the world around him. Like Anzaldúa, Güero is initially drawn to books and reading, becoming a founding member of los Derds, Diverse Nerds. The origin story, because all superheroes have to have one, is that los Derds were founded in sixth grade when a group of boys, all who love to read, wound up in the library. The mentor to the group is Mr. Soria, who in recognizing "what / major nerds we are" (29), provided the boys books by "all sorts of writers who look / and talk like us: Dominicans, / Koreans, Mexicans, Chicanos, / Black and Native folks, too" (29). The Bookworm Squad, another name for the Derds, was born on that day. Fancying themselves as superheroes, the boys believe that they are "heroes whose power / is traveling through these pages [from diverse books] / to distant times and spaces / to find our proud reflections" (29).

And then it happened: Güero, like Prieta, was called to write. In particular, he initially believes, like the boy in Gary Soto's poem, that he is called to write love poems. Güero, as it turns out, is madly in love with Joanna Padilla, who is "smart and rude, / takes judo classes after school, / helps her dad in his body shop, / loves superhero films and video games" (66). Following the advice of his Abuela Mimi, who tells him to find himself a *fregona*, "a tough one who doesn't need you at all / but wants you anyway" (66), Güero writes Joanna a long poem (66). Unfortunately, she takes the poem and sticks it in her back pocket, like it was an ordinary sheet of paper. As Güero says, "nothing works!" (67).

The additional bad news for Güero is that the school bully, Snake Barrera, later that day is set to "rearrange my face." Snake has it in for Güero, ever since Güero's father fired Snake's dad (26). Snake, who looks like he is fifteen, has been tormenting Güero ever since. On the day in question, Snake takes the bullying to the level of an intersectional identity put-down. Snake calls Güero a "güero cacahuatero," which is either a smackdown on Güero's eating habits (a *cacahuate* is a peanut) or a reinforcement of the idea that Güero, who has fair skin, looks like a peanut. In either case, Snake presses the issue by continuing: "Fancy house, / teacher's pet, / stupid poems, / and all these freckles— / you're just a gringo nerd" (63). Instead of fighting with Snake, Güero heads off for class and then yanks out his journal to "answer Snake / with words / instead of fists" (64). Ms. Wong, once she sees Güero is done with his poem, asks him to stand in front of the class and read it:

> Yo, bullies: lero, lero
> I'm the mero Güero
> a real cacahuatero,
> peanuts and chile
> all up in this cuero,
> this piel, this skin—
> it's white, that's true
> but I'm just as Mexican
> as you and you and you. (64)

Much as we discuss with *Gabi, a Girl in Pieces* in chapter 5, to be güero/a, or be fair skinned in Latinx, in this case Mexican American, communities is to stand apart from others who have darker skin tones. Difference is difference from the norm. Güero's sister, Teresa, is toasty brown; his brother, Arturo, is the color of honey (30); and his father is "deep brown like mesquite bark" (31). Only Güero and his grandmother have "lots of Spanish and Irish blood" (30). Colorism, which informs a hierarchy of human belonging in Latinx and Latin American communities, is a double-edged sword. As Güero's father instructs him, "pale folks catch all the breaks / here and in Mexico, too" (31). Thus, one side of the sword will allow Güero to catch all the breaks; unfortunately for him, the other side of the sword means that Güero is viciously taunted for his fair skin.

Güero's poem in response to bullying is insightful in the way it deconstructs Snake's taunts by reemphasizing them. In other words, he makes fair skin, the object of the ridicule, an asset. At the heart of Güero's rhetorical comeback is that he is "the mero," or the one and only, as in the foremost, güero and a "real cacahuatero." He proceeds with the reconstruction of the taunt by pointing out how his "cuero," his skin, looks like peanuts with red chile on it. In other words, Güero highlights his ties to Mexican and Mexican American street food that features fruit, nuts, or, in this case, peanuts with red chile on top. In this sense, Güero puts forward the argument that while he may look different from his Latinx peers and family because of his fair skin, he is as Mexican as "you and you and you" (64). Put simply, he remakes the taunt into a celebration of his intersectional identity. Much in the same way that Lupita in *Under the Mesquite* stresses that there is more than one way to think about language and translanguaging, Güero highlights the need to delink from racist hierarchies of colorism.

After reading the poem, Güero looks up to meet the eyes of the other students in the class. As he heads back to his seat, Bobby Lee, one of Güero's fellow Derds, bumps his fist and then whispers, "That was lit, / but he's [Snake's] gonna kill you" (65). In back of the room, one of Snake's friends has recorded Güero reading the poem. As luck would have it, just as Snake is set to rearrange Güero's face, Joanna walks by. Not knowing what else to do, Güero asks Joanna for help: "'Help me'! / I call. 'Help me, Joanna'" (67). Joanna takes Snake by the arm, then showing off her judo training, she throws him down. As she pulls Güero to his feet, she tells him that it "took guts to ask a girl for help" (67). She also says, "I liked your poem. Funny and sweet. / Okay, Güero. You can be my boyfriend" (67). Seeing love bloom in such an interesting way, the kids who have gathered around respond with oohs and aahs.

What starts out as a writing endeavor to win the heart of a young lady, ends with love blooming in the borderlands. The path to love, however, is not linear; it takes a circuitous route that involves poetry as a vehicle via which Güero lyrically enunciates his intersectional cultural identity. As Anzaldúa's Prieta also finds, choosing to write means "numerous visions and changes in the configuration of her identity" ("Memoir" 237). Thus, while Güero at various times has been troubled by the fact that he looks different than others in his family and ethnic group, poetry allows him to challenge this othering, and in the process he reclaims his connection to his cultural identity. In this, he, like Prieta, finds that writing brings about changes in how he understands identity. All of this is possible because of the books that allow him to survive and then to soar and because he answers the call to write. Fittingly, *They Call Me Güero* ends with Güero at his family's ranch listening to the sounds of nature in the borderlands, the water flowing in the river, the hum of bugs, and the trill of birds. Then, in the distance, he hears an ocelot growl. As Güero notes of this experience, "I know poetry when I hear it" (105). As we have discussed in this chapter, it is fun to be a border kid.

Conclusion

As a nepantlera-roman, *Under the Mesquite* showcases the journey of the young artist growing up to write the book that will describe the challenges and benefits of being a border kid. *They Call Me Güero* likewise presents the paradoxes inherent in the borderlands, what Anzaldúa explains as a position in which "we are detached (separated) and attached (connected) to each of our several cultures" (*Light / Luz* 56). She continues, "en este lugar entre medio, nepantla, two or more forces clash and are held teetering on the verge of chaos, a state of entreguerras. These tensions between extremes create cracks or tears in the membrane surrounding, protecting, and containing the different cultures and their perspectives" (56). As we have seen in *Under the Mesquite* and *They Call Me Güero*, this place can seem an *entreguerras*, a place between wars or warring parties. At the same time, as Anzaldúa posits, nepantla, the interstitial place in between, also reveals a third space, where languages, cultures, and perspectives merge. The key configuration present in *Under the Mesquite* and *They Call Me Güero* is that border kids enunciate from a location in which they are separated *and* connected, rather than a position in which they can be separated *or* connected. Put differently, border kids think and act and write within these paradoxical dichotomies instead of succumbing to their pressures.

Books like *Under the Mesquite* and *They Call Me Güero* give us hope. As a nepantlera-roman, *Under the Mesquite,* and *They Call Me Güero*, which has künstlerroman poetic overtones, enact a future vision in which young Latinx readers, by witnessing the ways in which border kids like Lupita and Güero have utilized conocimiento to great personal and cultural advantage, can trace their transformations. In this way, Lupita and Güero point the way forward to a future in which the 1,950-mile-long open wound that divides pueblos and cultures will be healed. In their lived experiences and in their creative acts, border kids bridge boundaries that divide communities; they construct new worlds in which one cultural imaginary unites both sides of the river—as it should be.

CHAPTER THREE

The Cultural Wealth of Diasporic Youth

> La negación sistemática de la cultura mexicana-chicana en los Estados Unidos impide su desarrollo, haciéndolo este un acto de colonización. As a people who have been stripped of our history, language, identity, and pride, we attempt again and again to find what we have lost by digging into our cultural roots imaginatively and making art from our findings.
>
> GLORIA ANZALDÚA / *Light in the Dark / Luz en lo oscuro*

In this chapter we investigate the processes at play when diasporic youth engage with their cultural wealth. We posit that *Maximilian and the Mystery of the Guardian Angel: A Bilingual Lucha Libre Thriller* (2011) by Xavier Garza and *Summer of the Mariposas* (2012) by Guadalupe García McCall utilize cultural wealth from their real and imagined homeland as a resource to challenge deficit thinking and to reveal, for their young readers, the possibilities entailed in being holders and creators of valuable cultural knowledge. In the process of establishing these transnational ties between and across nation spaces, we argue, these novels put forward a reparative theory that accounts for the way diasporic peoples can repair by rewriting "the stories of loss and recovery, exile and homecoming, disinheritance and recuperation, stories that lead out of passivity and into agency, out of devalued into valued lives" (Anzaldúa, *Light / Luz* 143). In our reading of *Maximilian and the Mystery of the Guardian Angel* and *Summer of the Mariposas*, we point to the movement from loss and disinheritance, in other words, deficit thinking, to forms of agency and cultural wealth. That is, these novels demonstrate how artfully assembling pieces gathered from many places, from over there as well as from here, reflect and project a lived experience that is necessarily intertwined in at least two nations. Further, they highlight the reparative value in knowing that one possesses great cultural wealth.

Maximilian and the Mystery of the Guardian Angel tells the story of a young lucha libre fan who discovers that his uncle is none other than the world-famous luchador, El Ángel de la Guarda (the Guardian Angel).[1] This newfound genealogical connection with luchador royalty allows Max to dream increasingly about becoming a luchador like his uncle. Dreams gain purpose as the novel proceeds and Max begins to think more earnestly about who will inherit the Guardian Angel mask when his uncle retires. Told in bilingual form, with alternating pages in English and Spanish, the novel signals its transnational intents linguistically. Further, in aligning Max's interests with lucha libre in general and with a luchador famous for his match exploits and for his reprisals in Mexican movies in particular, the novel points readers to Mexican cultural products and practices. In this way, we suggest, the novel highlights the interconnectedness between the United States and Mexico and the cultural wealth that can be derived from such entanglements.

The second novel for examination, *Summer of the Mariposas*, can be described as a mythological realist novel that reframes *The Odyssey* within a Latinx perspective. *Summer of the Mariposas* is both a literary and an intersectional adaptation, remapping the classical epic story along the US/Mexico borderlands and recasting the characters and obstacles within Latinx and Mexican mythologies, with La Llorona as spiritual counsel and Virgen de Guadalupe/Tonantzin as the central arbiter of life and justice. In offering a decolonized and localized *Odyssey*, the novel takes readers on a journey through the borderlands, the in-between spaces where languages meld, family inhabits both nations, and cultural construction emerges from an artful bricolage. In many ways, as La Llorona in the novel explains, "This is about all of you: your sisters, your parents, even your *abuela* . . . You must travel to the other side, into the land of your ancestors, to find each other again" (53). La Llorona's words, we argue, lead us into the processes of rewriting stories from disinheritance to recuperation, where cultural identity is constituted of materials here (*The Odyssey*) and special gifts from "the other side," that is, the "land of your ancestors." This journey, in which the personal, social, cultural, and political intersect across national borders, calls attention to the complex transnational components that form cultural wealth for diasporic youth. Transformations of self and of society emerge, we believe, from these processes of putting "our dismembered psyches and patrias (homelands) together in new constructions" (Anzaldúa, *Light / Luz* 21).

We title this chapter "The Cultural Wealth of Diasporic Youth" because of the possibilities engendered in understanding the importance of cultural wealth, where it comes from, and how it is artfully deployed. In this, our study is rooted in the work of Dolores Delgado Bernal and that of Tara Yosso, whose formulations of cultural wealth allow us to see Latinx youth and other young people of color as "holders and creators of knowledge" (Delgado Bernal 106). These vital forms of cultural wealth, Delgado Bernal informs us, are "taught to youth through legends, *corridos*, and storytelling. It is through culturally specific ways of teaching and learning that ancestors and elders share the knowledge of conquest, segregation, patriarchy, homophobia, assimilation, and resistance" (113). Tara Yosso, in her seminal essay "Whose Culture Has Capital? A Critical Race Theory Discussion of Community Cultural Wealth," echoes Delgado Bernal by noting that "Communities of Color nurture cultural wealth through at least 6 forms of capital such as aspirational, navigational, social, linguistic, familial, and resistant capital" (77). As Yosso further describes, these forms of cultural capital

> are not mutually exclusive or static, but rather are dynamic processes that build on one another as part of community cultural wealth. For example, as noted above, aspirational capital is the ability to hold onto hope in the face of structured inequality and often without the means to make such dreams a reality. Yet, aspirations are developed within social and familial contexts, often through linguistic storytelling and advice (*consejos*) that offer specific navigational goals to challenge (resist) oppressive conditions. (77)

At play in the work of both Delgado Bernal and Yosso is a challenge to conventional deficit thinking all too common in educational settings and in society at large that sees only deprivation in Latinx and other youth of color. Deficit thinking, that is, categorically denying value to the cultural wealth bestowed upon Latinx youth by elders and community members, to Yosso, is "one of the most prevalent forms of contemporary racism in US schools" (75). The ramifications of these forms of racism, Delgado Bernal states, is that youth "often feel as if their histories, experiences, cultures, and languages are devalued, misinterpreted, or omitted" (106).

Via the work of Yosso and Delgado Bernal, we are attentive to the cultural wealth that Latinx youth possess and, as such, we assert that these forms of cultural wealth endow Latinx youth with abilities to hold as well as to create knowledge. In contrast to deficit thinking, we believe that "culturally specific ways of teaching and learning" (Delgado Bernal 113) "offer specific navigational goals to challenge (resist) oppressive conditions" (Yosso 77). As Anzaldúa notes in the epigraph to this chapter, the United States has systematically attempted to erase the cultural capital of Latinx/Chicanx people (*Light / Luz* 48). And yet, as she continues to explain, Latinx/Chicanx people "attempt again and again to find what we have lost by digging into our cultural roots imaginatively and making art from our findings" (48). In this chapter, we examine the ways in which two contemporary Latinx young adult novels, *Maximilian and the Mystery of the Guardian Angel* and *Summer of the Mariposas*, imaginatively engage with these cultural roots and create art with these findings, demonstrating the power and possibilities of cultural wealth for diasporic youth.

We also must add that while the crux of our examination is powered by notions of cultural wealth as described by Yosso and Delgado Bernal, the novels chosen for our study, we argue, conceptualize Latinx cultural production and Latinx meaning making as diasporic in nature. In this way, our chapter also is propelled by Emma Pérez's insight that "immigrant" as a category, while it was meaningful for European immigrants who were mostly white and assimilable, is problematic when considering Latinx people. As Pérez notes, "immigrants are expected to become part of the dominant culture; they are urged to adopt its habits and forget their own—to erase. Diasporas, on the other hand, intervene, construct newness, and 'live inside with a difference'" (78). Further, Pérez understands Chicanx peoples as diasporic, as she further clarifies,

> The diasporic subject reminds us that Aztlán, the mythic homeland, shifts and moves beneath and around us. The mythic homeland is longed for, constructed, and rewritten through collective memories. Time is traversed, and a mythic past entwines with a future where a decolonized imaginary has possibilities. If diaspora, loosely defined, is a "history of dispersal coupled with myths and memories of a homeland," where "alienation in the host country" often fosters a "desire for eventual return" while a collective memory reconstructs the alienated group's history, whether real or imagined, then Chicanos/as are appropriately diasporic. (78)

Pérez's work on the decolonial imaginary veers our study in this chapter toward an understanding of Latinx youth as engaged with a transnational imaginary and, as such, holders and creators of knowledge where the mythic homeland and connections to it are "longed for, constructed, and rewritten" (78).

Within the study of children's and young adult literature, Carol Brochin and Carmen L. Medina propose in their article "Critical Fictions of Transnationalism in Latinx Children's Literature" that Latinx youth's "complex social networks transcend national borders, cultures, and languages. Sadly, however, the children's books used in schools rarely reflect the complex transnational identities of children and their families" (5). It is our objective, through Brochin and Medina's lens, to make "visible the complex dynamics and consequences of transnationalism in diverse Latinx communities in the US and across the US borders" and in this way ensure that critical literary mirrors will be available for diasporic young readers (5). These literary mirrors are vital, as they provide young readers with counter-stories that "disrupt notions of a linear path of migration while centering global politics of power" (6). Children's books that foreground diaspora and transnationalism challenge assimilationist practices and policies that reflect unilateral notions of immigration and deficit views of immigrants while simultaneously providing alternate ways of being that span national boundaries.[2]

Our objective in this chapter is to investigate the processes at play when diasporic youth engage with their cultural wealth, specifically, in this case, through literary works such as *Maximilian and the Mystery of the Guardian Angel* and *Summer of the Mariposas*. Such a venture, we believe, allows for a better understanding of the complex cultural networks that inform the lived experiences of Latinx youth. In other words, by being attentive to these diasporic imaginings, we better comprehend the way diasporic cultural wealth contests forms of nationalism, such as assimilationist policies and practices, and destabilizes deficit thinking. Furthermore, in our reading of *Maximilian and the Mystery of the Guardian Angel* and *Summer of the Mariposas* we argue that these novels situate diasporic cultural wealth as vital for Latinx cultural production and meaning making. Diasporic cultural wealth allows Latinx youth to be creators of knowledge, that is, to understand how this cultural wealth bestows on them the possibility of engendering new worlds where their lives are valued (Anzaldúa, *Light / Luz* 143).

Maximilian and the Mystery of the Guardian Angel

LOS TIEMPOS ENMASCARADOS

Luchador masks are ubiquitous now, even if they are a perplexing hodgepodge of designs that range from those that pay homage to luchadores to those that testify to national affiliation in their coloration or even sports teams. For children, a quick web search yields multiple templates that can be colored in, cut out, and then worn. Everybody, it seems, wants to be a luchador. As part of this contemporary phenomenon, luchador masks traverse cultures and nations while still retaining a strong identification with Mexico and with Mexican-ness. The irony of history is that luchador masks originated in 1934 when a bootmaker in Mexico City created a mask for a white American wrestler who was plying his trade in Mexico. As the story goes, Corbin James Massey, also known as Cyclone Mackey (el Ciclón McKey), asked respected bootmaker Antonio Martínez to make him a mask. Several years earlier, US wrestler The Masked Marvel had used a mask with great success, and Massey wanted to "use the Masked Marvel gimmick in Mexico" (Levi 110). In Mexican wrestling there are the good guys, the *técnicos*, and the bad guys, the *rudos*; Massey, a rudo, "wanted 'a hood, something you can put on, tie on, like the Ku Klux Klan'" (110). The rest, as they say, is history. Within a few years, masked wrestlers were everywhere in lucha libre.

The transnational journey of luchador masks followed, in many ways, the same path as Mexican wrestling. After watching a wrestling match in Eagle Pass, Texas, Salvador Lutteroth, along with his partner Francisco Ahumado, brought wrestling to Mexico on September 21, 1933. Much like the masks, lucha libre soon found its syncretic roots. In other words, it came to transcend the entertainment limits offered by its US form to become the fully Mexicanized amalgam of contradictions that it staged to great effect.[3] And now, this strange amalgam of contradictions seems to have found a place in the twenty-first-century United States, specifically with young Latinx people, as lucha libre and luchador masks move transnationally once again, this time (back) to El Norte.

Alongside Yuyi Morales's lucha libre picture books, *Niño Wrestles the World* (2013) and *Rudas: Niño's Horrendous Hermanitas* (2016), Xavier Garza's series—comprising *Maximilian and the Mystery of the Guardian Angel* (2011), *Maximilian and the Bingo Rematch* (2013), *Maximilian and the Lucha Libre Club* (2016), and *Maximilian and the Curse of the*

Fallen Angel (2020)—brings lucha libre to a whole new generation of Latinx readers. Most young readers of Max or Niño would, of course, be too young to remember the golden age of lucha libre when stalwarts such as El Santo, Blue Demon, and Mil Mascaras not only graced lucha libre rings but took their talents to the big screen. For young Latinx readers, therefore, Max and Niño allow them to more fully understand the importance of lucha libre in Mexican and Latinx history and culture, while also allowing them to participate in this modern age of lucha libre, which as noted above is transnational in scope. In this way, lucha libre becomes, for a new audience via these books, a notable component of Latinx artistic and cultural production.

MAX CONTRA LOS ADULTOS

The first thing to know about Max in *Maximilian and the Mystery of the Guardian Angel* is that he is an avid lucha libre fan. The fact that it is the summer before sixth grade or that he received straight As on his report card pale in comparison to his father's promise to take him to see lucha libre in Mexico. As fate would have it, however, the long-promised trip to Mexico gets canceled due to his father's work schedule. Max's plans seemingly are on the ropes until his Uncle Lalo (his mother's youngest brother) is talked into taking Max. Though Max ultimately makes it to the fights across the border in Mexico, the novel's opening provides readers an open-access view into the fracturing of his Mexican American family.

In this, the opening scenes of the novel show a family deeply at odds with each other, specifically as it affects Max. His father cannot take him to the lucha libre matches, seemingly disregarding how hard Max worked at school. Although Uncle Lalo will eventually take Max to the matches, as Max notes, "it's clear to me that my tío doesn't know a single thing about lucha libre! He wouldn't know the difference between a rudo and a técnico if they sat down in front of him" (24). Further, Lalo tries to demystify lucha libre for Max: "'You know, Max,' says Lalo, 'just because you see something in a movie doesn't mean that it's real. The Guardian Angel is just an old guy in a mask'" (10). Luckily, Max refuses to believe Lalo, even when his mom piles on by saying, "I bet you that he's ugly and bald" (10). To add to this insult, his mother repeats an often overheard rumor, one commonly uttered by Doña Alicia, owner of the corner convenience store, that the reason the Guardian Angel wears a mask is that in actuality the Guardian Angel is "Pedro Infante, the famed Mexican singer turned actor who died in a plane years ago" (12). At this point, it feels as though everyone is beating up on Max and he has no one to "tag in" for him.

Between a distracted father, a mother who puts down his interests, and an uncle who would not know a rudo if he sat in front of him, we surmise that Max desperately needs an intervention; he needs someone to help him and his family put the pieces together. Lucky for Max, an intervention by the Guardian Angel is coming. Before that point, though, readers are presented with how far Max has fallen. Upon arriving at the match Max charges into the arena, even before Lalo has bought the tickets, to "get to where the guy is who sells masks" (19). Max has his heart set on a Guardian Angel mask; however, he arrives too late and the masks are sold out. Then, because Lalo knows nothing about lucha libre but thinks he knows a good deal, Lalo purchases two sets of masks at a buy-one-get-one-free deal. When Uncle Lalo presents Max with a Diablo Rojo mask, while the other kids are wearing Guardian Angel masks, the one he so desired, Max is crestfallen: "I stare in disgust at the horned mask that Lalo is dangling in front of me. I give it the same look you would use for fresh roadkill" (24).

Temptation always beckons at the wrong time, and Max sees a girl wearing a Guardian Angel mask, a mask she has besmirched with a "six pink sticker hearts right on its forehead" (26). Thinking that she knows nothing about lucha libre, Max decides to trade her the four masks for the one Guardian Angel mask. As good as his intentions are (they are not), they turn worse when the girl refuses to even speak with him, even as he places the four masks in her hands. When she runs away, Max chases her down and proceeds to "pull [the mask] right off her head, but she grabs it and refuses to let go. We engage in a tug-of-war" (28). As it turns out, the girl is the daughter of the mask merchant and he does not take kindly to Max's actions. A fight ensues between Lalo and the merchant with "the crowd cheering Lalo, and booing the vendor" (30). The chapter ends with Max realizing that he tucked the Guardian Angel mask under his shirt: "I stare at the mask and admire it as it glistens in the glowing yellow light radiating from the dashboard of my uncle's red pickup truck. I pull the mask over my face. It falls into place perfectly. It was meant for me! My eyes stare out at the world through teardrop-shaped silhouettes" (32). Under the rules of lucha libre, Max is well on his way to becoming a rudo.

We pause for a few moments, an intermission between matches, if you will, to speak about the cultural geography of the novel. Max and his family live in Rio Grande City, Texas, which is on the United States side of the border with Mexico. Like many border towns, Rio Grande City has a Mexican counterpart, as we described in chapter 2 in the case of Eagle Pass and Piedras Negras in García McCall's *Under the Mesquite*. Although readers are not told how Lalo and Max traveled to the arena, it can be surmised that they crossed an international bridge either by vehicle or by foot. The ease with which an uncle and underage child cross the border into Mexico underscores the ease with which the characters in the novel live their everyday lives moving between countries.

This sense of fluid geographic movement between the United States and Mexico is echoed by the bilingual structure of the novel. *Maximilian* is marketed as a "bilingual thriller," thereby allowing for reading in English, Spanish, or in both languages, following its dual-page structure. As bilingual readers, we were hard pressed to stick to a single language in our reading, moving instead back and forth between the two versions. Often the Spanish version felt more plausible, especially with the name of the luchadores. For example, the Spanish name of a luchador, el Perro Aguayo, rolls off the tongue, largely because nicknames sound better in their cultural and linguistic provenance, in comparison to the English version, Dog-Man Aguayo. Further, the movement between Spanish and English impacts the poetry of the names. El Vampiro Velásquez, for example, becomes Vampire Velasquez, written without the signifying accents. Further, in its translated form, the name changes from six syllables to five syllables, thereby losing its parallel syllabic symmetry as well as its scansion. As we read the novel, we found richness in the Spanish version. At times, though, the immediate access to an English translation helped clarify specialized vocabulary. From these experiences, we suggest that *Maximilian* offers much to readers who are true bilinguals, readers accustomed to moving back and forth between the English and Spanish, between languages and cultures. In this regard, "bilingual thriller" implies a thriller for those who translanguage.

To these easy movements between nations and between languages we highlight one additional movement between two oft considered disparate spaces, the sacred and the secular. Latinx culture, in this regard, has strong affinities with "secular saints," that is, cultural and historical figures who have achieved a level of canonization. As Desirée Martín notes in *Borderlands Saints*: "a 'secular saint' may refer to someone who is venerated for their extraordinary actions or their contribution to a noble cause, but who is not recognized as a canonical saint by a religion" (3). Moreover, it is precisely because "they are not traditional saints that secular saints so clearly reveal the contradiction between the human and the divine. Secular saints are defined by their human qualities—whether heroic or fallible—instead of by their canonization into a pantheon of divinities or even by popular religious belief" (3). In her study, Martín considers such secular saints as Teresa Urrea (Santa Teresa de Cabora), Pancho Villa, César Chávez, Subcomandante Insurgente Marcos, and La Santa Muerte (4). Her findings show these cultural saints "produce and embody new forms of national, regional, and transnational identity for their devotees on both sides of the border" (4). Bridging the borders between nations as well as between the sacred and the secular, these figures not only are committed to social and political action, but also they "evoke the sacred, especially since they frequently draw upon the resources of the popular saint" (7).

For our study, we locate *Maximilian and the Mystery of the Guardian Angel* in this cultural geography in which secular saints play integral roles in the lives of Latinx people. By focusing on words in the title such as "mystery" and "guardian angel," we suggest that the novel highlights the deployment of a secular saint as a kind of cultural wealth. In this case, the secular saint appears in the form of the luchador, the Guardian Angel, to repair the fractures in Max's family as well as to heal Max of his desconocimiento. As the opening of the novel illustrates, the way that Max acquires his Guardian Angel mask and his pleasure in his ill-found gain suggest that he too needs healing. This intervention, we propose, comes in the guise of the Guardian Angel and the mystery that surrounds him. On a surface level, the mystery involves a long-lost uncle who has been estranged from the family. At a deeper level, the Guardian Angel (the luchador) functions as a protector of Max and his family, saving them in a variety of ways. Further, as we signal in our invocation of Martín's work on secular saints, the revelation of the Guardian Angel's identity, the way the family finds that he is a long-lost uncle, and his reparative role in the novel owes much to Martín's notions of secular saints.

As we return to *Maximilian*, the significance of the Guardian Angel becomes more prominent as the novel continues. Max and his family make a trip from the Rio Grande Valley to San Antonio in central Texas to attend lucha libre matches. As is the case in these bouts, the rudos are introduced first, what Max calls the "Trinity of Evil" (el Perro Aguayo, el Vampiro Velásquez, and el Cavernario). El Vampiro is only present as the wrestling manager for el Perro Aguayo, and he enters by holding el Perro by a leash.[4] Next, the Guardian Angel's tag-team partner el Príncipe Maya enters. The last luchador to enter the arena floor is the Guardian Angel. Thinking that he can touch the Guardian Angel as he passes by him, Max stretches as far as he can over the guardrails that hold back the crowd from the entranceway. He explains, "I reach out with my arms as far beyond the guardrail as I possibly can. But my arms don't go far enough. I can't touch him. I am going to miss this moment I had waited for all my life because my arms are too short" (70). Not to be deterred, Max climbs the guardrail. Unfortunately, or perhaps fortunately, he falls over the guardrail and lands at the feet of the Guardian Angel. As he looks up, Max notices the signifying scars on the Guardian Angel's chest: "My hero's chest is exposed, revealing—like medals of honor—the scars of his historic battles" (70). The Guardian Angel lifts up Max and delivers him into the arms of his father but not before the Guardian Angel seems to recognize Lalo: "There's a strange look in the eyes behind the mask—as if he recognizes Lalo! Lalo's face seems to startle him" (72).

As the scene unfolds, interplay between secular and sacred language increases. Drawing on Martín's analysis of secular saints, the scene evokes the sacred by foregrounding resources more commonly found in the veneration of saints or, in this case, of spiritual guardian angels, *los ángeles de la guarda*. In this sense, leaders do not simply watch a wrestling match; they witness a cosmic battle between the Trinity of Evil and the good guys, symbolically a prince and an angel, respectively the Mayan Prince and the Guardian Angel. The evocations of the sacred continue as Max believes he needs to touch the Guardian Angel and experiences it as a moment of self-realization and clarity: "I look up and witness a sight I know I will carry with me until the day I die" (70). And, of course, there is the stigmata, the signifying scars that prove the veracity of the Guardian Angel. What readers witness, therefore, is the careful staging of a ritual drama in which the Guardian Angel becomes more than a mere human wrestler; he becomes an embodied sacred figure.

THE REVELATION

These intersections of the secular and the sacred continue in the next scene as the Guardian Angel reveals his identity and part of the mystery is uncovered. After the match, which was won by the good guys, Max and his father, his brother, and Uncle Lalo are asked to meet with the Guardian Angel. They find the Guardian Angel in his dressing room, where he proceeds to ask them a set of questions. The first one is about Braulia, Max's mother, the next about Braulia's father, and the last about Braulia's sister and brother. These questions are deeply important to lucha libre, as the enterprise runs on secrets, from who will win the match to the identity of the luchadores. Before he will unmask, the Guardian Angel must make certain that he reveals his identity solely to his family. It is only after the family answers in accordance that he removes his mask to reveal that he is Rodolfo, son of Antonio (Max's grandfather) and brother of Braulia (Max's mother). Rodolfo, to everyone in the family, was presumed to have died many years ago. Thus, in keeping with the nature of the previous scenes, where the secular and the sacred intersect, Rodolfo has returned from the dead.

Actually, as we find out in the next chapter, Rodolfo ran away from home as a teenager. He did not believe himself called to a mundane life, so he went looking for fame and fortune in the big city of Monterrey. Instead of realizing his desires, however, the young Rodolfo finds only hardship. Then, one night, he starts a fight with a drunk man who not only stabs him in the chest (the stigmata attributed to lucha libre battles) but also leaves him for dead. Luckily, Rodolfo is saved by a passerby who (through fate) happens to train luchadores. Seeing potential in Rodolfo, Joaquin "Tempest" Anaya agrees to train him. Back in the day, Rodolfo learns, el Tempestad and Huracán Ramírez were world tag-team champions (94). Rodolfo also learns the ropes of lucha libre. Early in his training, he questions why he should train so hard: "It isn't like I'm going to be fighting anybody for real. It's all show, right?" (96). The gym suddenly grows quiet and Rodolfo is taken to task. First, he is informed as to the mutual interdependence of lucha libre: "one day your life could be in his hands. And vice versa. Every time you and your opponents go out into that ring, you're completely dependent on each other. You have to work together. One wrong move, one missed fall or slight miscalculation can send both of you to the hospital or worse" (96). Shortcuts in training, Rodolfo is told, can lead to careers cut short and lives lost. Second, Rodolfo learns what makes lucha libre magic. As Joaquin notes, "every man in this gym has a dream. They've all sacrificed for that dream. For you to belittle their efforts by making a mockery of what they do in the ring is an insult to them. Whether or not the outcome of a match is predetermined isn't the point. What matters is that you bring the crowd to its feet, that you make them chant your name" (98). Soon afterward, Rodolfo takes on the mask and becomes el Ángel de la Guarda. He also let his family back home believe that he died from the knife wounds. To his family, in many ways, he died.

This means that upon his return to Rio Grande City, Rodolfo has a lot of explaining to do. To everyone around him, he has returned from the dead. As a result, Doña Alicia, the corner convenience store owner, faints when she sees him. Naturally, she also wonders what happened. To this, Rodolfo explains that he had amnesia but that the sight of Lalo, because Lalo looks so much like him, brought all his memories back. However, as Max tells us, this story is actually the plot to *The Guardian Angel Versus the Crime Syndicate*, one of the many movies in which the Guardian Angel starred. Rodolfo, in this sense, answers as to his whereabouts by referencing a movie in which the Guardian Angel acted. Even as he comes back from the dead, therefore, Rodolfo continues to blur the line between fiction and reality and between the secular and the sacred, in this, adding more and more intrigue to the mystery of the Guardian Angel.

REDEMPTIONS

Another intermission—this time we explore the greater mystery of the Guardian Angel. While part of the mystery of the Guardian Angel is his hidden identity, we propose that the greater mystery has to do with the redemption of two characters in the novel, Max and Sonia Escobedo, the latter of which wrestles under the name of la Dama Enmascarada. When we first meet Sonia, she is the ex-girlfriend of Lalo. The relationship was fraught with Sonia's jealousies and violence, and ended in a traumatic breakup. In fact, there are still ill feelings. During Lalo and Marisol's wedding someone jammed a 2x4 between the seat and the gas metal and "launched" Lalo's red pickup into the church walls: "The people sitting in the front pews scatter out of the way as the truck comes to a screeching halt in front of the church piano" (124). All signs point to Sonia.

In order to raise funds to fix the damage to the church, Rodolfo proposes a lucha libre match. The first person to whom he proposes this idea is Sonia. Sonia, as it turns out, is the proprietor of a small restaurant, The Back Breaker Haven, in a neighboring town; after hearing Rodolfo's plan she cannot turn down the chance to participate in a match with her idol, the Guardian Angel, so she agrees. It should further be pointed out that the Haven is filled with photographs of luchadores, with the biggest and most prominent being the Guardian Angel. The other luchadores for the lucha libre match will be Dog-Man Aguayo and Vampire Velasquez, who along with la Dama Enmascarada will form the rudo side, and the Guardian Angel and the Aztec Princess will form part of the técnicos. The last técnico will be a newcomer who goes by the wrestling name of el Toro Grande, the Big Bull, and who also happens to be Lalo.

The match unfolds the way lucha libre matches unfold. The rudos come in, then the técnicos. Lalo, we are told, looks impressive, suggesting that his training has gone well. Appearances can be deceiving, and once the match begins Lalo finds himself "an easy target." It does not help that the rudos are doing what rudos do, which is cheat. El Perro Aguayo bites him so hard on the leg that Lalo stumbles, or at least tries to stumble to his corner so he can tag out. Dog-Man, instead, drags him over to their corner and he and la Dama proceed to beat him. Fighting between men and women luchadores is highly frowned upon, but as Max tells us, "rudos never follow the rules. They have no qualms about poking their opponents in the eyes or hitting them with a folding chair" (186). True to being a *ruda*, la Dama stomps on el Toro Grande and even humiliates him by doing a Mexican hat dance on his back. She then grabs him by the horns and plants a kiss on his lips, drawing a rebuke from Lalo's wife.

The fight continues, and no side is able to gain an upper hand, until, that is, Vampire Velasquez "delivers an illegal blow to the Guardian Angel's groin" (190). Finding the Guardian Angel dazed and staggering, the rudos move in for the kill, the unmasking of the Guardian Angel. At this moment, all seems dire, but then this is lucha libre, and, as we mentioned earlier, the greater mystery in the novel is the redemption of Max and Sonia. For Sonia, the moment has arrived, to pull the mask off the Guardian Angel or to prove that she can overcome her ruda-ness. Sonia refuses to pull the mask off the Guardian Angel and instead turns on the rudos. In the aftermath of Sonia's "conversion" the técnicos win easily. The Guardian Angel, it appears, is more than simply a wrestler. He looks out for people and even helps in their redemption.

As for Max, the novel ends with Rodolfo training him. As Rodolfo earlier learned, lucha libre training is more than techniques and holds and acrobatics; it is about larger life lessons. When Max asks Rodolfo if Lalo is to be the next Guardian Angel, Rodolfo says, "I don't know ... He might be, but at this point I can't say for sure" (200). Rodolfo adds that he would like the Guardian Angel to live on, after he retires. It is important in lucha libre to have an heir to the mask; although Rodolfo achieved his dream of fame and fortune, he also never married or had children. There are tinges of regret as he talks to Max. This may be the reason that Max then asks why Rodolfo never let anyone know he was alive, why he (Rodolfo) chose to distance himself from his family. Rodolfo says it was due to embarrassment: he could not be like his brother Antonio, who in Rodolfo's words, "sacrificed his own plans for the sake of the family" (202). Rather than deal with the shame of not being as good as Antonio, he left. Fame and fortune therefore came with a terrible price for Rodolfo, who finds himself alone and without an heir.

Perhaps guardian angels need guardian angels too, for the novel ends with two promises. Rodolfo promises to never abandon the family again: "I am your family's own personal Guardian Angel now" (202), the pun showcasing the way his role has brought families and communities together as well as the way he staged a place for Max and Sonia to find redemption through their actions. Max's promise comes after he has delivered a perfect flying dropkick. As he says, "Tío Rodolfo is taken by surprise. Like a colossal titan knocked off his perch by a young lion, he collapses down to the mat. I stare in disbelief. I have just knocked the Guardian Angel off his feet!" (204). If Lalo does not want to be the Guardian Angel (later novels tell us that he does not), then "I promise you that I will. I'll become the Guardian Angel" (206). The novel ends, therefore, with the passing of the mask from one generation to the next.

In our analysis of *Maximilian and the Mystery of the Guardian Angel*, we foreground the way in which cultural wealth, much like the tell-tale mask that is passed from Rodolfo to Max, from the current Guardian Angel to the future Guardian Angel, is diasporic in nature for Latinx youth. There is a complex transnational dynamic, to use Brochin and Medina's terminology, at play in the way that cultural wealth is inherited and the way that it is deployed in the lived experiences of diasporic youth, as the novel elucidates. This diasporic cultural wealth, we argue, is positioned to offset deficit thinking, namely, the idea that homelands such as Mexico are culturally impoverished. Much like Max in the novel, Latinx youth can contest these racist notions by turning to the stories, legends, and icons of their homelands. These forms of cultural wealth enable Latinx youth, as holders and creators of knowledge, to engender new worlds in which various forms of cultural wealth are acknowledged and valued. Understood from the narrative logic of the novel, Latinx youth can transform the world by donning the mask that is bequeathed to them by previous generations and from distant homelands.

Summer of the Mariposas

LATINX MYTHOLOGIES + MAGICAL REALISM = LATINX MYTHOLOGICAL REALISM

Madeline Miller, author of *Circe* and *The Song of Achilles*, uses the term "mythological realism" to describe her literary adaptations of Greek myths and stories. In the same vein as Rick Riordan, best known for his Percy Jackson series, and Neil Gaiman in *American Gods*, the cornerstone of Miller's project is adapting mythology-based stories for modern readers. As to these mythology-based retellings, she explains that adaptation allows her "to bring balance to the perspective—to say, 'Okay, we've had three thousand years of the male-hero tradition; can we just pull on that a little bit and bring the female voices up?'" (Plotz and Turrigiano). Indeed, whether in *Circe* or *The Song of Achilles*, Miller brings a much-needed corrective to the "single-narrative" usually associated with mythological (in this case Greek) male heroes. Thus, if the "mythological" part of the term is self-evident in the subject of her work, we are still left with questions regarding the "realism" part. In this, Miller goes on to add that the wellspring of her literary transfigurations stems from magical realism:

> I came out of a tradition as a young person [that involved] reading a lot of magical realism. I loved magical realism growing up, not just mythology. I loved Isabel Allende and I loved [Gabriel] García Márquez and Julia Alvarez and all these sorts of magical realist writers. They were books that I read again and again. It just felt very natural to have those [mythological] components in the story, and I think they're really doing something very interesting in the original. (Plotz and Turrigiano)

This, then, is the equation: Greek mythology x magical realism = mythological realism. In the course of our study, we propose to alter the equation, replacing Greek mythology with Latinx mythologies, where the new equation is Latinx mythology x magical realism = Latinx mythological realism. Latinx mythological realism, we posit, allows a critical entryway for exploring the role of Latinx mythologies and magical realism at play in Latinx literary productions, specifically as it informs Latinx young adult literature and Latinx young readers.

García McCall, attuned to such questions of mythology and Latinx identity, explains that the writing process for *Summer of the Mariposas* began for her after an eighth-grade female student in her class posed, "But why do boys get to have all the adventures? It's not fair. We need our own *Odyssey*" ("Teacher's Guide" 2). This inspiration led to the mixing of mythology and Latinx culture, as García McCall explains,

> She was right. Girls her age need to see themselves depicted in that light. They need to have books where they are wise and clever and brave . . . But why stop there? my brain asked. Why not really turn this thing on its ear and make it about Hispanic girls? Better yet, why not make it about our culture? We have myths and legends and monsters and heroes and ancient deities who are just as interesting as the ones in the original text. Suddenly it all came together for me, and I went home, took out the sticky notes, and outlined the entire adventure on my wall. ("Teacher's Guide" 2)

What García McCall outlined on her wall is a story of five sisters (teenage and younger) who live in Eagle Pass, Texas, but who, in finding a dead body floating in the Rio Grande, decide to take the body back to El Sacrificio, Coahuila, Mexico. In truth, the sisters want to return the body so afterward they can make the short trip from El Sacrificio to la Hacienda Dorada to visit their paternal grandmother, whose help they desire in locating their estranged father. The girls also seek an explanation for his absence from their home and lives.

True to the *Odyssey*, the sisters have to outsmart a witch (Cecilia/Circe) who gives them drugs to keep them in her home. They seek wisdom (the directions to their grandmother's house) from Teresita (Tiresias), wind up blinding the chupacabra (think Cyclops), and outduel lechuzas (sirens) to finally reach Abuelita Remedios, a *curandera*. Lastly, La Llorona is Athena to the sisters and La Virgen de Guadalupe/Tonantzin is the mother of humankind who oversees all things. The journey by the *cinco hermanitas* seems to be part of a larger plan and thus divinely inspired: "I have been sent here to help you find your way," La Llorona tells Odilia, the eldest of the girls and as such the Odysseus in the text. "There is a path designed for everyone and everyone must walk in his or her path. This is your path" (52). In this, we can interpret that La Virgen de Guadalupe/Tonantzin is troubled by what has become of her children, especially her children who migrated from Mexico to the United States and now find themselves adrift, so she sends La Llorona to guide them. La Llorona tells Odilia that she and her sisters "must travel to the other side, into the land of your ancestors, to find each other again" (53). This adventure, it appears, involves a transnational journey not only through the US/Mexico borderlands but also into the supernatural worlds of Latinx mythologies.

When asked why the radical change in La Llorona (who goes from wailing woman, a sort of bogeywoman, who abducts children to replace the ones she drowned) to Athena, García McCall notes that she was inspired by Rudolfo Anaya's *The Legend of La Llorona* ("David"). In Anaya's short novel, La Llorona gains historical and mythic dimensions. La Llorona, Anaya proposes, was Malintzin, consort to Hernán Cortés and mother to the first "Mexican" children. Thusly inspired, García McCall, in the author's note to the novel, states that by presenting Malintzin in a modern setting,

> I am giving her the occasion to tell "her side" of the story, to make us look into her heart and know that a mother's love is pure, not selfish or malignant. Using La Llorona as a mystical guide afforded me the opportunity to redeem her. After all, as parents, we all make mistakes and we all deserve a chance to make things right, much like Mamá does at the end of this book when she transforms herself. (337)

In *Summer of the Mariposas*, La Llorona first appears to Odilia when Odilia experiences grave doubts about taking the body back to Mexico. In fact, Odilia ponders sabotaging the enterprise by getting caught at the border. For now, though, she goes along with her sisters and drives to the river to pick up the body. It is at the river that La Llorona, or rather her children, first appear. Odilia notices two little boys running along the riverbank, who then fall into the water. She dives in after them, but they are already drowned. As their mother, La Llorona, states: "They drown before I can reach them. It is my nightmare, my destiny, my fate to search endlessly for them by night only to find them drowned with the sight of morning" (48). Although Odilia feels scared at first—"I had heard so many awful things about La Llorona that I couldn't help it, I pulled away from her and took a few steps back" (49)—she continues to listen and learns that La Llorona did not intentionally drown her children. Instead, the drowning was triggered by Hernán's decision to leave and in their fighting, "*mis hijos* were so scared, so confused, that they fled toward the river in darkness and drowned. It is a nightmare I experience every night, a memory I am forever reliving" (50). Further, La Llorona's punishment was self-imposed, as she goes on to explain: "A penance for my part in it. I should have been more careful, made sure they were always safe. I want them to come back to me, but they won't—or can't. I do not know the reason behind it, but they are being kept from me" (50).

Far from the malevolent figure depicted in didactic legends, La Llorona appears in this novel as a mother who refuses to rest, who from a self-imposed penance continues to search for her children for centuries (336). In this way, *Summer of the Mariposas*, we suggest, functions as a corrective not only to the traditional male heroic model in *The Odyssey* but also to traditional beliefs governing the role and function of La Llorona. As to this feminist turn, Cristina Herrera, in "Cinco Hermanitas: Myth and Sisterhood in Guadalupe García McCall's *Summer of the Mariposas*," argues,

> here La Llorona speaks as a way to model to Odilia the need to possess language to refute patriarchy. Odilia is left with the charge of questioning the narrative she has been told her whole life, a version that she learns is not only false, according to La Llorona's explanation, but one that positions all mothers as culpable for any harm that falls on their children, even in accidental cases. Odilia thus learns that women's stories are silenced and revised to fit within a system of patriarchy. (103)

From Herrera's lens, Odilia and her hermanitas learn the importance of recovering silenced voices in Latinx mythologies. In the process, the hermanitas also discover how transfiguring mythologies can be a powerful form of resistance, how the cultural collective of myths and other stories holds valuable purchase for modern identity reformulations that are more in concert with gender and racial equity.

Much like Madeline Miller in *Circe* or *The Song of Achilles*, García McCall in *Summer of the Mariposas* brings a much-needed corrective to the male hero tradition, recasting heroes, in this case the cinco hermanitas, within a more equitable framework of representation. The transfigured mythologies in *Summer of the Mariposas* allow for silenced voices, represented in the form of La Llorona, to come to the foreground to be heard. In the process, modern Latinx young readers—perhaps like the young woman in García McCall's class who did not see herself in the classical myths—can see themselves now in the Latinx mythological realism of *Summer of the Mariposas* and imagine a world where their culture and lived experience are treasured.

MAGICAL NEW REALITIES

With this understanding of Latinx mythological realism in mind, let us look at how *Summer of the Mariposas* deploys this genre as a way of helping young readers to know their cultural wealth. Here we will see the use of the genre, with its magical realist roots, as a decolonizing force that blurs binaries and calls for more openness to in-between spaces.

Summer of the Mariposas begins with a family tragedy, a natural disaster, and an enchanting, spectacular, and perhaps magical surprise:

> Almost a year after our father left the house, never to be heard from again, the long, miserable drought ended in Texas. The heavy summer rains had more than enchanted everyone; the days that followed had brought forth a most unexpected, spectacular surprise. To our delight, an unusually large brood of American Snout butterflies swarmed Eagle Pass by the billions. (1)

As readers, we are left to wonder if the drought is tied to the father leaving, as if nature mirrors the loss felt by the cinco hermanitas, and whether the butterflies are tied to both events with nature signaling some new beginning. In other words, we wonder if magic is present in the everyday, in our quotidian experiences. On one level, the butterflies appear as nothing more than a natural occurrence, a kaleidoscope emerging after the rains. And yet *Summer of the Mariposas* is not coy about announcing its magical realist roots, informing us in the teacher's guide that "it is recommended for teachers to explain that within this genre [magical realism], new realities are typically created. Inclusion of magical elements are organically weaved into the plot line, thus creating what appears to be realistic. Students must be able to draw the line between reality and what is unquestionably fantastic" ("Teacher's Guide" 2). The butterflies, on another level, therefore, appear to be magical elements "organically weaved into the plot."

In this regard, Wendy Faris tells us in *Ordinary Enchantments* that magical realist narratives conjure a space that "combines realism and the fantastic so that the marvelous seems to grow organically within the ordinary, blurring the distinction between them" (1). Faris adds that magical realism is an effective decolonizing agent that destabilizes conventions of realism based on empirical evidence by incorporating other kinds of perception, namely, the mysterious and the magical. She calls this conjured space the "ineffable in-between." By remystifying literary works, that is, bringing magic and mysteries that cannot be explained by scientific evidence, magical realism indeed opens a necessary space that counters what we are provided as real. It does so by accommodating in that space the presence of irreducible elements, which in the case of our study means mythological beings, culturally salient magical realms, and items with special properties and provenances.

Summer of the Mariposas, we argue, transforms the borderlands into an "ineffable in-between" space where La Llorona guides her children and where butterflies, as in Aztec times, are the cheerful souls of ancestors returning home to affirm and inspire the living. As the introductory page of the novel informs us,

> In almost every culture, butterflies are associated with transformation. The Aztecs held the butterfly, *papalotl*, in high regard and had a special celebration to welcome the migrating monarchs in early August every year. They believed that mariposas were the cheerful souls of their loved ones, the angels of women and children, their fallen warriors, their ancestors, returning home transformed to assure them that they were well and that life, however brief, was beautiful. (Introductory page)

Summer of the Mariposas, as we noted, begins with a family tragedy—the father has left and has not been heard of since—and a drought has plagued the land. After the enchanting summer rains, the *mariposas* arrive to inaugurate a new transformation, a new reality in which the ancestors come back to assure and affirm youths, their descendants, who live in the borderlands. It appears that the Aztecs, as a core element of

Chicanx and Mexican identity, have returned.⁵ And they have returned, via this mythological realist novel, to ensure that troubled children who may find themselves adrift can seek their own transformations, can grow their conocimiento so that they can create their own new realities.

In this light, the novel showcases the importance of Latinx mythological realism both at the beginning and the end of the cinco hermanitas' transnational odyssey. In order to cross into Mexico, for example, Odilia first attempts to convince the border guard that she and her sisters are taking a trip with their "father," who is seemingly asleep in the back seat. When the guard becomes suspicious, Odilia reaches up and gives her pendant earring a twist, earrings that were given to her as an aid by La Llorona. The earring begins to spin and she prays, "Aztec queen, Tonantzin, Holy Mother of all mankind, give me your magical assistance. Distract this man, make him forget what he has seen" (66). Thus entranced, the guard allows them to pass.

Significantly, the ear pendants resemble the likeness of Cihuacóatl, La Serpiente. Cihuacóatl, who as the novel's glossary informs the reader, is the Aztec "goddess of motherhood and fertility as well as midwives" (341). This invocation of Cihuacóatl resonates with the novel's endeavor to reconceptualize La Llorona in particular and mothers in general. It should be pointed out that in Aztec culture, mothers who died in childbirth, like warriors who died in battle, were transformed into butterflies. This, then, may be the reason why, as they are stopped at the border crossing, the butterflies "flittered around us, beating their wings gently against the windshield then sitting prettily on the dashboard. At least a dozen of them had flown into the backseat and settled on Pita. Four of them clung to her hair, opening and closing their wings in long, luxurious strokes, while the rest of them crawled delicately along her arms" (65). Cihuacóatl in this regard might denote the ways the cinco hermanitas are being taught new ways of being and doing, to see themselves "where they are wise and clever and brave" (Teacher's Guide 2). Furthermore, they are being taught to revise stories as counterspells to stories that do violence to mothers, such as La Llorona stories that harm Mexican American women. In this, Cihuacóatl, it could be argued, is "midwiving" a whole new way of being and doing for readers.

If the beginning of this transnational odyssey starts with this artfully rendered scene, the journey ends when the sisters have to get back "home" as quickly as possible; there are suspicions that the sisters have disappeared because their mother went "La Llorona" on them. With the help of their paternal grandmother, Abuelita Remedios, an apt name for a curandera, the sisters are first allowed to recuperate from their adventures with el Nagual, el Chupacabra, and las Lechuzas. Then, with Abuelita Remedios behind the wheel, they make their way back to the border. Upon arrival in Piedras Negras, on the Mexico side, they realize that in their haste to leave they forgot to get their birth certificates required to get back into the United States. Unwilling to go to the authorities, believing they will be detained unnecessarily or even made hostages for ransom, the girls and Abuelita Remedios seek magical help from La Virgen/Tonantzin. Together they go to church and pray: "*Virgencita Santa*, Holy Mother, we have done as you asked. We delivered a man to his wife and children and tried our best to stay humble and kind and gave mercy when it was asked of us. Aztec queen, Tonantzin, Holy Mother of all mankind, lend us your magical assistance one last time. Please help us cross the Rio Grande, deliver us home to our Mamá" (270).

After their prayer, the ear pendant begins to whiz and whirl and they are transported into a vision. In this vision-world they see "a youthful Tonantzin, the Goddess of Sustenance, the girl who had saved us from the *nagual*, lifted her arms to welcome us, her beloved daughters. And when I looked around, I saw that a flurry of magnificent mariposas swarmed around us as we stood waiting on the summit of the hill, awed by the surreal beauty that surrounded us" (271–72). La Virgen then gives them one more mission: "I need you to remind the mother that she is the flower, the bud, the giver of life. She needs to be honored with love and redemption" (274). Although they do not fully understand what this means, they pick up the *rosas de castilla* and begin to walk along a "moonlit trail toward a dark and misty shore, a surreal place, a place somewhere between sleep and wakefulness" (276). As Juanita notes, it is not so much a matter of where they are, as when. Even "when" is problematic as Abuelita's watch does not seem to work. They ask Ixtali, the young lady who graciously gives them a ride across the lake, where they are and if they have traveled back in time. She explains that they are not traveling back in time, but forward, across Texcoco Lake, to the place where their mother's people made their home. According to Ixtali, they are being given a vision "to always remember who you are, where you came from, as you develop a better future" (280). A few minutes later the mist clears and they find themselves at their old swimming hole. As with much of what has transpired in the novel, the ending blends the realism of the border, of finding themselves without their papers and thus trapped in Mexico and at the disposal of criminals, with the magical, a vision of Lake Texcoco that will allow them to remember who they are, by where they came from, as they move forward.

THE SHAMAN'S CURE

Summer of the Mariposas ends with the sisters making it back to Eagle Pass to stop their father from taking possession of their house and throwing out their mother, an artful twist on the fight with the suitors in *The Odyssey*. While this ends the sisters' adventure, the novel concludes with La Llorona rewarded for her help and divinely forgiven by La Virgen de Guadalupe/Tonantzin. La Llorona, then, is joined by her children in the sky. By forgiving and rewarding La Llorona thusly, La Virgen/Tonantzin heals the wound that opened at the Conquest in the birth of and then abandonment of the children born to Malintzin and Cortés. *Summer of the Mariposas*, in this sense, intertwines the cinco hermanitas' journey with the magical and mythological journey of La Llorona. The adventure ends with healing brought to both worlds, the real world of the cinco hermanitas, and the magical and mythological world of La Llorona.

As to ways in which magical realist, or in this case mythological realist, texts remystify narratives in the West, Wendy Faris notes that "magical realist narrative resembles a shaman's account of his activities, which seems as if it 'walks the "razor's edge" between the natural and supernatural universes and is therefore capable of entering and leaving them both at will'" (75). Faris further posits that

> Regardless of their specific political agendas, magical realist texts are often written in the context of cultural crises, almost as if their magic is invoked when recourse to other, rational, methods have failed. From this perspective, the shamanistic voice in magical realism represents the appeal to a power from a different place: ancient "guardians of life" are invoked in order to deal with present social atrocities. (83)

Summer of the Mariposas, in this regard, deliberately underscores the atrocities at the center of social crises in the borderlands, from the militarized border the cinco hermanitas have to cross and try to recross, to the influx of drugs and drug smuggling across the border, to fathers who abandon their children. *Summer of the Mariposas*, we argue, also deliberately foregrounds a cure to these social illnesses by tracing how "ancient 'guardians of life'" guide the cinco hermanitas in their journey through the real and magical borderlands. In the midst of these crises, in which other recourses have failed, *Summer of the Mariposas*, like other magical or mythological realist texts, deploys magic as a counterspell. As we have seen, *Summer of the Mariposas* is saturated with magic, in the form of the earrings, the butterflies, and the journey across Texcoco Lake, to name a few. From this, it is our argument that *Summer of the Mariposas*, as a mythological realist narrative, invokes ancient guardians of life and other Latinx mythological figures, as an epistemological cure to present social atrocities. In this endeavor, the shaman is vital.

According to Anzaldúa, in the past "the shaman and the poet were the same person. The role of the shaman is, as it was then, to preserve and create cultural or group identity by mediating between the cultural heritage of the past and the present everyday situation people find themselves in" ("Metaphors" 121). Akin to Faris's notions that magic is deployed in times of crisis, Anzaldúa further tells us that poet-shamans are able to see "'illness,' lo que daña, whatever is harmful in the cultural or individual body. I see that 'sickness' unbalances a person or a community. That it may be in the form of disease, or disinformation/misinformation perpetrated on women and people of color" (121–22). The cure to this sickness, whether caused by illness or disinformation perpetrated on women and people of color, may consist, according to Anzaldúa, of "removing something (disindoctrination), of extracting the old dead metaphors. Or it may consist of adding what is lacking—restoring the balance and strengthening the physical, mental, and emotional states of the person. This 'cure' leads to a change in our belief system, en lo que creemos" (122). Put another way, if realist narratives buoyed by empirical evidence are an important source for what we believe and thus how we organize the world, mythological realist narratives "cure" the system of destructive metaphors and debilitating racist stories by proposing a change in the ways we believe. This epistemological shift is highlighted, from our perspective, by occupying intermediary spaces between worlds, as nepantleras are wont to do, and by choosing "to move between worlds like the ancient chamanas who choose to build bridges between worlds, choose to speak from the cracks between the worlds, from las rendijas (rents). We must choose to see through the holes in reality, choose to perceive something from multiple angles" (*Light / Luz* 92).

If mythological and magical realist narratives resemble a shaman's account of their activities, as Faris informs us, these narratives do so in order to cure us of realistic stories that exclude other (magical) ways of seeing and elide important connections between the cultural heritage of the past and the present. In other words, mythological realist narratives, such as *Summer of the Mariposas*, heal these social sicknesses by (re)linking the everyday world with the world of the supernatural. For texts such as *Summer of the Mariposas* what this means is that the intentional deployment of La Llorona, the Virgen, or Ixtali allows young readers to see "the cracks between the worlds," to see "through the holes in reality" as a way of cultivating new realities, new epistemologies, whose role is to cure present social and cultural crises.

It is our understanding that the flowering of magical realism and mythological realism in children's and young adult literature stems from the realization that magical elements and mythological stories offer a curative counterspell to oppressions commonly found in the borderlands. Our reading of *Summer of the Mariposas* centers this idea that envisioning a more positive version of La Llorona, that seeing the Virgen as the mother of all children, and that reorienting *lo que creemos* are vital to *la curación*, the cure, of these crises. Our hope, in this, is that mythological realist texts, such as *Summer of the Mariposas*, continue to be read within this curative framework, for there is much daño in the world. Latinx mythologies, as found in *Summer of the Mariposas*, in this sense, cure.

Conclusion

Over the course of this chapter our endeavor has been to alight on the cultural wealth of diasporic youth. In our analyses, we highlight the significant role of lucha libre to Latinx culture and identity in *Maximilian and the Mystery of the Guardian Angel* and underscore the power of Latinx and Mexican mythologies to create decolonized epistemologies and thus new realities in *Summer of the Mariposas*. Such a venture, we believe, allows us to better comprehend the complex cultural networks that inform the lived experiences of Latinx youth. In other words, by being attentive to these diasporic imaginings, we better grasp the way diasporic cultural wealth contests forms of nationalism, such as assimilationist policies and practices, and destabilizes deficit thinking. In our reading of *Maximilian and the Mystery of the Guardian Angel* and *Summer of the Mariposas* we argue that these novels situate diasporic cultural wealth as vital for Latinx cultural production and meaning making. Diasporic cultural wealth, from this lens, allows Latinx youth to be creators of knowledge, that is, to understand how this diasporic cultural wealth bestows on them the possibility of engendering new worlds in which their lives and cultures are valued (Anzaldúa, *Light / Luz* 143).

CHAPTER FOUR

Kids' Agency and Empowerment in an Era of Family Deportation

Healing takes place in community, in the telling and
the bearing witness, in the naming of trauma and
in the grief and rage and defiance that follows.
AURORA LEVINS MORALES / *Medicine Stories*

Levántate, rise up in testimony.... Let's look at these
events as catalysts that allow us to reframe global disasters,
prompt us into remapping our priorities—figuring out
exactly what we believe in, what our lives mean, and what
our purpose is as individuals, as a nation, and as world citizens.
GLORIA ANZALDÚA / *Light in the Dark / Luz en lo oscuro*

When asked by his best friend why he did not share the devastating news that his mother had been deported, Efrén Nava, the protagonist of Ernesto Cisneros's young adult novel *Efrén Divided*, "pressed his lips together—felt them trembling" and said, "'I tried. It just hurt too much to say aloud'" (245). I (Jesus), too, know of the pain that haunts Efrén. I also know that the recovery from trauma, as Aurora Levins Morales informs us in the epigraph to this chapter, "takes place in community, in the telling and the bearing witness, in the naming of trauma and in the grief and rage and defiance that follows" (62). The first step, for Levins Morales, is to name the abuse. Then, from there, healing comes by "creating and telling *another story* about the experience of violence and the nature of the participants, a story powerful enough to restore a sense of our full humanity to the abused" (61, emphasis ours). In this way, we also must attend to the "grief and rage and defiance that follows" (62).

With Anzaldúa's call to "rise up in testimony" in mind, this chapter concerns bearing witness to what it means and feels like to be deported and/or to have a loved one deported, from the perspectives of Latinx children and young adults. We position deportation at the center of our discussion, first to recognize and acknowledge la herida, the wound, and, second, to bring light to a healing process for these heridas currently devastating Latinx children and families in the United States. In this, we believe that the young adult novels, *Efrén Divided* (2020) by Ernesto Cisneros and *Land of the Cranes* (2020) by Aida Salazar, and the picture book *From North to South / Del norte al sur* (2013) by René Colato Laínez and illustrated by Joe Cepeda, provide excellent testimonies that bear witness to the systemic, officially sanctioned, and nationally funded racism at the heart of the deportations of Latinx peoples in the United States. Our argument in this chapter is that these testimonies, beyond acknowledging the heridas, also serve as LatCrit counter-stories that intentionally foreground reparative tactics that challenge the dominant discourse on race and belonging. LatCrit counter-storytelling, in this sense, becomes a form of healing. As Levins Morales reminds us, "when the stories of the abused are transformed and push their way into public space, their power to undermine the dominant narrative and shake up how people perceive reality can be tremendous" (58). Our aim in this chapter is to focus our critical attention on stories of deportation and to push them into the public space, in this way undermining racist understandings of immigrants. The promise of these reparative processes is new realities constructed on foundations of belonging and racial equity.

These reparative processes, in many ways, emerge from the experience of authors. In the author's note to *Land of the Cranes*, Aida Salazar states that she wrote the young adult novel "with an understanding of the long and devastating history of raids, separations, deportations, incarcerations, and deaths my community has suffered" (244). She steps back, for a second, then reveals that she also wrote *Land of the Cranes* "from an intimate place. I, like Betita, was an undocumented child. I was born in Mexico and brought to the United States as a baby. My childhood fear of 'La Migra' (immigration enforcement) and how they could easily rip our family apart hung over me until we received our green cards" (244–45). Salazar's courage to speak from a space of intimacy weighs heavy on my mind (Jesus, here). Like Salazar, I lived part of my childhood in fear that at any moment our family could easily be ripped apart. Then, it was. When I was about five (first year of kindergarten), my father was caught by La Migra and deported. We lived in West Texas at the time. I do not remember much other than fleeting images of my mother crying incessantly. She later told us her story, though it was in whispers and only shared with my sisters and me. This is to say that she, to this day, is haunted by this deportation experience. A few years later—I was in third grade by then—La Migra caught me, my mother, and my middle sister. We were deported soon afterward. It was my father's time to grieve. He had recently received his green card and therefore could stay in the United States, along with my youngest sister, who was born in Texas. Our family was, once again, torn apart. When my sisters and I gather, we often remind ourselves of who we are and what we persevered by telling and retelling stories of our childhoods and of our deportations. In this way, bearing witness to our experiences has allowed us to know "exactly what we believe in, what our lives mean, and what our purpose is as individuals, as a nation, and as world citizens" (Anzaldúa, *Light / Luz* 21).

The promise of this chapter is that, in examining Latinx children's and young adult narratives on deportation, we can begin the reparative processes that will heal the heridas in people as well as in our nation. For this to unfold, we must grapple with the fact that deportations are founded on racist principles of desconocimiento. As Anzaldúa reminds us, the "path of desconocimiento leads human consciousness into ignorance, fear, and hatred. It succumbs to righteous judgment and withdraws into separation and domination, pushing most of us into retaliatory acts of further rampage, which beget more violence. This easier path uses force and violence to socially construct our nation" (*Light / Luz* 19). In this, the fight against ignorance, fear, and hatred cannot encompass retaliatory acts, in as much as these are often desired. Instead, we tread on the path of conocimiento, which "leads to awakening, insights, understandings, realizations, courage, and the motivation to engage in concrete ways with the potential to bring us into compassionate interactions" (*Light / Luz* 19). Our revolution, in this way, is empowered by ideas, and it "is fought with concepts, not with guns, and it is fueled by vision. By focusing on what we want to happen, we change the present" (Anzaldúa, "Now Let Us Shift" 5). The picture book and young adult novels chosen for this chapter, at their core, present ways to dismantle racism with conocimiento in mind, that is, with tactics that lead to the change we *want* to happen. I (Jesus) add my own testimonio to state, in what ways I can, that healing will transform our present as much as it will transform our future.

Finding Hope and Home

My story (Jesus) is not unique. In 2012 the Pew Research Center estimated that 4.5 million US-born children under eighteen live with at least one undocumented immigrant parent (Passel et al. 8). Further, increased immigration efforts in recent years, whereby the United States government has forcibly removed undocumented immigrants at the rate of 400,000 per year since 2009, has left many children who are US citizens without one or both parents (Dreby, "U.S. Immigration" 245). As these statistics indicate, the involuntary separation of family members via deportation and the fear of this possibility have become an everyday reality for myriad mixed-status immigrant families in the United States.[1]

It is important to examine the ways in which increased surveillance and seizures in recent years, in what Nicholas De Genova calls a "deportation regime" (34), have impacted Latinx children and young adults, with specific attention to living with heightened anxieties. As Joanna Dreby points out, "Indirectly, enforcement activities create a climate of fear" (*Everyday Illegal* 24). Further exacerbating this climate of fear has been the rhetoric emanating from government officials. We needed only listen to the exclusionary rhetoric of former US president Donald Trump, who associated Brown bodies with crime, drug abuse, and rape: "When Mexico sends its people, they're . . . sending people that have lots of problems, and they're bringing those problems with us. They're bringing drugs. They're bringing crime. They're rapists" (Lee). Not only are Mexicans entering the United States with drugs and crime, but also, according to Trump, they bring contagious disease: "Tremendous infectious disease is pouring across the border. The United States has become a dumping ground for Mexico and, in fact, for many other parts of the world" (Walker). We hear in these statements echoes of the rhetoric of disgust and the resulting need for separation, reminiscent of the segregation era in US history. This anxiety about mixing with immigrants becomes more pronounced in the president's comments on immigration in Europe, which he later associates to the United States, "I think what has happened to Europe is a shame . . . I think it changed the fabric of Europe and, unless you act very quickly, it's never going to be what it was and I don't mean that in a positive way . . . I think you are losing your culture" (Khan). There is a sense that Brown-bodied immigrants weaken the "fabric" of the nation; they taint the cloth and make the nation less than it was in its former glory. The danger in our present moment is that this disgust of Brown bodies and fear of contamination becomes part of the national imaginary. We already see how this exclusionary rhetoric plays out in laws and actions. And yet the real tragedy occurs when this hatred becomes inscribed in the minds of young Brown children.

This rhetoric of exclusion, specifically the forcible removal of immigrant parents, impacts Latinx communities, including children. According to a Pew Research Study, "about six-in-ten (59%) Hispanic immigrants and 46% of all Hispanics say they worry 'a lot' or worry 'some' that they themselves, a family member or a close friend could be deported" (Lopez et al. 6). Inasmuch as it is disturbing to know that many worry seriously about being deported, we are beginning to see the end point of such exclusionary practices. It is frightening to believe that this rhetoric of exclusion is leading to a place where many undocumented Latino immigrants support deportation relief over paths to citizenship by 61 percent to 27 percent (6). In other words, they are willing to trade away the rights that come with citizenship for respite from the fears that haunt them. Further, as Dreby notes, "The threat of deportation also has a negative effect on children of Mexican immigrants who fear the police, equate a stigma with immigration, and distance themselves from their heritage" ("U.S. Immigration" 246). These children struggle with fear, anxiety, depression, and difficulties at school, as well as the economic challenges that result from single-parent households (246, 250). Put simply, tragedy is unfolding before us.

There is hope, though, and we suggest it lies in our children. Inasmuch as children require our care in these desperate times, Aurora Levins Morales tells us in her essay "The Politics of Childhood" that it would be wise "to listen deeply and with respect to the ways they [children] experience the world, validate their sense of injustice, and help them understand the systemic nature of unfairness" (108). She goes on to add: "As adults, we need to listen to children more than we talk to them. We must back the initiative of children themselves, secure resources and share skills, respect their right and ability to lead themselves, and learn to let them lead us" (108). Our hope is funded by Levins Morales's entreaty that we "listen deeply" to our children as they make sense of injustices and unfairness. Moreover, we are heartened by her appeal to "back the initiative of children" and, in this way, "learn to let them lead us" (108). Children, if we listen to them and validate their experiences, can be our leaders.

In the texts chosen for this study we witness two present realities of

Latinx children: parent deportation and family detention. Both *From North to South / Del norte al sur* by René Colato Laínez and illustrated by Joe Cepeda and *Efrén Divided* by Ernesto Cisneros present the experience of children who confront the deportation of a parent. In the *Land of the Cranes* by Aida Salazar, Betita (the novel's protagonist), her mother, and the unborn "egg" that the mother is carrying are all placed in an Immigration and Customs Enforcement (ICE) hielera, or icebox, as the ICE detention facilities are called. Much like the real children affected by the racist deportation policies mentioned above, the children and young adults in these novels have to confront realities in which their families have been torn apart or in which they have been put in cages. At the same time, each of these books empowers their young protagonists to challenge and transform existing realities. Provided the agency to effect change in the world, José, Betita, and Efrén create new and more liberating worlds, not through violence or retaliation, but through conocimiento tactics that utilize knowledge, insights, and understanding as a healing process for the heridas caused by deportation.

Planting Seeds in *From North to South / Del norte al sur*

According to scholar Cristina Rhodes, America's reliance on graphic, jarring images concerning undocumented immigrants as criminals and as violent animals has reinforced racist notions toward undocumented immigrants and diasporic peoples.[2] What we need, according to Rhodes, are critical counter-narratives that destabilize racism and center agency in children. As she notes, "confronting the realities of undocumented immigration, movement, and diaspora in children's and young adult (YA) literature means rethinking the way childhood agency is constructed" ("Female Empowerment" 21).

We begin this section with Rhodes's imperative to rethink children's empowerment and agency as a way to enter our discussion on deportation narratives. Via picture book *From North to South / Del norte al sur*, we trace the way children deal with the loss of a parent to deportation, and therefore the pain and grief that grips young minds and hearts when faced with these heart-wrenching realities, as well as the way that children find bravery, gain agency, and begin the healing process, for themselves as well as for others.

Designed for readers in grades K–3, bilingual picture book *From North to South / Del norte al sur* recounts the story of José, a young US-born boy who lives in San Diego, California, with his parents. One day, the family's worst fear comes true when José's mother does not return from work: as José explains, "Mamá was born in Mexico and didn't have those papers. The men put Mamá and other workers in a van. In a few hours, Mamá was in Tijuana, Mexico" (7). Thankfully, José and his father are able to visit Mamá at a migrant center across the border in Mexico every weekend. They continue to contemplate what their future will be like—if Mamá will be able to come home and when.

In the introduction to the picture book, Salvadoran American author Colato Laínez highlights the inspiration for this story. In addition to his personal experiences as a young migrant, Colato Laínez explains how he hears stories like José's in the elementary classroom where he teaches in Los Angeles, California:

> One day, one of my students was crying because her father had been deported to Tijuana, Mexico. I discovered that many of the other children had cousins, uncles, or neighbors who had been deported, too. Most of my students had been born in the United States, and it is hard for them to see their loved ones forced to leave the country. For these children, family separation is a traumatic experience. (3)

Similar to children in earlier cited studies, José experiences a significant emotional loss. This trauma is expressed through contrasts between José's life with and without his mother as well as through his sorrowful emotions. For example, before her deportation, José experiences great joy as he gardens after school in the family yard with his mom and dad. On the day that she does not come home from work, José weeps with her over the phone as he learns what happened (7). Readers further see the significance of Mamá in José's life and the gaping hole of her absence when Papá and José visit her at Centro Madre Assunta, a Catholic shelter that aids women and child migrants in Tijuana, Mexico: "Mamá was waiting at the gate. I jumped out of my seat and gave her a hug, crying 'I missed you so much!'" (10). To underscore the impact of this moment, the illustration shows Mamá and José sitting on the floor of her bedroom locked in an embrace. Unable to verbalize his sadness completely, José complains about Papá's burnt tortillas and asks when his mom will be able to come home. In food, José finds a way to say that he misses her nurturing, an everyday way in which she provided comfort. Despite

Mamá's reassurance that everything will be OK because José's dad is a permanent resident and they have a lawyer working on the case (16), a sense of uncertainty remains. For readers, the fear is never assuaged. In fact, the closest we come to a reunification of José with his mom are his dreams on the final page of the picture book: "I dreamt that Mamá had the right papers and we crossed the border together. . . I was ready to eat Mamá's warm *tortillas*, to listen to her bedtime stories, and to hear her beautiful voice saying every single night, '*Buenas noches, mi José*'" (32).

In the midst of these challenges, we point to the ways that *From North to South / Del norte al sur* offers young readers ways of finding hope and agency. As Lauren Gulbas and Luis Zayas in their study on effects of immigration enforcement on children who are US citizens point out, current research on these children often focuses on detrimental effects. This "has led to generalized assumptions about the vulnerability of this population and overshadowed the evaluation of citizen children's strengths, agency, and capacity" (54). We see in *From North to South / Del norte al sur* the resilience of young people facing deportation. The creative tactics modeled in the picture book by José show how these can offer a sense of emotional well-being despite undesirable circumstances. In this, we suggest that these quotidian actions offer possibilities to young readers, especially the 4.5 million who live with at least one undocumented parent and fear or experience loss due to parent deportation. The actions, as modeled in the picture book, have incredible power to transform children's conception of the self (decolonizing the mind) and their place in the nation as the picture book offers alternatives of belonging. In this, *From North to South / Del norte al sur* presents a distinct national imaginary that is affirming and inclusive of children and their families regardless of their documentation status, all while offering useful tools for surviving and thriving.

One of the ways that José emotionally copes with the loss of his mother is through creativity with words and art as well as by gardening and painting. Creativity, in this way, becomes especially useful post-deportation since it helps him to manage powerful feelings and connect emotionally with his distanced parent. According to Kasia Kozlowska and Lesley Hanney in their study on art therapy for children traumatized by parental violence and separation, in addition to allowing children to express traumatic experiences and emotions in safe ways, "creating art is pleasurable and can lead to feelings of competence and hope. It is active rather than passive; uses externalized, concrete images which can be

FIGURE 4.1 Joe Cepeda, Mamá and José embrace. *From North to South / Del norte al sur* by René Colato Laínez and illustrated by Joe Cepeda. Permission arranged with Children's Book Press, an imprint of Lee & Low Books, Inc., New York, NY 10016. All rights not specifically granted herein are reserved.

FIGURE 4.2 Joe Cepeda, Planting seeds and playing games at the shelter. *From North to South / Del norte al sur* by René Colato Laínez and illustrated by Joe Cepeda. Permission arranged with Children's Book Press, an imprint of Lee & Low Books, Inc., New York, NY 10016. All rights not specifically granted herein are reserved.

shared with others; it is controllable and modifiable, and allows for free play and personal expression" (53).

While Kozlowska and Hanney attest to the importance of creativity in their field of child therapy, Sonia Rodríguez, in her essay "Conocimiento Narratives," highlights the power of creativity in challenging systemic oppression and providing a reparative path forward. As she notes, creative acts "serve as catalysts that allow them [Latinx youth] to develop their identity while disrupting and challenging various systems of oppression. Their creativity is born out of trauma and oppression and therefore functions as more than self-expression; instead, the young Latinas' creativity forges a path toward healing that impacts them and their communities" (9). In utilizing Anzaldúa's notions on conocimiento, specifically calling attention to the function of creative acts, such as "writing, art-making, dancing, healing, teaching, meditation, and spiritual activism—both mental and somatic (the body, too, is a form as well as site of creativity)" ("Now Let Us Shift" 542), Rodríguez posits that creative acts "offer both an opportunity to challenge and transform existing epistemologies and the possibility to create new, more liberating ones" (11). For our purposes, we are especially interested in the way that creative acts foster hope in dealing with the separation from parents and forge "a path towards healing that impacts them and their communities" (9). In *From North to South / Del norte al sur*, creative acts, we argue, sustain José post-deportation by providing a strong sense of togetherness with his mother, and, through such modeling, creative acts offer young readers dealing with similar traumas ways to heal.

The picture book foregrounds the use of creativity, especially gardening and painting, as a way to maintain connection and a sense of continuity during separation. Before the deportation, José's mom gardens with him at their home in San Diego each day after school. It is apparent that José experiences feelings of connection and pride in this creativity, as he explains: "Every day, I helped Mamá water her flowers and pull the weeds" (7). In the corresponding illustration, José and his mom face each other on hands and knees, smiling as they plant a blooming red flower in the ground (7). Post-deportation, gardening and other ways of being creative allow José and his mom to feel connected, regardless of their geographic location. During a visit to the center in Tijuana, José is still heartbroken that his mother will not be able to come home with them. Mamá then shows him the garden that she and children at the center take care of. When Mamá says that they will plant seeds that day, José suggests, "Let's play the seed game first" (20). The children then, as José explains, "curled up like seeds. We made rain sounds by clapping our knees together. We stretched one arm up towards the sun, like a sprout. Then, little by little, we stood up and reached for the sky like beautiful flowers" (20). Recalling our argument in chapter 2 that conocimiento can be likened to seeds that "survive and grow, give fruit hundreds of times the size of the seeds" (Anzaldúa, *Borderlands / La Frontera* 113), in this scene in *From North to South*, we find that the children enact (playfully) the processes of conocimiento. Even though most of the children at the center cannot see their parents because "they are so far away" (according to one of the little girls that José meets), they are transforming themselves and their circumstances (19). In their performance of the seed game, the children highlight their growing awareness as they transform from seeds, to sprouts, to beautiful flowers that reach for the sky. Thus, through the use of creative acts, the planting and the performance, the children create a space where they imagine their full potential as beautiful flowers. Moreover, this transformation not only empowers them by giving them agency over how they see themselves at this moment, but also it is a catalyst for how they imagine themselves going forward. In other words, they imagine new realities through these creative acts.

From North to South ends with José and his peers painting cans and getting them ready to use as pots for planting. To this, José adds, "I have an idea. Let's plant seeds in cans for our parents" (22). Thus, alongside the stars and happy faces, the children paint the name of their parents on the pots. It is their hope that they will be reunited with their parents when the seeds grow. The picture book, however, leaves these hopes unresolved, such as if or when José and his mother will be reunited. The other children at the center face these uncertainties. In this moment we are reminded of Rodríguez who warns us of the danger of easy binaries that pit "happy endings" against "sad endings." Instead of looking for resolutions as indicators of happy endings, Rodríguez posits that a better gauge for assessing happiness or resolution is whether conocimiento has taken place:

> The characters' happiness or the authors' resolutions are indicators that conocimiento has taken place, and the different stages the characters go through are probably the most significant aspect . . . Reading these children's texts as conocimiento narratives suggests that the conclusions of the texts are not guarantees of a

better future but instead offer Latinx children the possibility to imagine new realities. (27)

It is our argument that José and the children through creative acts have begun to harness the powers of conocimiento to imagine new realities. While a better future is not guaranteed in *From North to South*, we believe that the actions of painting the cans with their parents' names and planting the seeds, as well as envisioning themselves as seeds in their performance, are evidence that José and the children at the shelter are undergoing the processual stages of conocimiento. Further, as they wrap up their gardening day, "Mamá pointed to the can and said, 'I will take care of our seeds every day'" (27). With a newfound agency fueled by conocimiento, José promises Mamá, "I will take care of our garden at home, too" (27). Thus, even as the picture book leaves the situation unresolved with José and Mamá divided by a geopolitical border, creative acts allow José and the children to imagine new realities in which, like seeds, they will survive and grow into beautiful flowers.

Land of the Cranes and Retrofitted Memory

Land of the Cranes begins with an origin story, told to Betita Quintero, the fourth-grade protagonist of the middle-grade verse novel, by her papi:

> *Long ago, our people came from a place*
> *called Aztlán, the land of the cranes*
> *which is now known as the Southwestern US.*
> *They left Aztlán to fulfill their prophecy:*
> *to build a great city*
> *in the navel of the universe*
> *a small mound in the middle of a lake*
> *where they saw an eagle devour a serpent on a cactus.*
> *They called that place Mexica-Tenochtitlán.*
> *It was also prophesized*
> *our people would return to Aztlán*
> *to live among the cranes again.* (Introductory page)

Even as Huitzilopochtli informed the people of Aztlán that they would venture south to found a great city in the navel of the universe (Tenochtitlán, modern-day Mexico City), the Aztec god of war also prophesied that "our people would return to Aztlán / to live among the cranes again" (Introductory page). This component of the prophecy, the return to Aztlán, informs why many Mexican people emigrate to the US Southwest from Mexico and why Chicanx people have lived for many generations in the US Southwest, the mythical land of Aztlán. In this scenario, Latinx and Chicanx people are not intruders to the United States, but, instead, rightful heirs to their homeland.[3] Betita and her parents belong to these people coming "home," not as migrants fleeing, in this case drug violence in Mexico, but as people seeking to reclaim both the land and the history of their ancestors.

Unfortunately for Betita and her family, the US government has other plans for people who live in the United States *"sin papeles"* or undocumented, "a word that means / 'without permission'" (35).[4] One day, Betita's father is picked up by Immigration and Customs Enforcement and deported to Mexico. As a child, Betita is unable fully to grasp the situation. All she knows is that "Papi will be / put on a plane and flown / to Mexico" (41) and that ICE "are the ones doing 'round-ups' / collecting birds in cages / clipping their wings / and sending them back / to where they were born" (47).

Presenting the events from the perspective of a nine-year-old, *Land of the Cranes* utilizes her budding awareness to great effect. Specifically, Betita, influenced by the Aztec origin story, envisions herself and her parents as cranes. This understanding of the family as cranes allows Betita, when her father is picked up by ICE, to better grapple with complex geopolitical situations in her own way, by seeing ICE as "collecting birds in cages" and "clipping their wings" (47). The literary conceit continues throughout the novel: Juan Felipe Herrera, the first Latinx poet laureate of the United States, for example, is "a crane like us" (12) and her mother's unborn child is "our own egg" (46). Cranes also will inform her nom de plume, Plumita, an artful Spanish double entendre, as *pluma* is both a pen and a feather, in this case a crane feather.

It is our argument that by imaging herself and other Latinx people as cranes, a kind of mythohistorical intervention, Betita challenges the dominant narrative that immigrants should be rounded up and sent to their birthplaces. As Lee Bebout points out, "mythohistorical interventions—the seizing of historical agency to refashion the world and the ways in which experience is ordered—function as a significant strategy in identity-based social struggles. Through this discursive field, social movements can be mobilized and legitimated" (8). In this sense, mythological interventions both point to personal growth, in the form of agency, and, as Bebout posits, they can be used to mobilize and legitimate social movements. From this lens, Betita seizes historical agency to refashion her world, one in which families are separated, to reimagine a better world in which cranes, like the Quintero family, can move freely about their ancestral lands, following the origin story of Aztlán.

The crux of Betita's project is a reconceptualization of immigration, framed from a Latinx perspective, in which a network of stories from the past is woven into current social struggles and protest movements. While dominant narratives liken immigrants to intruders who must be removed from the national space, Betita envisions a world in which migration from Mexico to the United States, including the journey she and her family made, was preordained in the origin stories of Mexican and Latinx peoples. For Latinx young readers this mythohistorical intervention is vital, as it offers a resource for creative personal and societal transformations. Maylei Blackwell refers to this intentional restoration of older stories as a retrofitting of memory. To Blackwell, "retrofitted memory is a form of countermemory that uses fragments of older histories . . . [that] creates new forms of consciousness customized to embodied material realities, political visions, and creative desires for societal transformations" (2). Aztlán, in *Land of the Cranes*, emerges as a powerful retrofitted memory for contesting dominant and racist narratives and for creating, in their place, radical new ways of understanding immigration, on one level, and for immigrants to re-member themselves, on another. It thus is not surprising to see that cranes, and their allusions to Aztlán, become the foremost metaphor through which Betita sees the world. By linking the past with the present and future, Salazar provides a learning environment whereby Betita and young readers begin the processes of conocimiento that will allow them to reconfigure their world.

BETITA, THE WRITER AND ARTIST, ALSO KNOWN AS PLUMITA

Paying close attention to the artful and political roles of Aztlán and cranes allows us, further, to feel the foundation from which we will take our next leap. While the previous section focused on mythohistorical interventions and the importance of retrofitted memory for Latinx artistic and cultural production, in this section, we trace the growth of Betita the artist. As her nom du plume, Plumita, signals, she will use her plume, or pen, as well as her belief that she is a crane within the mythic frameworks of Aztlán, to make sense of the trauma endured by children separated from their parents by ICE. She will use it to challenge anti-immigration laws, heinous treatment in hieleras, or ICE facilities, and the racism that funds these oppressions. Plumita, we argue, gains agency by restorying the myths of Aztlán to our current situation in which children are separated from their parents and/or put in cages. Thus, while the first section of the novel is titled Aztlán, the next section is titled Mictlan, the Aztec land of the dead. In one of the most important Aztec stories of creation, Quetzalcoatl journeys to Mictlan to retrieve the bones of previous beings to generate humans for the current Quinto Sol (Fifth Sun) era.[5] Betita's journey through Mictlan in the middle section of *Land of the Cranes* has similar generative intentions. Instead of gathering bones, however, Betita gathers stories and, as her nom de plume portends, she uses these stories in her "picture poems" to bring forth the next world.

Betita first learned how to create picture poems, a rendered drawing with poetry underneath the image, from her fourth-grade teacher, Ms. Martinez (4). It is at her father's insistence, though, that Betita begins to create these poems on a daily basis. At the end of his workday, Betita's father asks her, "*What marvel did you make today, Betita?*" (11). Once she pulls the daily picture poem out of her backpack and uncrumples the edges, "he reads the rhyming poem I scribble below the picture: Recess / Running, sliding, climbing to reach the sky / up so high, I almost fly" (12). They then hang the picture poem "on what Mami calls / my 'laundry line gallery' / she strung across / the kitchen window" (12). This poem is dated September 7 and signed in her "best new cursive" (12).

Everything changes, however, after her father is taken by ICE and deported to Mexico. Instead of picture poems that describe the everyday life of a child, Betita's picture poems now have a new imperative, to comfort her father by "reuniting" the family through her art. To her father's insistence that Betita write to him—"*¡Escríbeme, Betita!*"—she responds, "I will, Papi. / I'll send you / crane poems / every time / I want to / fly with you" (57). Thus, even as the family is separated, via Betita's picture poems the family experiences togetherness. In the November 7 poem, this sense of being with each other becomes especially prominent, for example, as Betita writes, "Quiero volar / en el cielo azul / contigo, Papi" (61). Alongside the text describing Betita's wishes to fly in the blue sky with her papi, Betita draws "a huge brown nest / with big eyes and long eyelashes / like Mami's" and herself, holding the egg (62).

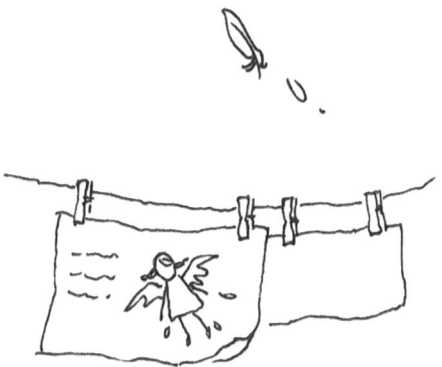

FIGURE 4.3 Aida Salazar, Betita's picture poems. *Land of the Cranes* by Aida Salazar. Reprinted by permission of Scholastic Inc.

FIGURE 4.4 Aida Salazar, Betita's picture poem of the nest. *Land of the Cranes* by Aida Salazar. Reprinted by permission of Scholastic Inc.

While Betita's picture poems show the anxiety a nine-year-old child would feel in such moments, they also reveal the processes of conocimiento. Specifically, we find that even as Betita's world is torn apart, she utilizes her art as a way to heal the wounds of deportation. The November 7 picture poem, from our perspective, highlights Betita's struggle "to reconstruct oneself and heal the sustos resulting from woundings, traumas, racism, and other acts of violation que hechan pedazos nuestras almas, split us, scatter our energies, and haunt us" (Anzaldúa, *Light / Luz* 1). Furthermore, the creative act of reimagining new worlds, as Anzaldúa offers, is "an agency of transformation. Using the creative process to heal or restructure the images/stories that shape a person's consciousness is a more effective way of healing" (35). Instead of allowing the trauma to split and scatter her, Betita turns to her picture poems to transform herself and the world around her.

In the novel, Betita and her mother are placed in Mictlan after a missed highway exit lands them at a border guard station along the San Diego/Tijuana border. They, along with other family members, were on their way to meet Betita's father at Friendship Park, where people on both sides of the border can connect with each other. Although Betita, as a brave Chichimeca warrior, tries to fight off one of the agents, she and her mother are detained and then sent to a family detention camp.

The ICE family detention centers are real-world versions of hell, Betita tells us: "Families captured / sad faced / worried faced / crying faced / distant faced . . . Coughs / babies crying" (84). The detained are held in cages: "In a cage with what looks / like thirty mothers and children / Mami and I find / a little spot on the concrete floor / enough for one to sit" (88). Betita, even in the midst of such brutality, begins to gather stories. From Josephina, a young mother separated from her children, Betita hears:

They took my niños from me
days after we arrived here the first time.
They called it "zero tolerance."

I'll never forget how they cried
as they pulled them away
with so much fear inside their tears
I could do nothing about. (102)

From Yanela, a young girl about the age of Betita, we are informed: "*There was a man who cooked our food / who would lock me in the closet with him. / He did things. / He told me it was supposed to feel good / but it didn't. It hurt me so so bad, I threw up*" (164). Betita previously had gained her trust by convincing Yanela that she (Yanela) is a crane who has returned to her ancestral lands. From this mythohistorical intervention, Yanela acquires new confidence as the two girls chase each other, pretending to be cranes flying home. Her laugh, we are told, "is as big as the sun" (140). Further, Yanela, with this retrofitted memory, begins her own conocimiento process by telling Betita of her wounds and trauma. We recall Levins Morales's words that "recovery from trauma requires creating and telling another story about the experience of violence and the nature of the participants, a story powerful enough to restore a sense of our full humanity to the abused" (61). By telling her story, Yanela begins the healing processes and her humanity is restored. Silence, Levins Morales tells us, is "imposed on us by perpetrators" and, as such, is part of the trauma itself (61). Healing, in this regard, begins with voice, "in the telling and the bearing witness, in the naming of trauma and in the grief and rage and defiance that follows" (62).

We pause for a moment to remind ourselves that readers, too, are invited to journey to Mictlan in *Land of the Cranes*. In varied ways, we, too, are asked to witness the inhumane conditions and the horrible events. Families separated, mothers in anguish, and children in cages gain force in the act of reading. At the same time, from our reading of *Land of the Cranes*, we find hope in Betita's project to collect stories and to utilize them in her picture poems. In a recent interview, Salazar states, "I wasn't interested in creating a victimizing narrative, but one that created action and activism" (Rasilla). Betita's picture poems, we argue, foreground how creative acts, such as writing and art, generate action and activism. As Levins Morales reminds us, the power "to undermine the dominant narrative and shake up how people perceive reality can be tremendous" (58). All that is needed are paper and crayons.

These simple tools of paper and crayons indeed go far in seeking justice when Fernanda, the family's lawyer who seeks asylum for them, steps in to help. From her, Betita receives two forms of aid: first, a two-hundred-page spiral notebook and crayons and, second, an invitation to create picture poems "*to tell us a little about / what has happened to you, to show the judge*" (173). With this mandate still ringing in her ears, Betita begins, as she notes, to *spell*, a double entendre that means to write words in correct sequence and to cast magical charms.

The spells that Betita conjures are presented in the novel in the form of a brief description of the picture, followed by the poem, and ending with Betita's name and the date of composition. For example, in one picture poem, Betita tells us:

> I drew a picture of Papi as a flying crane.
> > *You are the sound of*
> > *crane trumpets that*
> > *sing their love into the sky.*
> > *Betita-March 5* (182)

Other picture poems reflect the conditions under which the people live:

> I drew a maze of cages and crying cranes.
> > *Across from us there is another cage*
> > *with more cranes and their kids*
> > *and almost solitas kept from flying.*
> > *Betita-March 8* (182)

This poem tells readers about the food they are provided:

> I drew the food they expect us to eat.
> > *They give us black moldy burritos for breakfast*
> > *sometimes nothing for lunch*
> > *and frozen black moldy bread for dinner.*
> > *Betita-March 11* (183)

Lastly, Betita has readers look at the violent treatment at the hands of the guards, as well as resistance to such brutality:

> I drew Marisel after she got beaten.
> > *When you sing*
> > *the truth*
> > *not even a beating*
> > *will quiet it.*
> > *Betita-March 15* (184)

Thus, while the executive administration works best to occlude the horrors of Mictlan, Betita casts an unwavering light on hellish conditions and brutal treatment. As Marisel, the young Dreamer who is beaten by the guards, tells Betita, "these drawings might / be what people need to see / to understand how much we suffer" (214). *To understand* is the key point here, for the concept of understanding, specifically the kind of understanding and awareness fueled by conocimiento, has the power to transform how people feel, how they see, and what they believe. Anzaldúa notes that nepantleras "such as artistas / activistas help us mediate these transitions, help us make the crossings, and guide us through the transformation process—a process I call conocimiento" (*Light / Luz* 17). Betita, as a nepantlera artist/activist, helps readers of her poems, both formally within the novel and the readers of *Land of the Cranes*, facilitate passage between worlds. In other words, by creating alternative epistemologies that reframe how immigrants and, specifically, ICE detainees are seen, Betita radically transforms the current world in which oppressions prosper to a new and better world where, in this case, families can move freely on their ancestral lands.

The power of these picture poems, we argue, is their ability to alter how people see. As Marisel notes, the picture poems will help people "understand how much we suffer" (214). While the picture poems highlight key strategies for bringing to light the horrid conditions of ICE detention centers, Betita's picture poems also create new ways for those *inside* to see themselves. Specifically, we call attention to ways in which *Land of the Cranes* foregrounds the power of creative acts, such as writing and art, for detainees. The novel showcases the ways that they, too, want to become artists and activists in order to transform themselves and their world. In this, Betita, as a good nepantlera, becomes their teacher as the detainees begin their conocimiento transformations via creative acts:

> To make a picture poem
> first, close your eyes.
> I tell them.
> Then let your imagination
> lead to where your heart is
> and ask,
>   How are you feeling?
> Now sit with the answer
> and if it is sad or scary
> or happy or grumpy
> then ask yourself,

What does your feeling look like?
What shapes appear?
What words appear?
What story are you telling? (210)

With Betita mediating their conocimiento transformations into artists and activists, the detained children and mothers write picture poems. Marisel, for example, "draws a girl with thought-bubble swirls all around her head. / *I dream of a day when all migrants are / free and I am too*" (212). Yanela draws a girl flying over fields of flowers, with the poem, "*When I am a crane, no one can hurt me*" (213). Josefina "draws a woman reaching for three children on the other side of a fence. / *The day they took my children, I died inside*" (213). These picture poems show that counter-stories not only aid listeners, but also they are vital in the healing process for the teller. In other words, the picture poems by the ICE detainees empower them, allow them to gain agency, in the bearing witness, in the telling of their story. Rage and defiance, we believe, will follow their articulations.

POETRY NOW!

Near the end of the novel, readers see the power of the picture poems to make tangible change. Fernanda tells Betita, "*You should feel so proud for making / things really change here, Betita . . . Your picture poems have gone / across the country and have helped / so many people understand*" (228). As it turns out, the picture poems, from Betita as well as those by the detainees, were featured in an art exhibit to raise awareness and funds for legal fees as part of the larger campaign (219). Furthermore, the campaign is "starting to go viral! / AND, people are protesting because / they saw the pictures and words / of our nightmares / and it scared them too" (220). In response to the protest movement, by the end of the novel, the government begins the process of shutting down the detention centers. The children and mothers are free to go.

Now, it seems, comes the hard part, a reckoning that the real world will soon have to deal with how to heal from the tortures of Mictlan. As Betita experiences upon reuniting with her mother who has been away to deliver the "egg," "It [her memory] doesn't recognize the woman / hugging me, it doesn't / know her voice, her choking cry, / '*Mi niña, mi niña. Betita, I'm here*'" (237). Fortunately, Betita is able to remember and thus process that it is Mami "now sweeping large / golden-brown wings / around my own" (237–38). Mami also has brought the egg: "I don't believe what / I see / a baby crane / with little feathery ears / rounded lips / like a puckered beak / sleeping" (239). Her name, Betita's mother shares, is Alba: "*It means the first light of day*" (239).

As we have discussed in this section, via creative acts, Betita and those around her contest abusive treatment at the hands of ICE. In the process, they gain agency by transforming themselves from victims into artists / activists. The picture poems, in this sense, heal, for they acknowledge the trauma while simultaneously empowering the poet. As *The Land of the Cranes* elucidates, their creative acts also transform the world around them. In this, conocimiento propels the transformation of the current world, with its many and varied Mictlans, into new realities. While conocimiento makes no promises of a fairytale ending, the new baby crane's name, Alba, the "first light of day," signals that light is coming after a long, dark night.

Efrén Divided, the Secret Life of (Un)Documented Children

Efrén, the protagonist of *Efrén Divided*, calls his mother Soperwoman, because of the delicious sopes, "a thick corn tortilla topped with beans and fresh Ranchero cheese," that she makes (5–6). To Efrén and his younger sister and brother, they are "just one of the many milagros Amá performed on a daily basis" (6). As the novel begins, his mother indeed is making sopes for the family. Efrén, however, is still half-asleep, having stayed up late waiting for Amá to come home after a long night of overtime at the factory. What has been bothering Efrén for some time are the whispers:

> For the last couple of weeks, there'd been a whole lot of talk, a whole lot of chisme (especially around the laundromat) about various raids and stop points happening around town. Efrén tried not thinking about what he'd seen on the news, all the stories about families being separated, kids put in cages. But that was easier said than done. (4)

The good thing for Efrén is that miracle sopes do their job of calming him and he heads off to school.

Although Efrén is temporarily relieved of his worry, this early scene in the novel brings up one of the least studied aspects of the deportation crisis: young people's fear and anxiety of possible deportation. As we noted earlier in this chapter, deportation places a terrible burden on families. In her study "The Burden of Deportation on Children of Mexican Immigrant Families" Dreby reminds us that while we often pay more attention to actual deportations and family separations, the threat of deportation or deportability significantly impacts the lives of children ("Burden of Deportation" 842). Even hearing about raids, as is Efrén's experience, can sow uncertainty and panic in the community.[6] As Deborah Boehm notes, "deportability is a constant source of uncertainty for undocumented migrants and those connected to them" (31). Boehm describes deportability as a kind of "suffocation," the "repressive reality that can define daily lives for those living without documents" (32). As part of this repressive reality, Victor Talavera, Guillermina Gina Núñez-Mchiri, and Josiah Heyman add that the constant feeling of being a target, where all public spaces are deemed dangerous, "often leads to isolation and alienation, and many undocumented immigrants expressed sentiments of loneliness, despair, anxiety, and depression" (173). Thus, while our study, to this point, has focused on the devastating consequences of deportation on children's daily lives in *From North to South / Del norte al sur* and *Land of the Cranes*, with *Efrén Divided* we focus on the impact that the threat of deportation has on children. Our argument is that children are largely aware of deportability in their families, even though they are rarely invited into conversations on the subject. How they process (or not) their fears and anxieties is important for understanding the lives of children who are undocumented or who have a parent who is undocumented. Our hope is that by looking at the deportation crisis from the lens of children that *Efrén Divided* offers, we better are able to grasp the totality of how deportation and the threat of it can shatter young lives.

In the novel, the threat of deportation causes Efrén to stay up all night worrying about his mother. The *chisme*, or rumors, that Efrén hears around the laundromat and news stories about families being separated and children put in cages, along with helicopters incessantly flying overhead, have created a wave of terror that debilitates him. Not even a good book, *There's a Boy in the Girls' Bathroom* by Louis Sachar, or, for that matter, the numerous "threats of being on the receiving end of her chancla" (5), can stop Efrén from worrying. At the same time, Efrén has a right to be worried, not only about the deportation of his mother but also about the lack of discussion on the matter. A common theme of the novel, in this regard, is how children are left out of conversations on immigration: "As much as the adults liked keeping kids in the dark, Efrén had heard enough. He knew about the raids happening around the country. Around the state. Around his city" (48). Efrén further adds that he had "heard about ICE setting up checkpoints and literally taking people off the streets. He'd heard about ICE helicopters scaring people out of their homes and hauling them away. He'd even heard of ICE making stops at Mexican-geared supermarkets and handcuffing anyone who couldn't prove they belonged" (49). Even as he hears the "stories about nearby factories getting raided and somebody—usually someone's distant cousin—getting caught and deported," as Efrén acknowledges, "the word ICE wasn't something people liked to talk about—at least not around kids" (44). In all these instances, Efrén, we are told, *hears* about them. Thus, as he processes the possibility that his family will be separated, he faces these problems alone. This, for us, recalls Levins Morales's proclamation that children "need us to listen deeply and with respect to the ways they experience the world, validate their sense of injustice, and help them understand the systemic nature of unfairness" (108).

If we include children in conversations and, as Levins Morales instructs us, listen to them deeply and with respect about how they experience the world, we find that children are invested in finding viable solutions to the world's great problems. *Efrén Divided* shows us what this looks like in the form of Jennifer Huerta, a student in Efrén's school who, we are told, is the only other student who has checked out as many books as Efrén (27–28). While discussing translanguaging in *The House on Mango Street* with Efrén, and how from a representation standpoint Jennifer can see herself in the text, Jennifer reveals that while she is running for school president, she does not have much hope. Asked why by Efrén, Jennifer explains, "I was home watching a report on how undocumented families were being separated. They had kids in cages. Like animals. And that really hurt" (29). Then, she makes an interesting rhetorical leap: "Most of the eggs say they come from cage-free chickens. Which means people in this country worry more about chickens than they do about undocumented children. It makes me feel so—" (30). She begins to cry, then "with her head down, as if she was ashamed, she added: 'Mi mamá no tiene papeles'" (30). To Jennifer, that undocumented children could be put into cages perfectly captures how people feel about her mother and also how they feel about her, thus her hesitance about running for school president. When Efrén tells her that his "parents are here illegally too"

(30), Jennifer responds by showing him a brown paper lunch bag with the words *SOMOS SEMILLITAS* written across the front of it. Jennifer tells Efrén that this Mexican saying, "we are seeds," comes from the phrase *Nos quisieron enterrar, pero no sabían que éramos semillas / They tried to bury us, but they didn't know we were seeds.* Jennifer adds, "My mom likes to remind me of this *every* day. She's right though. That's why I'm running. Figured I could make a difference, even if just at school" (31, emphasis in original). Jennifer's mother, in this, validates her sense of injustice by giving her a Mexican saying that illustrates systemic unfairness ("They tried to bury us"), and provides a way forward ("somos semillas"). This scene ends with Efrén reading the first few pages of *Mango Street* and comparing the character Esperanza's neighborhood with his. When he gets to the line, *"But even so, it's not the house we thought we'd get,"* he stops reading, knowing that he had "hit the jackpot today" (32). Semillas, we propose, survive and grow and give fruit a hundred times the size of the seed. In other words, Efrén's insightful conversation with Jennifer on the topics of deportation and family separation leads to the profound realization that the current world can be transformed. Deportation and the threat of deportation is but another way that they want to bury us. What they did not know is that seeds, once planted, run for school president and create new realities.

The interactions between Efrén and Jennifer in *Efrén Divided* compel us to examine the secret lives of Latinx children amid this deportation crisis. As we notice at the beginning of the novel, Efrén is debilitated, in physical and emotional ways, by the "suffocation" of deportability. Without a proper channel to discuss what he knows and feels about deportability, Efrén is adrift in his own suffering. With the help of Jennifer, who like him is facing the threat of familial deportation, Efrén is shown a way forward. His newfound awareness of the transformational possibilities of semillas, such as Jennifer and him, empowers Efrén not only to change inwardly but also to begin to change the world around him. This is not the world, to echo *Mango Street*, we thought we would get, but it is the world that we will transform.

UNITED WHILE SEPARATED

One of the reasons we chose *Efrén Divided* as a key text to examine in our study of the deportation crisis in Latinx children's and young adult literature is because of the character Lalo, a taxicab driver in Tijuana who befriends Efrén when Efrén travels to Mexico to secure safe passage for his mother to the United States. In the same way that the novel casts a light on the secret lives of Latinx children facing the deportation of a family member, *Efrén Divided* also illuminates the parents, such as Lalo, in addition to Efrén's mom, who are deported and thus separated from their families.

Lalo appears in the narrative after Efrén's mother, having been caught in an ICE sting operation, is detained and then deported. After the money intended to pay a coyote to ferry Efrén's mother back to the United States is stolen, Efrén and his father draw up a plan to deliver the money directly to her. The plan involves Efrén journeying to Tijuana, finding his mother, and giving her the money. While Efrén's father is reticent at first, Efrén convinces his father by reminding him, "I've taken care of Max and Mía. I've taken them to school. Bathed them. Fed them, just like you needed me to. Please, Apá. Let me do this. For Amá" (165–66). Indeed, Efrén throughout his mother's absence has taken the role of primary caretaker of his brother and sister, even going so far as grabbing leftover food from his school cafeteria when they had little money. Having earned his father's trust with the significant work he has done in his mother's absence, Efrén is entrusted with delivering the money to her.

Things do not proceed as well as anticipated in Tijuana. Efrén quickly becomes disoriented by the hustle and bustle, and two men, seeing an easy target, begin to follow him. Lalo, who had previously given Efrén a taxicab ride from the international bridge, sees what is taking place and rescues Efrén just in time. The first thing that Efrén notices about Lalo is his voice: "while the voice itself wasn't familiar, the way the man spoke was. It reminded Efrén of Rafa, back in the neighborhood" (173). As it turns out, Lalo acquired this voice from having spent twenty-eight years in the United States, before he was deported. The second thing that Efrén notices about Lalo is the "detailed tattoo of a baby girl that curled around his neck" (173). Efrén, in the naïve yet curious way of kids, asks Lalo if his daughter is with him in Tijuana. Lalo's answer is very interesting. While the easy answer is no, Lalo goes on to say, "she knows I love her. If I didn't, I'd have my lady bring her over here. So I could be with her" (175). In other words, he loves her and, as such, wants her to stay in the United States, even though he cannot be with her: "It's simple. I love my girl. Want what's best for her. Look around. Do you really think *this* is a place to raise her? Nah, she's way better off in the US. There, she can make something of herself—be someone" (175, emphasis in original). Lalo, sensing that Efrén still does not fully understand, tells him, "This place is limbo, man. A place not quite Mexico, not quite the US. La Tierra de los Olvidados—the Land of the Forgotten" (175–76). Rather than raise his daughter in Tijuana, Lalo would rather live in the land of the forgotten, an apt term for those "left alone" or "left behind."[7] As Boehm notes, the fragmentation of families affected by deportation concerns both geography, living together or apart and in different nations, and emotions, "a family disposed of the possibility of reunification and unable to imagine, or actualize, a future path together" (93). Lalo feels forgotten, not because his daughter has no memory of him or keeps up with him, but because he is unable to "imagine, or actualize, a future path together." His life in limbo is just that, a life caught between wanting to be by his daughter but unable to live with her.

While Lalo's story shows the precarious position of fragmented families, it also illustrates how fortitude in keeping family connections alive can be, or needs to be, reimagined in the current deportation crisis. In this regard, Lalo becomes a case study on keeping these albeit fleeting connections going. Before Lalo gives Efrén a ride downtown to meet his mother, Lalo takes him to *el Muro*, the iron wall, which, as he tells Efrén, "separates us from the US side. It ends where the ocean waves begin to form" (188). El Muro, to Lalo, is also a place of memory: "Sometimes I come around here, buy myself a drink, and stare out into the ocean, thinking about my little girl" (188–89). Once activated, he recalls further memories.

> Lalo's jaw tightened. "You know what I miss most," he continued, while gazing out at the sea. "It's the way she used to look up at me . . . like she knew who I was. She didn't see a high school dropout, didn't see the tats on my arms or back. She just accepted me—unconditional love, bro. Anyway, my little Abby knew that I loved her and trusted that I would do anything and everything to protect her." (189)

While family ties can indeed fall apart after deportation, given the separation from loved ones and the improbability of futures together, Lalo demonstrates how relationships can be built across political borders. To this, Efrén looks over the unfolding scene at el Muro and he sees the many faces along the fence, each trying in some way, to foster family connections: "They came in all sorts. From babies to elderly folk with walkers—all different, beautiful shades of brown. Efrén began walking alongside the iron barrier. There were as many smiles as there were tears" (192). Returning to Lalo, Efrén encourages him not to give up. Lalo responds by saying, "trust me. If there's one thing I don't do, it's give up" (195).

We are encouraged by Lalo's resilience, as well as that of the many visitors to el Muro. We also are heartened that Cisneros intentionally provides a platform for the "forgotten" to articulate their experiences living in limbo. All too often we focus attention on the challenges that family members in the United States endure when families are separated. Very rarely do we listen to voices that present the perspectives of those who cannot return, yet who desire, in what ways are possible, to build and maintain familial relationships across national borders. A deportation regime would have us believe that those deported should be forgotten, erased from personal as well as collective memory. *Efrén Divided* offers a powerful dissent by foregrounding novel ways that families in deportation regimes are reimagined.

THE FIRST LATINX PRESIDENT

The journey to Tijuana proves transformative for Efrén. He meets up with his mother and with Lalo's help finds her a reliable coyote to ferry her to the United States. Efrén's transformation from powerless at the beginning of the novel to empowered after his trip to Tijuana reflects the way undocumented children and children whose parents are, or can be, deported gain agency as they actualize inner strengths despite the seemingly insurmountable obstacles. As Cristina Rhodes notes about undocumented border-crossers,

> Whereas children are often regarded as being in need of protection, the reality is that undocumented children are responsible for protecting themselves. The impetus for undocumented child border crossers' agency, then, is their ostensible powerlessness. Young border crossers must eschew a traditional childhood and develop a sense of power over themselves typically not associated with children or childhood. ("Female Empowerment" 21)

While Rhodes tracks childhood agency in undocumented children, we would like to expand her observations to include children whose family members are undocumented. In particular, we value Rhodes's thesis that this childhood agency comes from "embracing the hybridity that diaspora breeds" (22). For Efrén, his newfound impetus for embracing his hybridity can be traced to the realization that "he'd been born Mexican American. Only he'd forgotten about the Mexican part" (207). His journey to the land of the forgotten, or rather, to the land of people who the dominant narrative in the United States wants to be forgotten, creates a "strange mix of sadness and pride" in him: "for the first time in his entire life, he finally felt connected to this Mexican side" (208). In this regard, by embracing the liminal and nepantla space between Mexican and American, Efrén is transformed from a powerless young man into someone whose inner works leads directly to public acts, echoing Anzaldúa's concept of conocimiento.

By tracking agency in children who are facing the fear of deportation, for themselves or their family member(s), we purposefully destabilize what Aida Salazar calls "victimizing narratives" (Rasilla) and offer in their place counter-stories that foreground the creative ways that these children change the world. As we found in *From North to South / Del norte al sur* and *Land of the Cranes*, the antidote to toxic deportation narratives cannot be found in easy solutions to complex problems. While both the picture book and the young adult novel end in hope, neither text places a Band-Aid over la herida, the wound. *Efrén Divided* is no different in this regard: Efrén's mother is apprehended at a checkpoint and then placed in a detention center. The easy solution, in the novel, would have been the mother's safe return to the United States and a reunited family that lived happily ever after. When asked if he ever imagined an ending where Amá made it back, Cisneros responds by saying, "No, no. I [knew] from Page 1: She can't come back. Maybe 10 years ago, but right now, the way things are, you cannot do it. I had three students who were brave enough to let me know what's going on. Imagine how many didn't feel comfortable enough to share? I wanted to remain truthful" (Smith). What we gather from Cisneros is that it would have been "untruthful" to have Amá return safely. Instead, by being "truthful," the novel challenges young readers to empower themselves with knowledge and awareness of their circumstances as well as resources and, from this, to become activists, like Jennifer Huerta, engaged in changing the world.

Jennifer, we remember, is running for school president with the hopes of using the position to draw attention to the issue of deportation: "She wanted to start a campaign to raise awareness, maybe start a support group to help families" (141). Like Efrén, Jennifer faces her own set of daunting hurdles. Her mother, too, has been detained and deported.

However, when her mother is deported, the emotional upheavals compel Jennifer to drop out of the race. Understanding the importance of Jennifer's activist platform, Efrén decides that he should run for school president. With the help of his brother and sister, Efrén even comes up with a slogan to put on posters, "EFRÉN NAVA 4 ASB PRESIDENT 'THE CHANGE YOU WANT TO SEE'" (156).

By centering young people like Jennifer and Efrén who create change by becoming activists, Cisneros, in *Efrén Divided*, flips the script on what we often expect of children. Instead of powerless victims who need to be protected from challenging matters such as deportability, the novel posits that children, if provided avenues of conocimiento, that is, knowledge and awareness, can find means to empower themselves and those around them. Thus, even when Efrén's posters are vandalized to read, "Deport Efrén Nava, Non-Resident," Efrén is undeterred (239). As he states, "I can start a campaign to educate parents. Let them understand their rights. Maybe get a few schools to join us" (247–48). The novel ends, not with a Band-Aid happy ending, but with Efrén transformed into a social justice activist.

> There would be no quitting today. No, for all the semillitas like him, he couldn't stay buried any longer.
> The time had come for him to be the change he wanted to see.
> The time had come for him to be Soper too.
> To be . . . *Soperboy*. (248)

As Levins Morales reminds us about children, "We must back the initiative of children themselves, secure resources and share skills, respect their right and ability to lead themselves, and learn to let them lead us" (108). *Efrén Divided* illustrates that if offered the right to lead themselves, young readers, like the characters in the novel, can become their own form of super, or soper. Further, this transformation to soper will entail, if we learn to let children lead us, a transformation of the world for the better.

Conclusion

Not a day goes by that I (Jesus) am not reminded of the ways that living as undocumented as a child has marked my life. What racks my heart these days is not so much my own situation; instead, it is the way that fear, anxiety, and loss have been weaponized and aimed at young Latinx people. When I think of all the children currently living in fear and anxiety over deportability and the children currently being held in ICE detention centers, my heart truly and truthfully breaks.

Hope traffics in potentiality, in an anticipation of a better world. In this regard, I am hopeful, for unlike when I was child, we have powerful counter-stories that tell of oppression and resistance from the perspective of those affected by a deportation regime. The works examined in this chapter bear witness and tell of such violence from the viewpoint of the abused so that healing can take place. Moreover, *From North to South / Del norte al sur*, *Land of the Cranes*, and *Efrén Divided*, as well as other works like them, position us to look at the ways in which children, through creative acts and social justice activism, are leading the way. As these books have shown, incredible resistance can be found in young Latinx characters who deploy conocimiento tactics—countering by creative acts such as planting seeds, creating picture poems, or running for school president. Thus, while racist deportation narratives want to portray children experiencing deportability as victims to be silenced into further victimhood, José, Betita, and Efrén show us the possibilities of personal agency in the service of societal transformation.

CHAPTER FIVE

The Role of the Border Artista

> Border arte is an art that supersedes the pictorial. It depicts both the soul del artista y el alma del pueblo. It deals with who tells the stories and what stories and histories are told. I call this form of visual narrative "autohistorias." This form goes beyond the traditional self-portrait or autobiography; in telling the writer/artist's personal story, it also includes the artist's cultural history—indeed, it's a kind of making history, of inventing our history from our experience and perspective through our art rather than accepting our history by the dominant culture.
>
> GLORIA ANZALDÚA / *Light in the Dark / Luz en lo oscuro*

> So it began: her apprenticeship. The first stage was detribalization. She was forced to recognize the illusionary and arbitrary nature of social norms . . . Her training began. She attempted to strengthen her will, concentration, and memory. Every day she wrote in her journal . . . She wanted to know, to become a knower, while she turned away from society and towards herself. Gradually, too, she turned back to her community. As soon as she alleviated or came to understand her suffering, she tried to translate her insight into shareable form so that others could use it.
>
> GLORIA ANZALDÚA / "Memoir—My Calling; or, Notes on 'How Prieta Came to Write'"

Julia loves to read, and she loves to write. As the protagonist and first-person narrator of *I Am Not Your Perfect Mexican Daughter* (2017) by Erika L. Sánchez explains, "Ever since I could pick up a pen, I've wanted to be a famous writer. I want to be so successful that people stop me on the street and ask, 'Oh my God, are you Julia Reyes, the best writer who has ever graced this earth?'" (2). What readers first notice about Julia's storytelling is the way she captures her surroundings with a "border artista" eye for detail. Julia, for example, perfectly describes the inner workings of a Mexican birthday party, from the way that arriving at the home where the party is held means kissing every member of the family, to the wide variety of foods and drinks offered, and to the way that the party, largely because of the drinks, most likely will end in *morriña* tears that sum up the sadness and frustration that come from a deep longing for the homeland. At the same time, when Julia arrives at the party with J. D. Salinger's *The Catcher in the Rye* in hand, she draws on the literary reference strategically to express her sense of loneliness and alienation. Salinger's novel illustrates her growing sense of apartness from her parents, which can be attributed to normal teenage angst and, given that she is reading the novel at a Mexican party, also brings up questions of national and cultural belonging. As a budding border artista, Julia deliberately mixes two disparate entities, a typical Mexican party and a classic American literary work, and cohesively reimagines them together.

This is what border artistas do. As Julia shows us in the birthday scene described above, border artistas "cambian el punto de referencia. By disrupting the neat separations between cultures, they create a culture mix, una mestizada in their artworks," to use the words of Gloria Anzaldúa (*Light / Luz* 49). Instead of a neat separation between Mexican and American cultures, Julia presents us with a cultural mix, una mestizada, in her storytelling. At the same birthday party, she evokes Mexican culture, noting, for example, that the place smells of wet dog, which she finds curious given that the dog, Chómpiras, has been dead for some time. The dog, in this case, is named after a character in a popular Mexican television show.[1] Even as she engages specific Mexican cultural products and practices, via this reference to Chómpiras, for example, Julia's reading of *The Catcher in the Rye* at the party draws our attention to the in-betweenness of her experience. For Julia, we argue, the liminal space between cultures becomes "the locus of resistance, of rupture, of implosion and explosion, and of putting together the fragments and creating a new assemblage" (*Light / Luz* 49). Border artistas, in this sense, locate themselves in nepantla, "the place where at once we are detached (separated) and attached (connected) to each of our several cultures" (56), and in this border *lugar* begin the processes of "tearing apart and then rebuilding the *place* itself" (49). Border artistas put the pieces together in a new way, that is, they enact the processes of reconstruction and reframing and of making and unmaking to create a "new assemblage" (49).

In this chapter we demonstrate how this new assemblage, what Anzaldúa calls autohistorias, functions to bring healing and power to the Latinx characters considered. The form, Anzaldúa explains, "goes beyond the traditional self-portrait or autobiography; in telling the writer/artist's personal story, it also includes the artist's cultural history—indeed, it's a kind of making history, of inventing our history from our experience and perspective through our art" (*Light / Luz* 62). Our argument is that protagonists Julia, in *I Am Not Your Perfect Mexican Daughter* (2017) by Erika L. Sánchez, and Gabi, in *Gabi, a Girl in Pieces* (2014) by Isabel Quintero, are border artistas who utilize creative acts to share their autohistorias. These autohistorias, for Julia and Gabi, reveal their complex inner lives, specifically the struggles in negotiating Latinx identity and challenging gender norms imposed on them by parents and society. By connecting "experiencias personales con realidades sociales," that is, personal experiences with social reality, the characters find "a way of inventing and making knowledge, meaning, and identity through self-inscriptions" (*Light / Luz* 6). *I Am Not Your Perfect Mexican Daughter* and *Gabi, a Girl in Pieces* underscore the transformations inherent in the inner work that leads to public acts that are at the center of conocimiento. In this way, the novels function as studios in narrative form in which the young Latinx characters can artfully fashion themselves. How Julia and Gabi assemble themselves reveals the movement of their experiences and corresponding emotions into aesthetic forms, and these are as eclectic and wide-ranging as their creators. Evoking Anzaldúa's metaphor of the goddess Coyolxauhqui, Julia and Gabi put back together the pieces of their lives by utilizing multiple genres, ranging from journals, diaries, poems, and letters, in addition to more direct storytelling. Further, through their broad use of genres these budding creatives signal metonymically the multiple identity intersections at play, among these, gender, sexuality, ethnicity, language, religion, and cultural and national belonging. For Julia and Gabi, to be border artistas involves making knowledge through self-inscription, placing and blending together the pieces of identity in new ways. In this chapter, we trace how these autohistorias disrupt the seemingly neat separation between cultures and create a mestizada, a new cultural mix, through creative acts. Put another way, Julia and Gabi depict "both the soul del artista y el alma del pueblo" (*Light / Luz* 62), and in this the novels showcase the power of Latinx peoples in the artful creation of the self to social revolutionary and transformative ends.

I Am Not Your Perfect Mexican Daughter

INTERSECTIONAL BORDERLANDS—DETACHED AND
ATTACHED TO EACH OF OUR SEVERAL CULTURES

I Am Not Your Perfect Mexican Daughter begins with a death, in this case the death of the perfect Mexican daughter, Saint Olga, as Julia calls her. Sainthood in Mexican cultures equals conformity, as Julia explains, "Here she was, a grown-ass woman, and all she did was go to work, sit at home with our parents, and take one class each semester at the local community college" (2). Although twenty-two years old, Olga never moved out and never moved on from the family home in Chicago. Julia, the not-so-perfect Mexican daughter, in contrast, dreams of going away to college, preferably in New York. She questions rather than accepts what her parents and other authorities tell her, as she explains: "Ever since I was a little kid, I've questioned everything, which drove both my parents insane. Even when I tried to be good, I couldn't. It's as if it were physically impossible for me, as if I were allergic to rules. Things just got worse and worse as I got older. Stuff that's sexist, for example, makes me crazy" (21). At another moment Julia questions her mother's religion: "the Catholic church hates women because it wants us to be weak and ignorant" (21).[2] She also stands up to her math teacher, Mr. Simmons, who she suspects to be a "racist Republican" and who consistently mispronounces her name *Jewlia* (35–36). After one of these episodes, Julia ditches class, running off to The Art Institute of Chicago where she gazes at Artemisia Gentileschi's *Judith Slaying Holofernes* and imagines herself as Judith, with Mr. Simmons reprising the role of Holofernes (43–44). To be the perfect Mexican daughter, to Julia, means conforming to social norms with which she disagrees. As the title of the novel suggests, Julia refuses to acquiesce to these demands.

The problem for Julia is that these questions of identity and belonging are an intersectional sticky web of social identities. While teachers like Mr. Simmons want her to be "American" (adhering to the rules of whiteness), for others, such as her Tío Bigotes, "she can barely speak Spanish" even though she has a "cactus on her forehead" (84). In other words, Julia may look Mexican, but without the requisite language Spanish skills, she is not Mexican (enough). Then, of course, her parents wish her to conform to gender and social norms from a Mexican perspective, sometimes in direct opposition to American gender and social norms. For Julia these intersectional identity questions means she faces tremendous external pressures from a multitude of sides. Kimberlé Williams Crenshaw, who first coined the term "intersectionality," reminds us of the dangers of "single axis thinking" when considering identity. Along with coauthors Sumi Cho and Leslie McCall, she explains, "intersectionality has, since the beginning, been posed more as a nodal point than as a closed system—a gathering place for open-ended investigations of the overlapping and conflicting dynamics of race, gender, class, sexuality, nation, and other inequalities" (Cho et al. 787–88). Patricia Hill Collins adds that these overlapping and conflicting dynamics form a matrix that must be considered in its fullness (18). For Julia, in *I Am Not Your Perfect Mexican Daughter*, the interactions of gender, race, and other categories of social identity and the outcomes of these in terms of power, we argue, also play out along a border dynamic. In the open-ended investigation of gender, race, and ethnicity, we also must account for the ways that the border, "the place where at once we are detached (separated) and attached (connected) to each of our several cultures" (*Light / Luz* 56), informs the interactions of these overlapping and conflicting dynamics. By positioning intersectionality studies on the border, we advance the idea that border artistas, like Julia, expose systems of oppression that plague transnational and diasporic Latinx children and young adults. Border artistas, by disrupting the neat separations between cultures, provide unique ways of understanding the world within which they live. In the process, border artistas utilize liminal spaces between cultures as sites for putting together the intersectional fragments and creating a new assemblage.

At the heart of Julia's anger, her wish to "pack my bags when I graduate and say, 'Peace out, mothafuckas'" (2), are the complex contradictions and paradoxes that diasporic children and young adults face. Education, for example, is a minefield. On the one hand, many immigrant parents like Julia's want their children to do well in school, as Julia does. Because of their scholastic achievements, students like Julia begin to dream of future pathways available, namely, college and career. As Julia says, "I've been dreaming of going [to college] since I was little. I know I'm smart. That's why they skipped me ahead a year" (20). These pathways in turn lead to further dreams untethered by place, for example, world travel, as we see in this case: "I picture myself at the top of the Eiffel Tower, climbing pyramids in Egypt, dancing in the streets in Spain, riding in a boat in Venice, and walking on the Great Wall of China. In these dreams, I'm a famous writer who wears flamboyant scarves and travels all around the world, meeting fascinating people" (27). However, while parents such as Julia's often do not want their children to "work like a donkey like me" (121), they may fear deeply the Americanization of their children that will take them away and transform them via travel, college, and career.

Alejandro Portes and Rubén Rumbaut in their work on acculturation and second-generation immigrant children explain this anxiety: "the voices of immigrant parents speak in unison when it comes to the challenges of educating their children on American soil. They are less worried about racial discrimination and lack of opportunities than about their young doing themselves in because of excessive freedom and lack of institutional restraints" (98). To Amá, therefore, to be too Americanized means having excessive freedoms and little to no control, resulting potentially in dangerous and illicit behavior. According to Portes and Rumbaut, for immigrant parents the answer to a country full of permissive behavior resides in "only firm parental guidance and strong family and community ties [that] can lead to the hoped-for destination" (102). Many immigrant parents like Julia's often find themselves living with dissonance—with hopes of educational and career success for their children on one hand and fear of what will happen if their children follow these pathways on the other.

The answer for Julia's parents is thus to double down on parental guidance and ensure Julia does not Americanize too much. When Apá and Amá feel Julia is acculturating too rapidly, their solution is to hold the most Mexican of parties in Julia's honor—a quinceañera, an elaborate cultural ritual celebrating a young woman's fifteenth birthday. The absurdity is not lost on Julia: she is already fifteen. She begs her mother to cancel the party, to no success, perhaps because her parents never gave Olga a quinceañera and their guilt overwhelms Julia's concerns. The quinceañera will take place and to Julia, "the quinceañera hangs over me like the blade of a guillotine" (139).[3] She is made to perform the role of the perfect Mexican daughter.

Julia's quinceañera also performs quintessential Mexican culture in many ways. Following the procession of the quinceañera, her female "court," and their teenage male escorts, the partygoers waltz together with Julia and her *chambelán* at the center of the dance floor. Julia is then seated in the center of the dance floor and her parents, as she describes, "approach me with a pair of shiny white shoes on a satin pillow. They slip off my flat Mary Janes and replace them with the new heels"

(154). Metaphorically, the shoes represent her entrance into womanhood. Next, Julia is presented with a doll that she in turns hands over to her baby cousin Gabby, who wears a peach dress similar to Julia's—another part of the ritual drama. The dance with her father marks the end of this part of the ritual, as ceremonially the quinceañera takes her first step toward leaving her father and mother and preparing for marriage. The quinceañera party in this way enacts her parent's desire to control Julia's enculturation by making her perform her Mexican-ness. Further, as this scene elucidates, for Julia's family there is no way to separate Mexican cultural identity and gender norms.

When Julia's aunt suggests to her that Olga smiles down on the proceedings from heaven, Julia's suspicions that she is a mere stand-in for the perfect Olga are confirmed. This infuriates Julia, and, once the family returns home, a yelling match between Julia and her parents ensues. The fight quickly turns to questions of Mexican versus American identity, and Julia's father exclaims, "Maybe [Tío] Bigotes is right. Maybe this country is ruining you" (162). Julia counters with this: "Like living in Mexico would fix anything . . . My life sucks, but it would suck even harder in Mexico, and you know it" (162). Her mother, at her wit's end because Julia refuses to conform to Mexican cultural and gender norms, rebukes her by saying, "You know, Julia, maybe if you knew how to behave yourself, to keep your mouth shut, your sister would still be alive. Have you ever thought about that?" (162). For her parents, Julia's failure resides in her Americanization, and in particular her unladylike ways of misbehaving and talking back. Yet readers see the irony in this moment; it is not possible to be the princess of her parents' dreams. Just before the bust-up with her parents, before her mother's insinuation that Julia is responsible for Olga's death, the three walk into their apartment. During their absence, pests had come out of hiding. Julia notes wryly that she can use her new shiny white shoes to stomp on the cockroaches: "Apá flicks on the light, and the roaches scurry in all directions, looking for dark corners to hide in. We do the cockroach dance, which consists of stomping all over the kitchen floor, because they have a party whenever we're not home. This time I have to lift my dress and kill them with my new white shoes" (161). The scene has evolved into the absurd; what began as a Mexican tradition used to celebrate coming of age ends with another Mexican tradition, the hat dance. Instead of singing about *cucarachas*, however, the Reyes family "dances" due to an infested apartment. It is as if the ritual drama, the quinceañera, did not take. If anything, the proceedings evolved into farce and then tragedy. What was meant as a gesture to put things back together, to make Coyolxauhqui whole, revealed profound fractures. The contradictions are too strong to be overcome—Julia will not be made into a perfect Mexican daughter.

These tensions continue to rise as Julia cannot leave her oppressive home. She finally decides that the only way out is suicide. The events leading to Julia's attempt, as told through her artful storytelling, center on her mother's lack of respect for Julia's personhood and her mother's insistence on conformity to idealized Mexican womanhood. For example, Amá violates Julia's privacy by searching through Julia's room—disrespecting Julia's belongings, and by extension, her identity. In one instance, she finds Olga's racy underwear, hotel key, and a box of condoms—items that Julia tried to hide as she sought out the truth of Olga's life and death. When Julia denies ownership, her mother responds, "What must your sister think of you right now? What a disgrace" (204). In another instance, Amá takes it a step further, ransacking Julia's room, looking for "anything else that might be considered scandalous or immoral" (207). When Amá discovers Julia's journals, she tries to read them, even though she does not understand English, and then proceeds to tear out "all the pages that contained *fuck*, *bitch*, *shit*, and even *sex*, which were incredibly common, of course" (207). This devastates Julia, not only for the violation of her privacy, but also because Julia understands her writing as an extension of herself, her reason for living:

> I screamed and begged for her to leave my journals alone, but she went through them anyway and left me with only a dozen pages or so. I was hysterical and tried to swipe them from her hands, but Apá held me back. I cried on the floor in the fetal position for hours after. I couldn't find the motivation to get up, not even when a roach crawled near my head. Life without writing doesn't feel worth living to me. I don't know how I'm going to make it to graduation because I feel like a husk of a person these days. Some of the poems Amá destroyed I had worked on for years, and now they're gone. Poof. Just like that. I'll never see them again. The one thing I loved most in life has been taken away from me. What the hell do I do now? (207–8).

By attempting to read and then destroy Julia's journals, Amá attacked the deepest part of Julia—her love for words, her articulation of her feelings through language, her hopes and dreams. The violation shatters Julia, leaving her without a reason to live, and she attempts suicide.

In her true fashion, Julia discusses her inner turmoil and psychological descent via literary allusions: "In English class today, we discussed one of my favorite Emily Dickinson poems, and it felt as if something were splintering inside me. When we got to the part about the bees, my eyes ached from holding back tears" (209). The poem, "I Dreaded that First Robin, So," probes questions of suffering and death.[4] Rather than rejoicing at the return of spring and its bees, the poet longs for the bees' continued hibernation during winter. Finding solace in Dickinson's poem, Julia heads downtown after school to Millennium Park because "because it's the closest thing I can get to nature and because it's free" (209). Standing in the Chicago cold, Julia realizes, "I can't keep going like this anymore. What is the point of living if I can't ever get what I want? This doesn't feel like a life; it feels like a never-ending punishment" (210). The chapter ends with Julia repeating to herself, "Go home, go home, go home" (210).

There is a glimmer of light, though. In the midst of conflicting expectations that Julia succeed in America but still remain Mexican, Julia possesses literature and art—her writing and her creativity. Even if her mother destroys her journals, she cannot take away these passions and abilities. Her mother, in other words, cannot keep Julia from being a border artista, who will make a mestizada of her art and her life.

DISMEMBERMENT AND HEALING FOR MEXICAN DAUGHTERS

Anzaldúa tells us that "nepantleras such as artistas/activistas help us mediate these transitions, help us make the crossings, and guide us through the transformation process—a process I call conocimiento" (*Light / Luz* 17). Rather than see herself as solely Mexican or American Julia begins to envision a kind of third path that, as Anzaldúa articulates, allows for both belonging and leaving. This conocimiento process emerges from struggle, from thought and creativity; it comprises a form of spiritual inquiry / activism that is "reached via creative acts—writing, art-making, dancing, healing, teaching, meditation, and spiritual activism—both mental and somatic (the body, too, is a form as well as site of creativity)" ("Now Let Us Shift" 542). We suggest that following her suicide attempt, Julia embodies this conocimiento epistemology as she uses art as a way of rearticulating a multifaceted self and ultimately learning to love herself.

Drawing on Anzaldúa, we affirm that the transformation process of conocimiento entails honesty about pain, suffering, and loss, specifically as it concerns the border, whether the geopolitical one that stretches between the United States and Mexico or the emotional one between immigrant parents and their children. In *I Am Not Your Perfect Mexican Daughter* readers see characters divided by these borders. On one side, Amá, Apá, and Olga function as stereotypical characters in an immigrant novel: the controlling mother obsessed with keeping her girls at home, the emotionally disconnected father, and the perfect other sister. On the other side, Julia is the rebellious "American" daughter, and Amá, Apá, and Olga only serve as foils to Julia, as obstacles she must overcome, and as people she must leave.

But Coyolxauhqui must be put back together. By drawing on Coyolxauhqui, goddess of the moon, in Aztec mythic history, Anzaldúa illustrates the process of dismemberment and healing. In the story, Coyolxauhqui attempts to kill her mother, and in response her brother Huitzilopochtli throws her down the sacred mountain, shattering her body into a thousand pieces. For Anzaldúa this Aztec goddess comes to represent "light in the darkness"—the pain of fragmentation and the possibility of transformative healing (Keating xxi). Coyolxauhqui is "both the process of emotional psychical dismemberment, splitting body/mind/spirit/soul, and the creative work of putting all the pieces together in a new form" (*Light / Luz* 124). It is in this dismemberment and the struggle of putting back together in new, creative ways, that the possibility of healing and transformation begins:

> Coyolxauhqui personifies the wish to repair and heal, as well as rewrite the stories of loss and recovery, exile and homecoming, disinheritance and recuperation, stories that lead out of passivity and into agency, out of devalued into valued lives. Coyolxauhqui represents the search for new metaphors to tell you what you need to know, how to connect and use the information gained, and, with intelligence, imagination, and grace, solve your problems and create intercultural communities. (*Light / Luz* 143)

For Julia, like Anzaldúa's Coyolxauhqui, conocimiento is the path that leads toward healing. In order to fully understand what the novel means by healing, we turn to Olga, Amá, and Apá. By growing in her understanding of her family, Julia gains a new awareness and begins to put back the pieces. In this regard, the path of conocimiento leads to a new and more profound awareness of her family, and this path also will lead to a more robust understanding of herself.

Shortly after her suicide attempt and against her wishes, Julia is sent to Mexico. As she notes, "some people think that shipping their children back to the motherland when they get out of control will solve everything . . . Maybe parents think their kids have lost their values, that they've become too Americanized. So is Mexico supposed to teach me not to have sex? Is it supposed to teach me not to kill myself?" (228). In Mexico Julia comes to see family members she previously saw as flat characters, immigrant stereotypes straight from central casting, in a new way. She discovers they were once dynamic and artistic. For example, Julia learns from her grandmother that Amá "was always the rebellious one. She was the first one in the family to move to the other side. But you knew that, didn't you? I told her not to go, but she said she wanted to live in Chicago, where she could work and have her own house" (248). Then, of her father, she discovers that, according to her grandmother, "he was the town artist. He drew everyone, even the mayor. Haven't you seen that drawing of your tía Fermina hanging in her living room? Your father drew that, too" (251).

Puzzled by this information regarding her wild mother and artistic father, Julia asks questions of her family in Mexico and gains new insights. The longer she stays in Mexico, the more she realizes the vastness of the immigration tragedy, as she explains:

> All of my father's brothers and sisters are scattered across the United States—Texas, Los Angeles, North Carolina, and Chicago. His parents died right after he and Amá left Los Ojos. My grandfather got a tumor that ate away his lungs, and my grandma followed him a few months later. They say she died of sadness. Can I miss people I've never met? Because I think I do. (255)

Further, Julia learns that those who were left behind suffer as much as those that left. In this case, Julia's paternal grandmother dies from heartbreak, from the sadness that comes from loneliness. What Julia finds in Mexico is that the border is a giant wound, evoking Anzaldúa's concept of the border as *una herida abierta* (*Borderlands / La Frontera* 25). Julia exclaims to her friend and love interest Esteban before she leaves Mexico, "'The border . . . The fucking border.' I feel a wildness spreading through me. 'It's nothing but a giant wound, a big gash between the two countries. Why does it have to be like that? I don't understand'" (280).

What Julia finds in Mexico is that many have to risk their lives crossing that "giant wound" and that crossing the "fucking border" can make them go from dynamic and rebellious to fearful and controlling. It can even make artists put down their pencils and paints.

Julia develops an even deeper compassion for Amá and Apá when she learns of the tragedy of her parents' border crossing from Tía Fermina. Her mother, her tía explains, was raped by the coyote who helped them cross the border while her father, "They held him down with a gun. There was nothing he could do" (274). Tía Fermina tells Julia in secret so that she can reassess her parents: "See, mija, that's why I want you to know. So when you and your mother fight, you can see where she's come from and understand what's happened to her. She doesn't mean to hurt you" (275). These conversations indeed help Julia to understand her parents in new ways. While Julia long believed she and her mother shared nothing in common, she learns that Amá was rebellious and had dreams just like her. She likewise discovers that her father shares her love for art. As such, Julia realizes she is a perfect combination of her parents, and therefore their perfect Mexican daughter. This knowledge yields a greater understanding; the conocimiento process allows Julia to find wholeness, to love her parents, and to love herself as she is. Where once Julia devalued her parents and herself, she uses the information gained in Mexico to put Coyolxauhqui together, with "intelligence, imagination, and grace" (*Light / Luz* 143). In such a process, Julia, among the many fractures, is still round and whole, much like moon goddess Coyolxauhqui.

Julia also finds a sense of wholeness by coming to peace with her sister Olga, who she learns is not perfect after all. By breaking into Julia's computer and email, Julia learns about Olga's affair with Dr. Castillo at the office where she worked. And, as Julia finds out, Olga was pregnant. In a meeting with Dr. Castillo at a diner near his office, he confesses to the affair, one that both hoped would end with him leaving his wife and marrying Olga. He then gives Julia a copy of Olga's ultrasound. The baby, according to him, changed everything—marrying Olga was now an imperative. He also tells Julia that in Olga's last texts, she said that if it was a boy, she wanted to name him Rafael, like her father (312). If readers believe Dr. Castillo that he was going to leave his wife and start a new life with Olga, perhaps that explains why she was smiling when she was hit by the semi. She smiled as she read the text messages that signaled her new beginning with her beloved.

Perspectives change when we are given vital information regarding how to assess. Most times this allows us to look differently, perhaps with empathy, toward others. Perhaps, as Julia notes, "These last two years I combed and delved through my sister's life to better understand her, which meant I learned to find pieces of myself—both beautiful and ugly" (340). Instead of a stereotypically perfect Mexican daughter, what Julia believes of Olga, it turns out that Olga was involved in a complicated relationship. In this, Julia finds that her sister was not a saint, and, accordingly, maybe perfect Mexican daughters are fictions. Revelations such as these, though painful, allow Julia to see her sister as something more than a cutout figure; they enable her to see Olga as human.

AUTOHISTORIAS: TOWARD THE POWER AND POSSIBILITIES OF BEING LATINX

Julia succeeds because she is not your perfect Mexican daughter. Her story is not about stereotypical Mexican mothers and fathers or about saintly daughters. To a world that often portrays Latinx people as carbon copies of worn-out stereotypes, Julia's story counters such assumptions. Her autohistoria pushes the boundaries of what it means to be the perfect Latinx daughter. As a border artista, Julia finds ways to bring the many intersectional pieces together. Her story is thoughtful, artistic, and creative, drawing on great literature and art, including works by Lorca, Salinger, Dickinson, Camus, Gentileschi, and Hopper, among others, to "show" instead of "tell" her experiences. At the same time, her story stays close to its roots, thus allowing readers a window or a mirror onto the lives of Mexican immigrants in the United States and their second-generation children. Julia's story thus holds both her Mexican identity and her broader American identity.

By interrogating social and cultural questions at personal and familial levels, Julia enacts the processes of transformation, of conocimiento. Julia's autohistoria thus is not one of leaving family or of leaving life; it is one of healing via rewriting "the stories of loss and recovery, exile and homecoming, disinheritance and recuperation" (*Light / Luz* 143). Her autohistoria is a story about healing self and family by rewriting the lives of Amá, Apá, Olga, and ultimately herself to show the ways in which Coyolxauhqui personifies the wish to tell stories that "lead out of passivity and into agency, out of devalued into valued lives" (143). This rewriting with honesty and compassion allows Julia an integrated sense of self in the midst of many intersections of culture, language, religion, gender, and family. Julia understands this complexity and offers it lovingly to her family: "I think that part of what I'm trying to accomplish—whether Amá really understands it or not—is to live for her, Apá, and Olga. It's not that I'm living life *for* them, exactly, but I have so many choices they've never had, and I feel like I can do so much with what I've been given" (339, emphasis in original). As her words signal, Julia defines success not as personal gain but as a benefit to others. Julia, like a true border artista, translates her insights into "shareable form" so that others can know the power and possibilities of being Latinx.

Gabi, a Girl in Pieces

INTERSECTIONAL QUESTIONS—TOO MUCH AND NOT ENOUGH

Like Julia in *I Am Not Your Perfect Mexican Daughter*, Gabi Quintero in *Gabi, A Girl in Pieces* finds herself in the midst of intersectional questions of ethnicity, race, language, and gender, among others. The first time that readers are introduced to Gabi via the journal that traces her senior year of high school, she tells the origin of her name, Gabriela; Gabi is named after her maternal grandmother, who did not want to meet her because her mother was pregnant and unmarried. As Gabi explains, "My mom has told me the story many, many, MANY times of how, when she confessed to my grandmother that she was pregnant with me, her mother beat her. BEAT HER! She was twenty-five. That story forms the basis of my sexual education" (7). Gabi learns from this story and many like it that to be Mexican and a woman, she should not have sex outside of marriage: "Every time I go out with a guy, my mom says, 'Ojos abiertos, piernas cerradas.' Eyes open, legs closed" (7). Gabi's mother's lax expectations for her brother Beto infuriate her even more. Before Beto leaves for a date "all she says is 'Make sure you take a condom with you?' Really, Mom, what the hell is that about?" (236). Her mother's gendered ethnic notions, that girls must remain pure *virgencitas* and that "boys will be boys," leaves Gabi writhing within herself.

These intersections of gender and ethnicity are further underscored when Gabi complains in her journal about her mother's fear that she is becoming like a *white* girl—going off to college, sleeping around, and becoming pregnant. Gabi writes in her journal "Seriously, Mom? Only White girls sleep around? Let me introduce you to my friend Cindy, to Georgina, to Tomasa, to Kanisha, and all the non-White girls at my school who have already had sex. And guess what? None of them are in college! But some of them will be soon" (184). As with Julia's parents in *I Am Not Your Perfect Mexican Daughter*, to many immigrant parents, including Gabi's mom, "white" connotes permissiveness—and, in this case, sexual immorality. These tensions create dissonance within Gabi as her passionate words underscore; she loves her Mexican culture and mother and simultaneously abhors these gendered double standards.

Asking Gabi to be *Mexican* has its problems as well since she wrestles with her ethnic identity, especially as it intersects with nationality and her perceived race. Is she Mexican, American, two much of one or the other, or both? Gabi writes in her September 16th entry, "Today is Mexican Independence Day. While I know we don't live in Mexico, and I am not technically Mexican, there is still a sense of pride that swells in my chest during this day. Being Mexican-American is tough sometimes. Your allegiance is always questioned. My mom constantly worries that I will be too Americana" (34). These questions of ethnic identity and belonging become even more challenging as Gabi considers the role of her physical appearance: "The other problem with being me—and my Mexican ancestry—is that people don't believe that I am any kind of Mexican. They always think I'm White, and it bugs the shit out of me. Not because I hate White people, but because I have to go into a history lesson every time someone questions my Mexicanness" (34–35). While some people of Mexican descent receive their "Mexican card" based on appearance of darker skin and hair, others like Gabi have to insist on it or be questioned. This questioning comes not only from white people but also from other Mexican Americans, as the nicknames she offers indicate: "My skin is there for all the world to see and point at and judge. Güera. Casper. Ghost. Freckle Face. Ugly. Whitey. White girl. Gringa. I've been called all of those names" (35).[5]

For Gabi, as these examples have shown, the many facets of her identity intersect in curious but oppressive ways. They set up stark contradictions that pull Gabi in different directions, in some instances to the point of breaking her. The novel's author Quintero explains: "living on the hyphen is a complex cultural existence at times, and we're often pulled in many directions where allegiance is always demanded. It is a fractured state of being" ("2015 Morris Award"). Gabi indeed feels these tensions and finds herself unable to change her reality simply by desiring to do so. She cannot, for example, change the color of her skin to be more "Mexican."

As if these intersectional struggles were not enough, Gabi faces a multitude of challenges during her senior year of high school: her father dies from a meth overdose, her mother becomes pregnant at an advanced age (an accident from the brief period Gabi's father was sober), her friend Cindy is raped and becomes pregnant, her friend Sebastian comes out and is rejected by his family, and her friend Georgina needs Gabi's support in seeking an abortion. All of these challenges would seem to leave Gabi devastated and hopeless. Yet, as readers see via their access to Gabi's intimate thoughts in her journal, Gabi finds ways of putting together in beautiful ways her brokenness and that of those around her. This creative reconfiguring of painful experiences is presented in an inclusive variety of genres—letters, zines, dramatic dialogues, and poems—all in a mixture of English and Spanish. While seemingly fragmented, or as the novel's title suggests, "in pieces," we argue that Gabi, as a border artista, puts the pieces together through her creative acts to alleviate and come to understand her suffering from oppressive gender and cultural norms so that she can "translate her insight into shareable form so that others could use it" (Anzaldúa, "Memoir" 237).[6]

FINDING VOZ IN (CREATIVE) WRITING, OR TRANSLANGUAGING

Gabi, though she does not know it at the beginning of the novel, is a border artista who utilizes creative acts to challenge, disrupt, and transform the world around her. Gabi is first introduced to her creative talents by her English teacher, Ms. Abernard. As Gabi tells us, "She taught me about e.e. / cummings— / that dead white guy changed my life . . . Now I sleep with / cummings / dream in words / think in meter / and spit up ink" (140–41). Playful sexual innuendos aside, Gabi realizes that poetry changes her life: "I can't stop writing. / I write about trees. / I write about love. / I write about my brother. / I write about me. / I write about my mom. / I write about my dad" (141). Given all fragmentation in her life, Gabi utilizes her creative acts to find healing: "Poetry helps heal wounds. / Makes them tangible" (141). While many of her poems touch on her relationship with her brother and mother as well as her father's addiction and overdose, Gabi also writes poems to disrupt the neat separations between cultures and, in the process, create una mestizada in her artwork. Gabi, we argue, strategically locates herself on the border in her poetry. She then utilizes her nepantla position as "the locus of resistance, of rupture, of implosion and explosion, and of putting together the fragments and creating a new assemblage" (*Light / Luz* 49).

For Gabi, this new assemblage includes translanguaging, that is, using both Spanish and English in her poems.

Gabi first learns that it is possible to use both Spanish and English in her poems by reading poets Michele Serros and Sandra Cisneros: "We [Gabi and her boyfriend, Martin] have been practicing using two languages in writing since after we read some poems by two superpoets: Michele Serros (who is still alive AND from California!) and Sandra Cisneros (she's still alive too, but not from California). Before we read their poetry, I didn't even know you could use two languages in a poem" (67). By expressing herself with her full linguistic repertoire, Gabi experiences freedom to showcase the complexity of herself. According to Shannon Daniel and Mark Pacheco, options for young people like Gabi who translanguage in speech and writing include code-switching, translating, and language brokering (translation by youth for parents or older adults), as well as interpreting between individuals of various linguistic and cultural backgrounds (654). In Gabi's case, and in those of many young readers, English-only education continues to be the norm in the United States, even though many students speak other languages in their homes and communities. This diversity of practices within, between, and beyond two languages allows for Gabi's increased creativity with words and ideas and also affirms her linguistic and cultural identities. Quintero notes that the reason for paying homage to Serros in the novel is that Serros was "one of the reasons I write. I was writing [before] but she gave me permission to be as Chicana and Mexican as I wanted to be. Before that I only wrote in English. After reading her work, I realized I could write in Spanish too. Like, oh I could write about chicharrones. I could write about the body. I could write about sex. Just so many different things" ("Interview"). Much like for Quintero, Serros "gives" Gabi permission to be as Latinx as she wants to be.

An openness to diversity of expression, in particular via translanguaging, opens Gabi, and Quintero likewise, to new possibilities in the articulation of identity and the struggle for social justice. As Quintero explains, "language, too, is political. Specially, speaking Spanish . . . I am bilingual, Gabi is bilingual, and therefore the book is bilingual" ("Morris"). By foregrounding the use of multiple and mixed codes, *Gabi, a Girl in Pieces* draws specific attention to the ways in which translanguaging is a political act with a social justice imperative. According to Suzanne García-Mateus and Deborah Palmer, translanguaging can "potentially contribute to constructing . . . [and] empowering bilingual identities" as well as "potentially address language-related social justice issues" (253). This occurs, in many ways, because via language the speaker (or writer in this case) attempts to share language—and, "at the same time, they are co-constructing their sense of identity and positionality within a certain context" (248). Translanguaging thus allows writers, real author Isabel Quintero and fictional author Gabi, to fashion a positive sense of self that celebrates all parts of the diverse Latinx world. Ashley Hope Pérez and Patricia Enciso affirm this connection between language and identity in their analysis of the novel: "How and when Spanish is used relates to the novel's broader engagement with identity as strategic improvisation. Languages and cultures are shown to be plural, complex in their interactions, and often in tension with one another" (4). Border artistas, such as Serros and Quintero, as well as Gabi, showcase translanguaging as a powerful tactic to disrupt neat separations between cultures and to put the pieces together in ways that more accurately portray the complex cultural existence of living on the hyphen.

WRITING TO BE THE CHANGE IN THE WORLD

Beyond developing a strong sense of identity via writing, the novel foregrounds the role of writing as a way of exploring challenging issues, naming and questioning injustice, and ultimately of making change. As Quintero explains,

> I had always talked about the power of writing and how it could change things, because it had changed my life. Other writers' work changed how I saw the world and how I thought about things like patriarchy and white supremacy. It taught me to call those things by their name. Most importantly, their work taught me to question everything. I would like my work to do that; to have readers question things they had otherwise accepted. ("'My Writing'")

If the goal of *Gabi, a Girl in Pieces* is to have readers identify injustice, question it, and then change their worlds, as Quintero says other writers' works did for her, Gabi is a dynamic role model. This power of writing becomes evident to readers when Gabi uses writing to work through her relationship with her father and the pains his addiction cause, when she uses her zines to reenvision the female body, and when she writes out her feelings in her journal about the challenges her friends face around abortion and homophobia. What *Gabi, a Girl in Pieces* points to, then, is that while we do not always have school programs to deal with these challenging issues and complex intersections of gender, ethnicity, sexuality, and cultural belonging, we do have writers and artists and activists. As Anzaldúa reminds us, "nepantleras such as artistas/activistas help us mediate these transitions, help us make the crossings, and guide us through the transformation process—a process I call conocimiento" (*Light / Luz* 17).

Readers see Gabi model this process in her journal as she writes through the many fractures in her life—moving from desconocimiento to conocimiento. As Cristina Herrera points out in her article on "chicaNerds," "Through her diary, and later, through poetry, Gabi discovers power in using creative means to find agency and voice" (318). One of the greatest fractures Gabi deals with in this process is that of unintended pregnancies, which include the experiences of sexual violence, abortion, and the accompanying gendered expectations around pregnancy. The three unintended pregnancies (Gabi's mom, her friend Cindy, and her classmate Georgina) cause significant challenges, not only for practical and emotional reasons, but also because of societal responses to these women.

When Gabi learns about her best friend Cindy's pregnancy, she finds herself in a place of fracture and desconocimiento.

> PREGNANT? What the hell? . . . I was so pissed at the situation. Pissed and disappointed. Not at the fact that she had sex, but that she hadn't been careful. That she had just become another statistic: Hispanic Teen Mom #3,789,258. Or some ridiculous actual number that we had been lectured about last year and had sworn we would never become. We [Gabi and Cindy] had even criticized the girls who showed and called them stupid. (11)

Like many of her peers, Gabi enacts the ways society has normalized her, shaming those who transgress social gender norms. Faced with the teen pregnancy of her peer, she repeats the internalized response of criticism and mockery. Through her journaling, however, Gabi begins to take notice of Cindy's emotional pain. Gabi realizes that alongside mockery, Cindy suffers from malicious gossip and isolation.

Not long after the school finds out about Cindy's pregnancy, Gabi's mother insists that she avoid Cindy: "You can't hang out with her anymore. She is a bad influence. She's a bad, bad girl. I knew that she would come to this. Always so desperate and siempre de ofrecida, no se daba a respetar. No respect for herself at all" (20). Although Gabi's mother concedes and allows Gabi to be friends, Gabi learns that Cindy is also ostracized at home: "She told us that her dad won't even speak to her yet and that her grandmother told her that maybe it was time to quit school, that she shouldn't pretend to be a good school girl anymore because—obviously—she isn't" (49). That Gabi refuses to ostracize Cindy at this point when others do is telling. In this, readers see Gabi's development from criticism to compassion; she is able to learn and adapt. This, in turn, positions readers to trace an arc that starts with an acknowledgment of complicity and moves toward understanding, toward conocimiento.

Significantly, Gabi's newfound conocimiento moves her from aiding one person to helping others who are hurt by conventional ways of looking at the world. Her journal entry detailing the photo they took after sending off college applications elucidates this progression: "And I know Cindy doesn't like to have pictures with her pregnant belly showing, but you know what? Who cares! Everyone knows you're pregnant, and that's part of your life now and part of our life. I don't want us to be ashamed anymore . . . of being pregnant or gay or poor or having a crackhead dad! I want us to be fucking proud of ourselves" (127). Gabi sees that changing the world is in order, beginning with Cindy and extending to others. As the novel reveals, these others include Gabi and Cindy's arch nemesis Georgina.

When Georgina tells Gabi that she needs help, Gabi first notes what she could do: "I should say, 'Well, now she'll know what she put Cindy through,' but being treated as a pariah is not something that anyone deserves—especially for having sex because everybody does it. It sounds cliché, but sex is a natural human function. I mean we shouldn't do it with everyone, but maybe it isn't as bad as parents make it seem" (162). Instead of ostracizing Georgina, Gabi offers compassion and she offers to help. As it turns out, one of the reasons Georgina turns to Gabi is that Georgina feels she is in danger of physical violence. In this, Georgina fears what would happen if her conservative Jehovah's Witness parents find out about the pregnancy; as she tells Gabi, "They'd kill me. My dad would really kill me. When he found out I had sex with Joshua, he kicked the shit out of me. That's why I wasn't here that whole week" (176). This is why Gabi suggests to Georgina that she terminate the pregnancy and why she accompanies Georgina to the abortion clinic.

Rather than shaming Georgina, Gabi offers kindness and affirmation with her witty words, "Georgina must have ovaries of steel to do this. I had never thought of her as strong" (182). Gabi reimagines and re-genders the cliché, making sure readers understand the strength that choice takes. Further, as Gabi explains, "It had never occurred to me that strength was needed to make this choice. I am sure that this will not be the last day she will think about it" (182). Whereas at the beginning of the novel, Gabi called Georgina *payasa* or clown, Gabi recognizes the strength that it takes to make "this choice."

From assisting individual friends like Cindy and Georgina, among others, Gabi begins the next part of the transformation. She starts to see the insidiousness of the system that places blame on women while not responding similarly to men. Gabi asks:

> Why did Georgina have to make the choice about her baby? And then live with the guilt and the fear of being found out and being labeled slut and baby killer while Joshua Moore [Georgina's boyfriend] paraded around like nothing ever happened? . . . Now he doesn't have a responsibility and is free to go and play football or soccer or wrestle bears or whatever it is he is doing to get college scholarships. And she's the one who's wracked with guilt. It makes me mad. Why are we always screwed? (204)

Gabi's answers to these questions can be found in her zines, her art, and her writing.

CHOOSING THE ROUTE OF INTERCONNECTIVITY

Anzaldúa tells us that in moments like this one,

> A heightened consciousness or awareness that I call "conocimiento" and some call "love" (which may be the same thing) stirs the artist to take action, propels her toward the act of making. This conocimiento initiates the relationship between self-knowledge and creative work. Because the artist must keep watch on her inner responses, she becomes more aware, more alive, and thus she "makes" the story of herself as she makes her art (*Light / Luz* 40).

Gabi's zines, composed of cutouts of different female body parts that are assembled alongside text, resemble short graphic novels in their presentation and style. Gabi repurposes images from *All About Your*

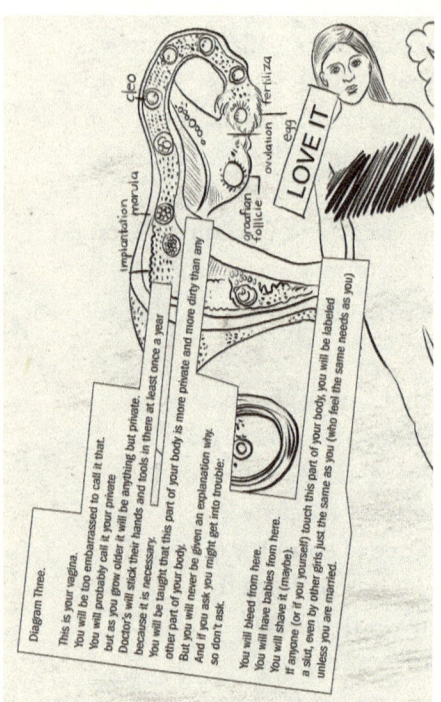

FIGURE 5.1 Zeke Peña, Gabi's zine page of female anatomy. *Gabi, A Girl in Pieces* by Isabel Quintero. Illustration by Zeke Peña with Isabel Quintero (Cinco Puntos Press, 2014).

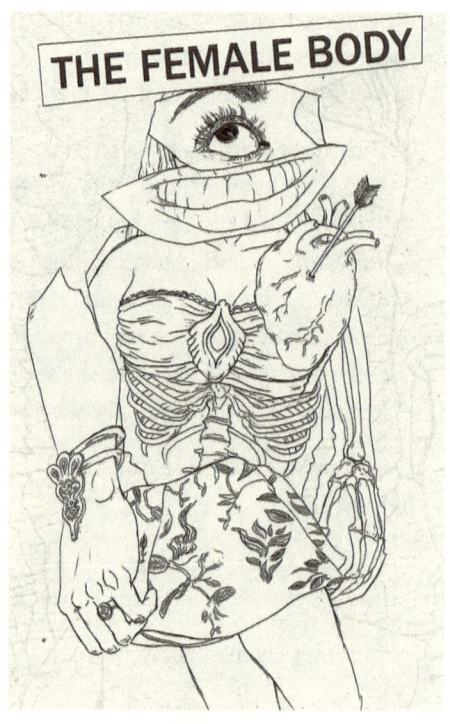

FIGURE 5.2 Zeke Peña, Gabi's zine cover. *Gabi, A Girl in Pieces* by Isabel Quintero. Illustration by Zeke Peña with Isabel Quintero (Cinco Puntos Press, 2014).

Body, a book her mother had given her during fifth grade. Although the book had "diagrams, see-through pictures with descriptions of what our body parts do," it did not cover "how cramps would make you want to roll around on the floor. Or that you would get chills so bad that you'd wish you could sleep in the sun. Or how pads feel like diapers that you are always worried are leaking all over the place" (191). Gabi's intention, therefore, is to make the book much more informative in her zines: "I decided that my zine would have all the information that that book left out—the truth about the female body from a female point of view. Because, really, the older I get, the more I realize how full of crap that book was" (191–92). The zine on the vagina, along with an image of a bisected vagina, directly addresses readers and notes:

> You will be taught that this part of your body is more private and more dirty than any other part of your body.
> But you will never be given an explanation why.
> And if you ask you might get into trouble: so don't ask. (198)

The accompanying text box reads "LOVE IT" (198). All told, the eight-page zines net her fifteen dollars when, after she presented them at a local coffee shop as part of a poetry reading, some of the guests, mostly college students, wanted to buy a copy (205). Gabi tells us, with a bit of glee, that she is now a published poet. In this, readers see how Gabi becomes more aware, more alive, and thus she "makes" the story of herself as she makes her art. Gabi's growing self-awareness and creative works act in concert to showcase her conocimiento in the final scenes of the novel.

The novel ends with Gabi suspended from her high school graduation ceremony. Although she will receive her degree and thus be able to attend college, she is not allowed to "walk" at graduation because she assaults German, the father of Cindy's baby. While Gabi initially thought the sex between German and Cindy was consensual, Cindy tells Gabi that in fact it was a rape. What had started out as kissing and petting turned violent: "He held her down, and she cried the whole time" (229). Cindy, out of shame and because she did not think anyone would believe her, kept the assault a secret. Frustrated and angry, Gabi decides to do what border artistas are called to do: "The whole way home I just kept thinking about what I've heard all my life from my mom and other women whenever boys have done something stupid and/or wrong: 'Boys will be boys,' and what a load of bullshit that is. I had to write about it" (229). Gabi then proceeds to pen a long list of what happens when boys are allowed to be boys. While her zines speak to the ways girls are supposed to see their bodies according to society (a sort of double consciousness), this list of "boys will be boys" concerns society's permissiveness of guys. In her list, for example, boys are allowed to be predators and need not worry about wearing condoms—which proved especially heinous for Cindy. As Gabi ironically states, "because boys will be boys, he's not going to use a condom (he likes the real deal), so you might just get pregnant. But hopefully, you won't get AIDS or herpes or chlamydia. So you should feel good about that. Besides, babies are cute" (230).

Having rendered her anger into art, Gabi is ready to go. Rather than assaulting German for Cindy alone, Gabi resorts to violence only after seeing German with another possible victim and after thinking about how this new victim would likewise be afraid to speak up. It was then that "the levee broke. I hurricane. I flood. I baptismal waters. God the punisher. Ancient being full of wrath. Hammer of Thor. Bolt of Zeus. Huitzilopochtli emerging from Coatepec—recently birthed and thirsty for vengeance. Chola from the barrio that I could never be" (260). Gabi, therefore, only assaults German—kneeing him in the crotch, pinning him down and beating him—after thinking deeply about injustices in which any number of women could be hurt. While what German did to Cindy was present in Gabi's attack, the text positions the reader to see the fuller social picture, in which boys are granted impunity and as such all women can be victims.

No matter how good it may feel to us as readers that German got what was coming to him, the text seems to imply otherwise. Cindy stops talking to Gabi since the fight revealed Cindy's secret about the rape. Gabi should have sought help for Cindy—choosing the route of interconnectivity instead. As Gabi herself notes,

> What I should have done instead—and realized after researching on the internet (apparently a tool that can also be used for good, not just evil)—was to just be there for her and suggest she talk to someone (a teacher, the police, a counselor). I looked this info up before I went to her house and made a list of rape crisis hotline numbers and websites so that if she didn't want to talk to me anymore, she would have options. (269)

Gabi, as with prior confessions, is honest. She first chose the path of desconocimiento, the easy path of violence. Having recognized this,

Gabi turns to professionals to help, for them to use their conocimiento for Cindy. The scene ends with Gabi explaining in her journal that she eventually chose that route with Cindy, listening to her and offering referrals to professional counselors: "We sat and talked for hours. Cindy hadn't talked to anyone about how she felt. I mean she had told us what had happened but not how she felt. I had never seen her so sad . . . I gave her the list of hotlines I had made from my internet research and suggested she call one" (270). In her arc, Gabi moves from a complicit member of society who enforces traditional gender constructs to a bold activist that challenges these norms in healthy ways—via her zines and offering support to her friends.

While the novel begins with a girl in pieces, it tells of the creative process of making pieces of art. Quintero explains that "when I wrote the book, I was having Gabi tell herself things that I wish I would have been able to tell myself before" ("An Interview"). Gabi provides the sort of insights Quintero now has but also wished she had as a teenager. This growth that Quintero notes and which *Gabi, a Girl in Pieces* enacts, we suggest, exemplifies Anzaldúa's notion of gathering insight and translating it into "shareable form" ("Memoir" 237). The healing process begins with Quintero creating a character who tells herself (via writing in her journal) the kinds of insights gained in Quintero's real-world experiences. It continues as Gabi enacts these insights by questioning and changing perceptions of what it means to be and do Latinx. This is completed as readers see Gabi developing as a writer who uses writing for social justice, thereby inviting readers to grow in the way that Quintero was transformed by other writers' work. What *Gabi, a Girl in Pieces* traces, we argue, is the way creative acts are a catalyst for change, for the transformation of this world into a better one that more accurately represents the lived experiences of Latinx children and young adults.

AUTOHISTORIAS, THE NEXT BORDER TO CROSS

Julia, at the end of *I Am Not Your Perfect Mexican Daughter*, leaves for New York University (NYU). As she is driven to the airport by her parents, her father is wearing the same shirt he wore the day he found her attempting to commit suicide. Also, in her hands, as the plane takes off for New York, is Olga's ultrasound. In the last words of the novel, Julia notes, "these last two years I combed and delved through my sister's life to better understand her, which meant I learned to find pieces of myself—both beautiful and ugly" (340). Her autohistoria, as she heads off to college, is complete: Julia "was forced to recognize the illusionary and arbitrary nature of social norms" and from her "apprenticeship" she "came to understand her suffering" (Anzaldúa, "Memoir" 236–37). Then, as a border artista, she narrates her own counter-story, so as "to translate her insight into shareable form so that others could use it" (Anzaldúa, "Memoir" 237). Gabi also deals with significant intersectional identity issues, not to mention a multitude of struggles during her senior year of high school. As a border artista, Gabi creates her autohistoria in a mishmash of journal entries, zines, poems, and telephone conversations recorded in this composite novel in a mixture of Spanish and English. To mark her conocimiento understanding, *Gabi, a Girl in Pieces* ends, we are led to understand, with Gabi heading off to the University of California, Berkeley. She, therefore, celebrates her past achievements and how they portend future success in a way that only Gabi can, by eating with her family at Pepe's House of Wings.

Reading *I Am Not Your Perfect Mexican Daughter* and *Gabi, A Girl in Pieces* as autohistorias that depict "the soul del artista y el alma del pueblo" (*Light / Luz* 62) allows us better to understand the processes of self-inscription for border artistas. Crossing the border between personal lived experiences and public social realities, as Anzaldúa informs us, is a "way of inventing and making knowledge, meaning, and identity through self-inscriptions. By making certain personal experiences the subject of this study, I also blur the private/public borders" (*Light / Luz* 6). As we have discussed in this chapter, Julia and Gabi open a nepantla (in-between) space for inventing and making new knowledge "from our experience and perspective through our art rather than accepting our history by the dominant culture" (*Light / Luz* 62). Autohistorias, in this sense, attest to the transformational possibilities of putting the pieces from "our" experiences and perspectives together via "our" creative acts. This is to say that crossing this new borderland terrain between personal experiences and social reality provides us vistas from which to see how the dualities, contradictions, and struggles of Latinx everyday life are synthesized in an artful mestizada. The promise of these novels is that Julia and Gabi, as border artistas, demonstrate for others the power of intertwining their artistic souls with communal ones.

Afterword

A work of art, Gloria Anzaldúa tells us, "represents and reveals" (*Light / Luz* 178). She goes on to add that because art "brings about a new interrogation that goes against the existing order, art is revolutionary. Art has a political purpose: to push the world in a certain direction, to change others' ideas of reality, and to tell them what reality to strive for" (178). For us, the children's and young adult books considered in this study constitute art for young people. These books indeed represent, reveal, and change our notions of reality. We wrote this book to highlight the necessity of this art, in particular, to represent in positive and more accurate ways the lived experiences of Latinx children and young adults. Our motorcycle ride, following the metaphor we employed for reading *Tactics of Hope* in the introduction, has allowed us to feature the works of Latinx authors and illustrators in such works as *Tomás and the Library Lady*, *Side by Side / Lado a lado*, *Under the Feet of Jesus*, *They Call Me Güero*, *Under the Mesquite*, *Maximilian and the Mystery of the Guardian Angel*, *Summer of the Mariposas*, *From North to South / Del norte al sur*, *Land of the Cranes*, *Efrén Divided*, *I Am Not Your Perfect Mexican Daughter*, and *Gabi, a Girl in Pieces*. We also drew inspiration in our introduction and this afterword from *My Papi Has a Motorcycle*.

Art also reveals, as Anzaldúa posits, by casting a light on the existing order, an everyday America in which desconocimiento is not only rampant but also, in these last few years, celebrated. What this means for many Latinx children and young adults is that their everyday world tells them to forget their multiple languages, both Spanish and English as well as vernacular and translingual expressions, and their stories, which include mythologies and other narratives from across the Americas. Even as US policies and practices present assimilation as an aspirational goal for Latinx children and youth, the art of Latinx children's and young adult literature, we suggest, reveals oppressions to be contested and proposes alternatives fueled by conocimiento. This critical awareness is revolutionary, according to Anzaldúa, as it creates new epistemologies by which to see the world and ourselves in it. Conocimiento, in this way, pushes in the direction of equity and justice. With conocimiento we move toward a place where belonging is measured by the complexity of affiliations and variety of relationships rather than by a simple binary organized around whiteness.

Latinx children's and young adult literature propels young readers to strive for this new reality by showcasing literary mirrors in which Latinx young readers can see themselves and literary windows via which young readers can grow in their awareness of Latinx cultures and peoples. Fundamental to our study is the understanding that Latinx children's and young adult literature allows young readers to experience within themselves the processes of conocimiento as modes of resistance and as sites of transformation. From this we gather, with instructions from Aurora Levins Morales, that children and youth lead the way toward this new world.

As we conclude our book, we loudly call for more sustained critical analyses on Latinx children's and young adult literature, that is, that scholars turn regularly to it as part and parcel of Latinx studies and that academic journals and university presses open widely their doors to these studies. The academy has marginalized children's and young adult literature in general, and has doubled its efforts for children's and young adult literature of color. The academy, in what it deems worthy of scholarship, holds great sway in the United States and beyond. What students in colleges and universities read and how they read it has a direct relationship to future research. In addition, what teachers are trained to teach and how they are trained to teach comes from their professors and from the types of scholarship professors engage.

Since we began writing this project, there has been an increase in the separation of migrant children from their parents, the rhetoric of hatred has become more pronounced, more emboldened, and the processes of assimilation have become more insidious, targeting those most vulnerable, our youngest, by attempting to define, then contain, and finally eliminate Latinx peoples. As scholars, professors, teachers, and activists we can do what we do best: write, teach, and fight for change. Further, we can teach others to do the same and we can work to get these books into the hands of young readers. These, indeed, are the tactics of hope. ¡Sí, se puede!

Notes

INTRODUCTION

1. See Bernstein for more information on notions of childhood innocence.

2. John Beverley notes "in oral history it is the intentionality of the recorder—usually a social scientist—that is dominant, and the resulting text is in some sense 'data.' In testimonio, by contrast, it is the intentionality of the narrator that is paramount. The situation of narration in testimonio has to involve an urgency to communicate, a problem of repression, poverty, subalternity, imprisonment, struggle for survival, and so on, implicated in the act of narration itself" (14).

3. An early iteration of our title was *Movidas of Hope*. Movidas, as Tomás Ybarra-Frausto tells us, are "coping strategies you use to gain time, to make options to retain hope" (86). While we moved on from installing movidas in the title of our book, we hold onto the notion that movidas and tactics retain hope, for the ways they fund conocimiento as well as the ways they contest gatekeeping mechanisms in the publishing industry. Tactics, in this sense, mean kicking down the gates that keep Latinx works out.

4. The numbers reflect "data on books by and about Black, Indigenous and People of Color published for children and teens compiled by the Cooperative Children's Book Center, School of Education, University of Wisconsin–Madison." For more information see: https://ccbc.education.wisc.edu/literature-resources/ccbc-diversity-statistics/.

5. For more discussion on the term "Latinx," see Milian, in the *Cultural Dynamics* journal's special issue *Theorizing LatinX*.

CHAPTER ONE

1. For more on migrant farmworkers in the United States and their struggles, see Holmes and *United Farm Workers*.

2. United Farm Workers of America (UFW) was founded in 1962 by César Chávez, Dolores Huerta, and other organizers under its original name, National Farm Workers Association (NFWA). The union creates contracts with agricultural industries to protect workers and improve governmental regulations to prevent heat-related deaths and improve immigration processes, among other issues. Farmworker Justice is a nonprofit organization that empowers migrant and seasonal farmworkers. The organization began in 1981 and in 1996 became a subsidiary corporation of National Council for La Raza. Many other groups like The Coalition for Immokalee Workers also aid farmworkers in their struggles for

fair wages and working conditions. For more information see *United Farm Workers*, *Farmworker Justice*, and *The Coalition of Immokalee Workers*.

3. While not a historical figure, Estrella may be based on the experiences of Viramontes's parents, who worked as migrant laborers in the grape harvest during her youth. For more on Viramontes's life and work, see Gutiérrez y Muhs.

4. See Serrato, "Conflicting Inclinations." Serrato wisely cautions that Chicanx children's literature, while offering a view into the lived experiences of Chicanx children, sometimes falls short of fully addressing real conclusions to the problems.

5. See Rodríguez's "Conocimiento Narratives," with specific attention to her notion that conocimiento challenges and then transforms, as part of its process, epistemologies of oppression.

6. For in-depth biographical information, see García on Dolores Huerta and Levy on César Chávez.

7. For detailed biographical information on Tomás Rivera, see Olivares and Lattin et al.

8. For more information on questions of language education in the United States for students that do not speak English as their native language, see Adamson.

9. For a detailed analysis of the artist-activist in Tomás Rivera's *. . . y no se lo tragó la tierra / . . . And the Earth Did Not Devour Him* (1971), see Postma-Montaño.

10. Examples of künstlerroman works include: James Joyce's *A Portrait of the Artist as a Young Man*, Willa Cather's *The Song of the Lark*, Rodolfo Anaya's *Bless Me, Ultima*, and Sandra Cisneros's *The House on Mango Street*. For more on the Chicanx künstlerroman, see Eysturoy.

11. Shea suggests that memory is important in the novel as it provides "the resources for survival, for personal healing, and for collective struggle" (142). While this may be true, Estrella takes on an analytical role as artist-activist instead of functioning solely as a memory keeper.

12. Beck and Rangel suggest that the novel critiques traditional Catholicism through its association of the religion with colonial oppression (17). While this critique can be seen in the novel through the replacement of the Savior (Jesucristo icon) with Estrella, there is no direct questioning of God as can be seen in Rivera's *. . . y no se lo tragó la tierra*.

CHAPTER TWO

1. In the poem, Lupita contrasts the United States and English with Mexico and Spanish. While she struggles with the language and customs of the United States, she finds comfort in Mexico and Spanish. The poem ends with the family joyfully going to Mexico, thereby enacting physically their daily use of language and cultural practices (38–41).

2. Our sentence paraphrases the poem "En Los Estados Unidos": "The chain-link fence on the bridge / was like a harp, and our fingers / would play a joyful tune upon / its rib cage as we traipsed along, / looking down at the laughing / waters of the Rio Grande / until we reached that other world, / the one we missed so much" (40).

3. For an example of the way this text is being integrated into school literacy programs in Texas, see Rodríguez, Murillo-Sutterby, and Cummins.

4. The künstlerroman form has much to offer ethnic American writers and by that same token, young Latinx readers. Künstlerromans have a long and pronounced history in Chicanx literary history and culture. Works such as . . . *y no se lo tragó la tierra / . . . And the Earth Did Not Devour Him* by Tomás Rivera, *The House on Mango Street* by Sandra Cisneros, and *The Circuit* by Francisco Jiménez are a few of the more well-known künstlerromans in Chicanx literary heritage. For more on the Chicanx künstlerroman, see Eysturoy.

5. As Dina Gavrilos notes, "studies point to the function of whiteness as silent 'strategic rhetoric,' constituting an invisible, universal, and normative racial position in everyday practices. This scholarship (from rhetorical scholars) helps explain the unspoken, taken-for-granted symbolic link between English and national identity that enacts hierarchical ethnic and racial divisions. English functions so powerfully as a culturally unifying symbol of national identity in mainstream national culture that its white, Anglo-specific roots seem invisible" (116).

CHAPTER THREE

1. The character of the Guardian Angel seems to be most closely influenced by El Santo, one of the most famous luchadores of all time. The Guardian Angel's name, Rodolfo, appears to be a homage to Rodolfo Guzmán Huerta, the name of El Santo. For more information, see Rubenstein.

2. Diaspora, as Thomas Faist explains, normally denotes groups living outside an imagined homeland, while transnationalism refers "to migrants' durable ties across countries—and, more widely, to capture not only communities, but all sorts of social formations, such as transnationally active networks, groups and organisations" (9). At the same time, as Faist explains, there is much overlap (33). In our study, we use "diaspora" to refer to the group, which sees Aztlán as the imagined homeland, and transnationalism as the ties that bind people across national borders. For more information, see Faist.

3. For more information on lucha libre as cultural performance, see Levi, who notes that wrestlers see lucha libre as both sport and spectacle; "their job is not to win or lose, but to put on a satisfying show" (49). Levi goes on to explain that this "ritual drama in which good and evil (or at least bad) struggle for domination" becomes more complex due to the way wrestlers take on fictional identities and often times "represent the social world" (49).

4. El Perro Aguayo and el Cavernario (Galindo) were real-life luchadores, as was El Príncipe Maya. El Vampiro is an artful play on the real-life Murciélago Velásquez.

5. See Alarcón, *The Aztec Palimpsest*; Hidalgo, *Revelation in Aztlán*; and Vásquez and Gómez-Quiñones, *Making Aztlán*. In young adult literature, see Bowles, *Feathered Serpent, Dark Heart of Sky* for Aztec mythologies and his Garza Twin Series for further examples of Aztec mythologies in Latinx mythological realist texts.

CHAPTER FOUR

1. It is also important to note that involuntary separation occurs in other moments. For example, families have been separated from their children at border crossings as seen in the news headlines of 2018 and subsequent protests. Separation also occurs in situations when parent(s) migrate without children for economic reasons or when unaccompanied minors are sent by their parents, many times fleeing violence or economic hardship. For more on the effects of deportation on immigrant families, see Dreby's *Everyday Illegal*, and for more on undocumented child arrivals, see Terrio.

2. For more information on negative metaphors, such as "illegal," "criminal," and "animalist," in public discourse concerning Latinx people, see Otto Santa Ana, *Brown Tide Rising*. Chapters 7 and 8 pay specific attention to the use of these metaphors as well as discuss ways to contest and challenge them.

3. Volumes have been written on the role of Aztlán in Chicanx cultural and artistic production. As a primer for understanding its historical and cultural relevance, see part 1, "Quest for a Homeland" in Ruiz, *Chicano!: History of the Mexican American Civil Rights Movement*. For civil rights matters, see Vásquez and Gómez-Quiñones. For aesthetics, see Gaspar de Alba. For environmental issues, see Ontiveros's *In the Spirit of a New People*, specifically chapter 2, "Green Aztlán: Environmentalism and Chicano/a Visual Arts." For spiritual matters, see Hidalgo.

4. The novel italicizes passages when a person is "speaking" in Spanish, even though the words are in English in the novel.

5. For the significance of transformations and movements in Aztec philosophy, see Maffie.

6. It is important to note that regardless of the legal status of the child in question, "children in Mexican immigrant households describe fear about their family stability and confusion over the impact legality has on their own lives" (Dreby, "Burden of Deportation" 829). Moreover, stress and anxiety of deportation occurs even when the threat of deportation does not directly affect their immediate family (838).

7. "Left alone" and "left behind" are terms that Boehm uses to illustrate the hazards of being undocumented in the United States. One can be left alone, in

Mexico or in the United States, if others are deported. The same holds true for left behind. See Boehm, pp. 74–96.

CHAPTER FIVE

1. This is a deep cultural reference, even for those who grew up watching the various comedy sketches in the *Chespirito* television program. For more information on the television program, see www.chespirito.com.

2. For more on the mother-daughter relationship in *I Am Not Your Perfect Mexican Daughter*, see Cantú-Sánchez.

3. In an earlier part of the novel Julia takes Albert Camus's *The Stranger* along on a class field trip to Warren Dunes (132). In this regard, Julia's comment about the quinceañera hanging over her like a guillotine closes the loop on this literary allusion. Like Mersault, Julia has grasped the absurdity of the world: Mersault is punished because he does not perform accordingly at his mother's funeral, just as Julia is punished for refusing to perform the role of the perfect Mexican daughter at her quinceañera.

4. Erika L. Sánchez's poem "The Poet at Fifteen," also alludes to Dickinson's poem. In Sánchez's, the speaker describes what happened to her at fifteen: "*I dreaded that first robin, / so, at fifteen you slash / your wrists*" (40).

5. Lighter skin in Latinx cultures is complex and multifaceted. From an intersectional standpoint, lighter skin confers privileges along common race lines. Within a border understanding, lighter skin, as Gabi finds out, also can be perceived as *different* within-group. For more information, see Chavez-Dueñas et al. and Quiros et al.

6. See also Ellis's chapter "Chicana Teens, Zines, and Poetry Scenes: *Gabi, A Girl in Pieces* by Isabel Quintero," which highlights writing and performative outlets in the novel as tools of agency and transformation for Chicana geeks, and, in the same edited volume, Santos's chapter "Broken Open: Writing, Healing, and Affirmation in Isabel Quintero's *Gabi, A Girl in Pieces* and Erika L. Sanchez's *I Am Not Your Perfect Mexican Daughter.*"

Works Cited

"About." *Cooperative Children's Book Center*. School of Education, University of Wisconsin–Madison, 2021, https://ccbc.education.wisc.edu/about/. Accessed 2 Feb. 2021.

"About Us." *We Need Diverse Books.* 2021, https://diversebooks.org/about-wndb/. Accessed 2 Feb. 2021.

Adamson, H. D. *Language Minority Students in American Schools: An Education in English*. Routledge, 2005.

Alarcón, Daniel Cooper. *The Aztec Palimpsest: Mexico in the Modern Imagination*. U of Arizona P, 1997.

Alba, Francisco. "Evolving Migration Responses in Mexico and the United States: Diverging Paths?" *Mexican Migration to the United States: Perspectives from Both Sides of the Border*, edited by Harriett D. Romo and Olivia Mogollon-Lopez, U of Texas P, 2016, pp. 17–36.

Aldama, Frederick Luis. *Latino/a Children's and Young Adult Writers on the Art of Storytelling*. U of Pittsburgh P, 2018.

Anguiano, Claudia. "Dropping the 'I-Word': A Critical Examination of Contemporary Immigration Labels." *The Rhetorics of US Immigration: Identity, Community, Otherness*, edited by E. J. Hartelius, Pennsylvania State UP, 2015, pp. 93–111.

Anzaldúa, Gloria E. *Borderlands / La Frontera: The New Mestiza.* 1987. Aunt Lute, 1999.

———. "Let Us Be the Healing of the Wound: The Coyolxauhqui Imperative—la sombra y el sueño." *The Gloria Anzaldúa Reader*, edited by AnaLouise Keating, Duke UP, 2009, pp. 303–17.

———. *Light in the Dark / Luz en lo oscuro: Rewriting Identity, Spirituality, Reality*, edited by AnaLouise Keating, Duke UP, 2015.

———. "Memoir—My Calling; or, Note for 'How Prieta Came to Write.'" *The Gloria Anzaldúa Reader*, edited by AnaLouise Keating, Duke UP, 2009, pp. 235–37.

———. "Metaphors in the Tradition of the Shaman." *The Gloria Anzaldúa Reader*, edited by AnaLouise Keating, Duke UP, 2009, pp. 121–23.

———. "Now Let Us Shift . . . The Path of Conocimiento . . . Inner Work, Public Acts." *This Bridge We Call Home: Radical Visions for Transformation*, edited by Anzaldúa and AnaLouise Keating, Routledge, 2002, pp. 540–78.

Bebout, Lee. *Mythohistorical Interventions: The Chicano Movement and Its Legacies*. U of Minnesota P, 2011.

Beck, Scott A., and Dolores E. Rangel. "Representations of Mexican American Migrant Childhood in Rivera's . . . *y no se lo tragó la tierra* and Viramontes's *Under the Feet of Jesus.*" *Bilingual Review*, vol. 29, no.1, 2008–9, pp. 14–24.

Bernstein, Robin. *Racial Innocence: Performing American Childhood from Slavery to Civil Rights.* NYU Press, 2011.

Beverley, John. "The Margin at the Center: On Testimonio (Testimonial Narrative)." *MFS: Modern Fiction Studies,* vol. 35, no. 1, 1989, pp. 11–28.

Bishop, Rudine Sims. "Mirrors, Windows, and Sliding Glass Doors." *Perspectives: Choosing and Using Books for the Classroom,* vol. 6, no. 3, 1990, pp. ix–xi.

Blackwell, Maylei. *¡Chicana Power!: Contested Histories of Feminism in the Chicano Movement.* U of Texas P, 2011.

Boehm, Deborah A. *Returned: Going and Coming in an Age of Deportation.* U of California P, 2016.

"Books by and/or about Black, Indigenous, and People of Color 2018–." *Cooperative Children's Book Center.* School of Education, University of Wisconsin–Madison, 2021, https://ccbc.education.wisc.edu/literature-resources/ccbc-diversity-statistics/books-by-and-or-about-poc-2018/. Accessed 2 Feb. 2021.

Bowles, David. *Feathered Serpent, Dark Heart of Sky: Myths of Mexico.* Cinco Puntos Press, 2018.

———. *They Call Me Güero: A Border Kid's Poems.* Cinco Puntos Press, 2018.

Braden, Eliza G., and Sanjuana C. Rodriguez. "Beyond Mirrors and Windows: A Critical Content Analysis of Latinx Children's Books." *Journal of Language and Literacy Education,* vol. 12, no. 2, 2016, pp. 56–83.

Brochin, Carol, and Carmen L. Medina. "Critical Fictions of Transnationalism in Latinx Children's Literature." *Bookbird: A Journal of International Children's Literature,* vol. 55, no. 3, 2017, pp. 4–11.

Brown, Monica. Interview. *Latino/a Children's and Young Adult Writers on the Art of Storytelling,* by Frederick Luis Aldama, U of Pittsburgh P, 2018, pp. 41–48.

———. *Side by Side / Lado a lado: The Story of Dolores Huerta and Cesar Chavez / La historia de Dolores Huerta y César Chávez.* Illustrated by Joe Cepeda, translated by Carolina Valencia, Harper Collins, 2010.

Butler, Judith. *Excitable Speech: A Politics of the Performative.* Routledge, 1997.

Cantú-Sánchez, Margaret. "'The Fourth Choice': Forging the Future of Chicanx Mother/Daughter Relationships through Storytelling and the Path of Conocimiento in Erika L. Sánchez's *I Am Not Your Perfect Mexican Daughter* and Barbara Renauld González's *Golondrina, Why Did You Leave Me?*" *Label Me Latino/a,* vol. 8, 2018, pp. 1–17, https://labelmelatin.com/wp-content/uploads/2018/09/Margaret-Cantu-Sanchez-The-Fourth-Choice-Forging-the-Future-of-Chicanx-MotherDaughter-Relationships-1.pdf. Accessed 2 Dec. 2019.

Chavez-Dueñas, Nayeli, Hector Adames, and Kurt Organista. "Skin-Color Prejudice and Within-Group Racial Discrimination: Historical and Current Impact on Latino/a Populations." *Hispanic Journal of Behavioral Sciences,* vol. 36, no. 1, 2014, pp. 3–26.

Cho, Sumi, Kimberlé Williams Crenshaw, and Leslie McCall. "Toward a Field of Intersectionality Studies: Theory, Applications, and Praxis." *Signs,* vol. 38, no. 4, 2013, pp. 785–810.

Cisneros, Ernesto. *Efrén Divided.* Quill Tree, 2020.

The Coalition of Immokalee Workers. 2018, http://www.ciw-online.org/. Accessed 14 June 2018.

Colato Laínez, René. *From North to South / Del norte al sur.* Illustrated by Joe Cepeda, Children's Book Press, 2010.

Collins, Patricia. *Black Feminist Thought: Knowledge, Consciousness, and the Politics of Empowerment.* Routledge, 2000.

Cooper, Lydia R. "'Bone, Flesh, Feather, Fire': Symbol as Freedom in Helena María Viramontes's *Under the Feet of Jesus.*" *Critique,* vol. 51, 2010, pp. 366–77.

Cooperative Children's Book Center. School of Education, University of Wisconsin–Madison, 2021, https://ccbc.education.wisc.edu/. Accessed 2 Feb. 2021.

La Cosecha / The Harvest. Directed by U. Roberto Romano, Global Vision/Cinema Libre, 2011.

Cotera, María Eugenia, Maylei Blackwell, and Dionne Espinoza. Introduction. *Chicana Movidas: New Narratives of Activism and Feminism in the Movement Era,* edited by Espinoza, Cotera, and Blackwell, U of Texas P, 2018, pp. 1–32.

Daniel, Shannon M., and Mark B. Pacheco. "Translanguaging Practices and Perspectives of Four Multilingual Teens." *Journal of Adolescent & Adult Literacy,* vol. 59, no. 6, 2016, pp. 653–63.

de Certeau, Michel. *The Practice of Everyday Life.* U of California P, 1984.

Deciu Ritivoi, Andreea. "Reading Stories, Reading (Others') Lives: Empathy, Intersubjectivity, and Narrative Understanding." *Storyworlds: A Journal of Narrative Studies,* vol. 8, no. 1, 2016, pp. 51–75.

De Genova, Nicholas. "The Deportation Regime: Sovereignty, Space, and the Freedom of Movement." *The Deportation Regime,* edited by De Genova and Nathalie Peutz, Duke UP, 2010, pp. 33–65.

Delgado, Richard, and Jean Stefanic. *Critical Race Theory: An Introduction.* NYU Press, 2001.

Delgado Bernal, Dolores. "Critical Race Theory, Latino Critical Theory, and Critical Raced-Gendered Epistemologies: Recognizing Students of Color as Holders and Creators of Knowledge." *Qualitative Inquiry,* vol. 8, no. 1, Sage Publications, 2002, pp. 105–26.

deOnís, Catalina (Kathleen) M. "What's in an 'x'?: An Exchange about the Politics of 'Latinx.'" *Chiricú Journal: Latina/o Literatures, Arts, and Cultures,* vol. 1, no. 2, 2017, pp. 78–91.

Des Moines Performing Arts. "Tomás and the Library Lady Experience." *Pat Mora: Author, Presenter, Literacy Advocate,* 12 Feb. 2014, http://www.patmora.com/books/tomas-and-the-library-lady/. Accessed 20 June 2018.

DignidadLiteraria. 2021, http://dignidadliteraria.com. Accessed 2 Feb. 2021.

Donahue, Alice. "¡Mira! Look!: *Tomás and the Library Lady.*" *Vamos a Leer: Teaching Latin America through Literacy,* 12 Sept. 2016, https://teachinglatinamericathroughliterature.wordpress.com/2016/09/12/mira-look-tomas-and-the-library-lady/. Accessed 4 June 2018.

Dreby, Joanna. "The Burden of Deportation on Children in Mexican Immigrant Families." *Journal of Marriage and Family,* vol. 74, no. 4, 2012, pp. 829–45.

———. *Everyday Illegal: When Policies Undermine Immigrant Families*. U of California P, 2015.

———. "U.S. Immigration Policy and Family Separation: The Consequences for Children's Wellbeing." *Social Science and Medicine*, vol. 132, 2015, pp. 245–51.

Dyrness, Andrea, and Enrique Sepúlveda III. *Border Thinking: Latinx Youth Decolonizing Citizenship*. U of Minnesota P, 2020.

Ellis, Amanda. "Chicana Teens, Zines, and Poetry Scenes: *Gabi, A Girl in Pieces* by Isabel Quintero." *Nerds, Goths, Geeks, and Freaks: Outsiders in Chicanx and Latinx Young Adult Literature*, edited by Trevor Boffone and Cristina Herrera, UP of Mississippi, 2020, pp. 15–30.

Eysturoy, Annie O. *Daughters of Self-Creation: The Contemporary Chicana Novel*. U of New Mexico P, 1996.

Faist, Thomas. "Diaspora and Transnationalism: What Kind of Dance Partners?" *Diaspora and Transnationalism: Concepts, Theories and Methods*, edited by Faist and Rainer Bauböck, Amsterdam UP, 2010, pp. 9–34.

Faris, Wendy. *Ordinary Enchantments: Magical Realism and the Remystification of Narrative*. Vanderbilt UP, 2004.

Farmworker Justice. 2018, http://www.farmworkerjustice.org/. Accessed 14 June 2018.

Fish, Stanley. "Interpreting the 'Variorum.'" *Critical Inquiry*, vol. 2, no. 3, 1976, pp. 465–85.

García, Mario T. *A Dolores Huerta Reader*. U of New Mexico P, 2008.

García-Mateus, Suzanne, and Deborah Palmer. "Translanguaging Pedagogies for Positive Identities in Two-Way Dual Language Bilingual Education." *Journal of Language, Identity, and Education*, vol. 16, no. 4, 2017, pp. 245–55.

García McCall, Guadalupe. "Belpré Author Award Acceptance Speech." *Children & Libraries: The Journal of the Association for Library Service to Children*, vol. 10, no. 2, 2012, pp. 15–16.

———. "David Bowles with Guadalupe Garcia McCall, *Feathered Serpent, Dark Heart of Sky: Myths of Mexico* and *El Verano de Las Mariposas* (*Summer of the Mariposas* Spanish Edition)." 28 June 2018, The Twig Book Shop, San Antonio, TX. Reading.

———. *Summer of the Mariposas*. Tu Books, 2012.

———. "Teacher's Guide: *Summer of the Mariposas*." Lee & Low Books, 2017, https://www.leeandlow.com/uploads/loaded_document/572/Summerofthe Mariposas_TG.pdf. Accessed 5 July 2018.

———. *Under the Mesquite*. Lee & Low, 2011.

Garza, Xavier. *Maximilian and the Mystery of the Guardian Angel: A Bilingual Lucha Libre Thriller*. Cinco Puntos Press, 2011.

Gaspar de Alba, Alicia. "There's No Place Like Aztlan: Embodied Aesthetics in Chicana Art." *CR: The New Centennial Review*, vol. 4, no. 2, 2004, pp. 103–40.

Gavrilos, Dina. "'American' Children's Success and Global Competitiveness: The Racial Paradox of Bilingualism as Cultural Capital." *The Rhetorics of US Immigration: Identity, Community, Otherness, edited by E. J. Hartelius, Pennsylvania State UP, 2015, pp. 112–32.

Griswold de Castillo, Richard, and Richard A. Garcia. *César Chávez: A Triumph of Spirit*. U of Oklahoma P, 1995.

Guidotti-Hernández, Nicole. "Affective Communities and Millennial Desires: Latinx, or Why My Computer Won't Recognize Latino/a." *Cultural Dynamics*, vol. 29, no. 3, 2017, pp. 141–59.

Gulbas, Lauren, and Luis Zayas. "Exploring the Effects of U.S. Immigration Enforcement on the Well-Being of Citizen Children." *RSF: The Russell Sage Foundation Journal of the Social Sciences*, vol. 4, no. 3, 2017, pp. 53–69.

Gutiérrez y Muhs, Gabriella. *Rebozos de Palabras: An Helena María Viramontes Critical Reader*. U of Arizona P, 2013.

Herrera, Cristina. "*Cinco Hermanitas*: Myth and Sisterhood in Guadalupe Garcia McCall's *Summer of the Mariposas*." *Children's Literature*, vol. 44, 2016, pp. 96–114.

———. "Soy Brown y Nerdy: The ChicaNerd in Chicana Young Adult (YA) Literature." *The Lion and the Unicorn*, vol. 41, no. 3, 2017, pp. 307–26.

Hidalgo, Jacqueline M. *Revelation in Aztlán: Scriptures, Utopias, and the Chicano Movement*. Palgrave Macmillan, 2017.

Holmes, Seth M. *Fresh Fruit, Broken Bodies: Migrant Farmworkers in the United States*. U of California P, 2013.

Jiménez García, Marilisa. "En(countering) YA: Young Lords, Shadowshapers, and the Longings and Possibilities of Latinx Young Adult Literature." *Latino Studies*, vol. 16, no. 2, 2018, pp. 230–49.

Khan, Mariam. "Immigration Is 'Changing the Culture' of Europe: Trump." *ABC News*, 13 June 2018, https://abcnews.go.com/Politics/immigration-changing-culture-europe-trump/story?id=56564695. Accessed 20 Dec. 2018.

Keating, AnaLouise. "Forging El Mundo Zurdo: Changing Ourselves, Changing the World." *This Bridge We Call Home: Radical Visions for Transformation*, edited by Gloria Anzaldúa and Keating, Routledge, 2002, pp. 519–29.

———. "From Borderlands and New Mestiza to Nepantlas and Nepantleras: Anzaldúan Theories for Social Change." *Human Architecture: Journal of the Sociology of Self-Knowledge*, vol. IV, pp. 5–16.

———. "Re-Envisioning Coyolxauhqui, Decolonizing Reality: Anzaldúa's Twenty-First Century Imperative." *Light in the Dark / Luz en lo oscuro: Rewriting Identity, Spirituality, Reality*, by Gloria Anzaldúa, Duke UP, 2015, pp. ix–xxxvii.

Keen, Suzanne. "Narrative Empathy." *Toward a Cognitive Theory of Narrative Acts*, edited by Frederick Luis Aldama, U of Texas P, 2010, pp. 61–93.

Kozlowska, Kasia, and Lesley Hanney. "An Art Therapy Group for Children Traumatized by Parental Violence and Separation." *Clinical Child Psychology and Psychiatry*, vol. 6, no. 1, 2001, pp. 49–78.

Latimer, Dan. "The La Brea Tar Pits, Tongues of Fire: Helena María Viramontes's *Under the Feet of Jesus* and Its Background." *Soundings: An Interdisciplinary Journal*, vol. 85, nos. 3–4, 2002, pp. 323–46.

Latinx Pitch for Kid Lit. https://latinxpitch.com. Accessed 2 Feb. 2021.

Lattin, Vernon, Rolando Hinojosa, and Gary Keller. *Tomás Rivera, 1935–1984: The Man and His Work*. Bilingual Review/Press, 1988.

Lee, Michelle Ye Hee. "Donald Trump's False Comments Connecting Mexican Immigrants and Crime." *The Washington Post*. 8 July 2015, https://www.washingtonpost.com/news/fact-checker/wp/2015/07/08/donald-trumps-false-comment-connecting-mexican-immigrants-and-crime/. Accessed 10 Nov. 2018.

Levi, Heather. *The World of Lucha Libre: Secrets, Revelations, and Mexican National Identity*. Duke UP, 2008.

Levins Morales, Aurora. *Medicine Stories: Essays for Radicals*. Duke UP, 2019.

Levy, Jacques. *Cesar Chavez: Autobiography of La Causa*. U of Minnesota P, 2007.

Lopez, Mark Hugo, Paul Taylor, Cary Funk, and Ana Gonzalez-Barrera. "On Immigration Policy, Deportation Relief Seen as More Important than Citizenship." *Pew Research Center: Hispanic Trends*, 19 Dec. 2013, https://www.pewresearch.org/hispanic/2013/12/19/on-immigration-policy-deportation-relief-seen-as-more-important-than-citizenship/. Accessed 10 Aug. 2018.

Maffie, James. *Aztec Philosophy: Understanding a World in Motion*. UP of Colorado, 2014.

Martín, Desirée A. *Borderlands Saints: Secular Sanctity in Chicano/a and Mexican Culture*. Rutgers UP, 2014.

McCracken, Ellen. *New Latina Narrative: The Feminine Space of Post-Modern Ethnicity*. U of Arizona P, 1999.

Medina, Carmen L., and Carmen Martínez-Roldán. "Culturally Relevant Literature Pedagogies: Latino Students Reading in the Borderlands." *Celebrating Cuentos: Promoting Latino Children's Literature and Literacy in Classrooms and Libraries*, edited by Jamie Campbell Naidoo, Libraries Unlimited, 2011, pp. 259–72.

Mickenberg, Julia L., and Philip Nel. "Radical Children's Literature Now!" *Children's Literature Association Quarterly*, vol. 36, no. 4, 2011, pp. 445–73.

Mignolo, Walter. *Local Histories / Global Designs: Coloniality, Subaltern Knowledges, and Border Thinking*. Princeton UP, 2012.

———, and Catherine E. Walsh. *On Decoloniality: Concepts Analytics Praxis*. Duke UP, 2018.

Milian, Claudia. *Theorizing LatinX*, special issue of *Cultural Dynamics*, vol. 29, no. 3, 2017.

Mora, Pat. "Library Magic." *Pat Mora: Author, Educator, Literacy Advocate*, http://www.patmora.com/a-poem-for-summer-reading/. Accessed 20 June 2018.

———. *Tomás and the Library Lady*. Illustrated by Raúl Colón, Knopf-Random House, 1997.

———. "*Tomás and the Library Lady*." *Pat Mora: Author, Educator, Literacy Advocate*, http://www.patmora.com/books/tomas-and-the-library-lady/. Accessed 23 June 2018.

Nikolajeva, Maria. "Picturebooks and Emotional Literacy." *The Reading Teacher*, vol. 67, no. 4, 2013, pp. 249–54.

Olivares, Julián, ed. *International Studies in Honor of Tomás Rivera*. Arte Público Press, 1986.

Ong, Walter. *Orality and Literacy*. Routledge, 2013.

Ontiveros, Randy J. *In the Spirit of a New People: The Cultural Politics of the Chicano Movement*. New York UP, 2014.

Passel, Jeffery S., D'Vera Cohn, Jens Manuel Krogstad, and Ana Gonzalez-Barrera. "As Growth Stalls, Unauthorized Immigrant Population Becomes More Settled." *Pew Research Center: Hispanic Trends*, 3 Sept. 2014, https://www.pewresearch.org/hispanic/2014/09/03/as-growth-stalls-unauthorized-immigrant-population-becomes-more-settled/. Accessed 10 Aug. 2018.

Pérez, Ashley Hope, and Patricia Enciso. "Decentering Whiteness and Monolingualism in the Reception of Latinx YA Literature." *The Bilingual Review / La Revista Bilingüe*, vol. 33, no. 5, 2017, pp. 1–15.

Pérez, Emma. *The Decolonial Imaginary: Writing Chicanas into History*. Indiana UP, 1999.

Plotz, John, and Gina Turrigiano. "Madeline Miller on 'Circe,' Mythological Realism, and Literary Correctives." 6 June 2019, https://www.publicbooks.org/madeline-miller-on-circe-mythological-realism-and-literary-correctives/. Accessed 3 Jan. 2021.

Portes, Alejandro, and Rubén G. Rumbaut. *Legacies: The Story of the Immigrant Second Generation*. U of California P, 2001.

Postma-Montaño, Regan. "Creative Words, Creative Acts: Tactics of the Artist-Activist in Tomás Rivera's . . . *y no se lo tragó la tierra* and Helena María Viramontes' *Under the Feet of Jesus*." *Border-Lines: Journal of the Latino Research Center*, vol. 10, 2016, pp. 69–90.

Pratt, Mary Louise. "Harm's Way: Language and the Contemporary Arts of War." *PMLA*, vol. 124, no. 5, 2009, pp. 1515–31.

Quintero, Isabel. "2015 Morris Award: An Interview with Finalist Isabel Quintero." By Faythe Arredondo, *The Hub: Your Connection to Teen Collections*, 26 Jan. 2015, http://www.yalsa.ala.org/thehub/2015/01/26/morris-award-finalist-interview-isabel-quintero/. Accessed 5 Aug. 2018.

———. *Gabi: A Girl in Pieces*. Cinco Puntos Press, 2014.

———. "Interview: Isabel Quintero, Author of *Gabi, A Girl in Pieces*." By Kelly Duarte, *The Strange is Beautiful*, http://thestrangeisbeautiful.com/interview-isabel-quintero-author-of-gabi-a-girl-in-pieces/. Accessed 5 Aug. 2018.

———. "An Interview with Isabel Quintero!" By Pamela Penza, *Teen Services Underground*, https://www.teenservicesunderground.com/an-interview-with-isabel-quintero/. Accessed 5 Aug. 2018.

———. "Morris Award Finalist Interview: Isabel Quintero, Author of *Gabi, A Girl in Pieces*." By Stephanie Kuehn, *Stephanie Kuehn*, 15 Jan. 2015, http://stephaniekuehn.com/morris-award-finalist-interview-isabel-quintero-author-of-gabi-a-girl-in-pieces/. Accessed 5 Aug. 2018.

———. *My Papi Has a Motorcycle*. Illustrated by Zeke Peña, Kokila, 2019.

———. "'My Writing Is My Activism': An Interview with Isabel Quintero." By

Jackie Rhodes, *Los Angeles Review of Books*, 1 Feb. 2017, https://lareviewof books.org/article/my-writing-is-my-activism-an-interview-with-isabel -quintero/. Accessed 5 Aug. 2018.

Quiros, Laura, and Beverly Araujo Dawson. "The Color Paradigm: The Impact of Colorism on the Racial Identity and Identification of Latinas." *Journal of Human Behavior in the Social Environment*, vol. 23, no. 3, 2013, pp. 287–97.

Rasilla, Azucena. "Aida Salazar's 'Land of the Cranes' Is an Immigrant Tale of Hope." *The Oaklandside*, 15 Sept. 2020, https://oaklandside.org/2020/09/15 /aida-salazars-land-of-the-cranes-is-an-immigrant-tale-of-hope/. Accessed 14 Dec. 2020.

Rhodes, Cristina. "Female Empowerment and Undocumented Border Crossing in Bettina Restrepo's Illegal." *Bookbird: A Journal of International Children's Literature*, vol. 55, no. 3, 2017, pp. 20-26.

———. "Processes of Transformation: Theorizing Activism and Change through Gloria Anzaldúa's Picture Books." *Children's Literature in Education*, 2 Nov. 2020, https://doi.org/10.1007/s10583-020-09429-2. Accessed 4 Nov. 2020.

———. "'Seemingly on the Inside . . . but Really on the Outside': Reading for Mirrors in Mexican Whiteboy." *Research on Diversity in Youth Literature*, vol. 1, no. 1, 2018, https://sophia.stkate.edu/cgi/viewcontent.cgi?article=1006&context =rdyl. Accessed 4 Feb. 2020.

Rivera, Tomás. . . . *y no se lo tragó la tierra/ And the Earth Did Not Devour Him*. 1971. Translated by Evangelina Vigil-Piñón, Arte Público Press, 1987.

Rodríguez, Rodrigo Joseph, Sandra Murillo-Sutterby, and Amy Cummins. "Literacies in Practice through Literature: Teaching with Guadalupe Garcia McCall's *Under the Mesquite* and *Summer of the Mariposas*." *Literacy Summit Yearbook*, vol. 2, 2016, pp. 100–107.

Rodríguez, Sonia Alejandra. "Conocimiento Narratives: Creative Acts and Healing in Latinx Children's and Young Adult Literature." *Children's Literature*, vol. 47, 2019, pp. 9–29.

Romo, Harriett. "Policies, Dynamics, and Consequences of Mexican Migration to the United States." *Mexican Migration to the United States: Perspectives from Both Sides of the Border*, edited by Romo and Olivia Mogollon-Lopez, U of Texas P, 2016, pp. 1–9.

Rubenstein, Anne. "El Santo's Strange Career." *The Mexico Reader: History, Culture, and Politics*, edited by Gilbert M. Joseph and Timothy J. Henderson. Duke UP, 2002, pp. 570–78.

Ruiz, Jose Luis. *Chicano! History of the Mexican American Civil Rights Movement*. NLCC Educational Media, 1996.

Salazar, Aida. *Land of the Cranes*. Scholastic, 2020.

Saldívar, Ramón. *The Borderlands of Culture: Américo Paredes and the Transnational Imaginary*. Duke UP, 2006.

Salvadore, Maria. "Meet David Bowles, author of *They Call Me Güero*." *Reading Rockets*. 6 May 2019, https://www.readingrockets.org/blogs/page-page/meet -david-bowles-author-they-call-me-g-ero. Accessed 14 Jan. 2021.

Sánchez, Erika L. "Amá." *Lessons on Expulsion: Poems*, Graywolf Press, 2017, pp. 8–9.

———. *I Am Not Your Perfect Mexican Daughter*. Knopf, 2017.

———. "The Poet at Fifteen." *Lessons on Expulsion: Poems*. Graywolf Press, 2017, pp. 40–41.

———. "Three Questions for Erika L. Sánchez regarding Her YA Novel, 'I Am Not Your Perfect Mexican Daughter.'" By Daniel Olivas, *Los Angeles Review of Books*, 9 Oct. 2017, https://lareviewofbooks.org/article/three-questions-for-erika-l-sanchez-regarding-her-ya-novel-i-am-not-your-perfect-mexican-daughter/#!. Accessed 5 Aug. 2018.

Sandoval, Chela, and Guisela Latorre. "Chicana/o Artivism: Judy Baca's Digital Work with Youth of Color." *Learning Race and Ethnicity: Youth and Digital Media*, edited by Anna Everett, MIT Press, 2008, pp. 81–108.

Santa Ana, Otto. *Brown Tide Rising: Metaphors of Latinos in Contemporary American Public Discourse*. U of Texas P, 2002.

Santos, Adrianna M. "Broken Open: Writing, Healing, and Affirmation in Isabel Quintero's *Gabi, A Girl in Pieces* and Erika L. Sanchez's *I Am Not Your Perfect Mexican Daughter*." *Nerds, Goths, Geeks, and Freaks: Outsiders in Chicanx and Latinx Young Adult Literature*, edited by Trevor Boffone and Cristina Herrera, UP of Mississippi, 2020, p. 45–59.

Schreiber, Rebecca M. *The Undocumented Everyday: Migrant Lives and the Politics of Visibility*. U of Minnesota P, 2018.

Serrato, Phillip. "Conflicting Inclinations: Luis J. Rodríguez's Picture Books for Children." *Ethnic Traditions in American Children's Literature*, edited by Yvonne Atkinson and Michele Pagni Stewart, Palgrave Macmillan, 2009, pp. 191–204.

———. "Not Quite Heroes: Race, Masculinity, and Latino Professional Wrestlers." *Steel Chair to the Head: The Pleasure and Pain of Professional Wrestling*, edited by Nicholas Sammond, Duke UP, 2005, pp. 232–59.

Shea, Anne. "Don't Let Them Make You Feel You Did a Crime: Immigration Law, Labor Rights, and Farmworker Testimony." *MELUS*, vol. 28, no. 1, 2003, pp. 123–44.

Shuldiner, David. "The Politics of Discourse: An Applied Folklore Perspective." *Journal of Folklore Research*, vol. 35, no. 3, 1998, pp. 189–201.

Smith, Vicky. "Ernesto Cisneros: Seeing Wrongs, Finding Hope." *Kirkus*, 30 Aug. 2020, https://www.kirkusreviews.com/news-and-features/articles/ernesto-cisneros-efren-divided-interview/. Accessed 15 Dec. 2020.

Sólorzano, Daniel G., and Tara J. Yosso. "Critical Race Methodology: Counter-Storytelling as an Analytical Framework for Education Research." *Qualitative Inquiry*, vol. 8, no. 1, 2002, pp. 23–44.

Stone-Mediatore, Shari. *Reading across Borders: Storytelling and Knowledge of Resistance*. Palgrave Macmillan, 2003.

Talavera, Victor, Guillermina Gina Núñez-Mchiri, and Josiah Heyman. "Deportation in the U.S.-Mexico Borderlands: Anticipation, Experience, and Memory."

The Deportation Regime, edited by Nicholas De Genova and Nathalie Peutz, Duke UP, 2010, pp. 166–95.

Terrio, Susan. *Whose Child Am I? Unaccompanied, Undocumented Children in US Immigration Custody*. U of California P, 2015.

Terrones, Lettycia, "Técnica Con/Safos: Visual Iconography in Latino Picture Books as a Tool of Cultural Affirmation." *Multicultural Literature for Latino Bilingual Children: Their Words, Their Worlds*, edited by Ellen Riojas Clark, Belinda Bustes Flores, Howard L. Smith, and Daniel Alejandro Gonzalez, Rowman & Littlefield, 2015, pp. 241–64.

Texas Department of Transportation. "Texas-Mexico Border Crossings." 2018, https://www.txdot.gov/inside-txdot/projects/studies/statewide/border-crossing.html. Accessed 5 July 2018.

Tuck, Eve, and K. Wayne Yang. "Decolonization Is Not a Metaphor." *Decolonization, Indigeneity and Society*, vol. 1, no. 1, 2012, pp. 4–42.

United Farm Workers. 2018, http://www.ufw.org. Accessed 14 June 2018.

Vásquez, Irene, and Juan Gómez-Quiñones. *Making Aztlán: Ideology and Culture of the Chicana and Chicano Movement, 1966–77*. U of New Mexico P, 2014.

Viramontes, Helena María. *Under the Feet of Jesus*. Dutton, 1995.

Walker, Hunter. "Donald Trump Just Released an Epic Statement Raging against Mexican Immigrants and 'Disease.'" *Business Insider*, 6 July 2015, https://www.businessinsider.com/donald-trumps-epic-statement-on-mexico-2015-7. Accessed 10 Aug. 2018.

Walsh, Catherine. "'Other' Knowledges, 'Other' Critiques: Reflections on the Politics and Practices of Philosophy and Decoloniality in the 'Other' America." *Transmodernity*, vol. 1, no. 3, 2012, pp. 11–27.

———, and Edizon León. "Afro-Andean Thought and Diasporic Ancestrality." *Shifting the Geography of Reason: Gender, Science and Religion*, edited by Marina Paola Banchetti-Robino and Clevis Ronald Headley, Cambridge Scholars Press, 2006, pp. 211–24.

We Need Diverse Books. 2021, https://diversebooks.org/. Accessed 2 Feb. 2021.

Ybarra-Frausto, Tomás. "Rasquachismo 1989: A Chicano Sensibility." *Chicano and Chicana Art: A Critical Anthology*, edited by Jennifer A. González, C. Ondine Chavoya, Chon Noriega, and Terezita Romo, Duke UP, 2019, pp. 85–90.

Yosso, Tara J. "Whose Culture Has Capital? A Critical Race Theory Discussion of Community Cultural Wealth." *Race Ethnicity and Education*, vol. 8, no. 1, 2005, pp. 69–91.

Index

Page numbers in *italic* text indicate illustrations.

activism, 4; in *Efrén Divided*, 127–28, 132–33. *See also* social justice activism
adaptations, 78, 154; of Greek myths and stories, 92–93
Afro-Andean cultures, 65–66
agency, 62, 167n6; in *Efrén Divided*, 131–32; in *Land of the Cranes*, 118, 120, 124
Aguayo, El Perro (fictional character), 85, 87, 90, 166n4
Alba, Francisco, 5–6
Aldama, Frederick Luis, 9, 11
ancestrality, 23, 149; *Land of the Cranes* and, 116–17, 121, 123; in *Summer of the Mariposas*, 78–79, 94, 97–98; in *They Call Me Güero*, 65–68
Anzaldúa, Gloria, 1, 2, 14, 15, 23, 34; on art, 135–36; on artistas/activistas, 143–44, 161; on autohistorias, 35, 37; on balancing, 101; on border artista, 135, 136; on conocimiento, 4, 40, 113, 155, 161–62; on cultural capital, 77, 80; on deportation, 104; on education, 26; on histerimonia, 42–43; "Memoir—My Calling" by, 72; metaphor of, 137; on nepantla, 52; on paradoxes, 75; on testimony, 18, 104–5
artist/activists (artivist), 25, 164n11; Anzaldúa on, 143–44, 161; in *Land of the Cranes*, 123–25; in *Under the Feet of Jesus*, 42–44, 47–49. *See also* creativity and art; *Side by Side / Lado a lado*
assimilation, 17–18, 21, 79, 81, 161; in *They Call Me Güero*, 69, 71; *Under the Mesquite* and, 55, 57, 59–60

autohistorias, 6, 7, 19–20, 135, 137; in *Mexican Daughter*, 147–48, 159–60
Aztecs, 98–99
Aztlán, 80, 115–16, 165n2, 166n3

Bebout, Lee, 116–17
Beck, Scott A., 164n12
belonging, 17, 19, 22, 53, 60, 64, 105; intersectionality of, 136, 137, 138, 143, 153, 161–62; physical appearance and, 74, 149; in *They Call Me Güero*, 65–68
Beverley, John, 163n2
bilingualism, 40, 78, 85. *See also specific topics*
Blackwell, Maylei, 11, 117
Boehm, Deborah A., 126, 130, 166n7
border artista, 19–20; autohistorias in, 135; community in, 135; detail in, 135–36; detribalization in, 135; self-inscription in, 137; soul in, 135. *See also I Am Not Your Perfect Mexican Daughter*
border checkpoint, 15–16, 63–64
border educators, 69, 71–72
borderlands, 52–53. *See also Under the Mesquite*; *They Call Me Güero*
Borderlands / La Frontera (Anzaldúa), 1, 26, 40, 52
Borderlands Saints (Martín), 86
Bowles, David, 2, 13, 17–18
Brochin, Carol, 81, 91
Brown, Monica, 16–17, 24, 26
"The Burden of Deportation on Children of Mexican Immigrant Families" (Dreby), 126
Butler, Judith, 48

Camus, Albert, 167n3
cancer, 42, 54–55
The Catcher in the Rye (Salinger), 136
Catholicism, 110, 138, 164n12
el Cavernario (Galindo), 87, 166n4
CCBC. *See* Cooperative Children's Book Center
Cepeda, Joe, 6, 16, 19, 29, *29*
Chávez, César, 24, 33, *33*, 163n2. *See also Side by Side / Lado a lado*
Chespirito television program, 167n1
Chicana Movidas (Cotera, Espinoza, and Blackwell), 11
Cho, Sumi, 139
Cihuacóatl, 98
"Cinco Hermanitas" (Herrera, C.), 95
The Circuit (Jiménez), 62–63
Cisneros, Ernesto, 3, 6, 19. *See also Efrén Divided*
Cisneros, Sandra, 62–63, 165n4
Coalition for Immokalee Workers, 163n2
code-switching, 1, 151
Colato Laínez, René, 6, 19. *See also From North to South / Del norte al sur*
Collins, Patricia Hill, 139
Colón, Raúl, 24, 36, *36*, 38, *38*
community, 37, 71, 135
community building, 41, 45–46
conocimiento, 53, 133–34, 164n5; Anzaldúa on, 4, 40, 113, 155, 161–62; definition of, 4; desconocimiento compared to, 5, 6, 16, 25, 161; in *From North to South / Del norte al sur*, 113–15; in *Gabi, a Girl in Pieces*, 153, 154, 155, 157, 158–60; of *Land of the Cranes*, 120, 123–24; in *Mexican Daughter*, 143–44, 146, 147; negation compared to, 15; in *They Call Me Güero*, 68–72, *70*; of *Tomás and the Library Lady*, 34, 35, 36–42, *38*; in *Under the Feet of Jesus*, 43–44, 46, 50, 51

conocimiento children: autohistorias in, 6, 7; creative acts of, 7; healing of, 6–7; #LatinxPitch for, 13–14; mirrors for, 12–13, 14; movida of, 11–12; nepantla and, 4–5; 9/11 and, 5–6; normative whiteness and, 14; problem solving by, 3–4; publishing for, 14; social justice activism by, 7–8; transformation of, 7–8
conocimiento mirrors, 16–17, 25–26, 49–51; *Side by Side / Lado a lado* as, 28, 31, 34
"Conocimiento Narratives" (Rodríguez), 25–26, 113
contestation, 15
Cooperative Children's Book Center (CCBC), 13
La Cosecha / The Harvest (documentary), 23
Cotera, María Eugenia, 11
counter-storytelling, 19, 43, 53, 64, 105, 160
Coyolxauhqui, 137, 144, 146, 147
creativity and art, 9, 135–37, 160; body in, 143; healing in, 144; in poetry, 150
Crenshaw, Kimberlé Williams, 139
"Critical Fictions of Transnationalism in Latinx Children's Literature" (Brochin and Medina), 81
cultural capital, 77, 79, 80
cultural geography, 85, 86
cultural wealth: in *Maximilian*, 78, 86, 91–92, 102–3; in *Summer of the Mariposas*, 78–79, 96, 102–3. *See also* diasporic
Cummins, Jeanine, 13
cure, 100–102
Cyclone Mackey (el Ciclón McKey), 82

Daisy (fictional character), 1–2, 8–9, 10, *10*
Daniel, Shannon, 151
Danny (fictional character), 12

el daño, 6, 15, 102
decolonial/decolonization/
  decolonizing, 69, 78, 96–97, 102, 111;
  ancestrality and, 65–66; Pérez, E.,
  on, 80–81
deficit thinking, 18, 77, 81, 91–92,
  102–3; in diasporic, 79–80
Delgado Bernal, Dolores, 79–80
Del norte al sur. See *From North to
  South / Del norte al sur*
deportability, 126, 128, 134–35
deportation, 18–19, 118, 120, 126;
  empowerment related to, 109;
  fear, stress, anxiety about, 104–8,
  166n6; paths to citizenship or, 108;
  public space and, 105; social justice
  activism related to, 134; testimonies
  on, 104–6; Trump and, 107; wound
  of, 105. See also *Efrén Divided*; *From
  North to South / Del norte al sur*;
  Land of the Cranes
deportation regime, 107, 134
desconocimiento, 53, 86, 153;
  conocimiento compared to, 5, 6, 16,
  25, 161
diaspora, 18, 165n2. See also
  *Maximilian and the Mystery of the
  Guardian Angel*; *Summer of the
  Mariposas*
diasporic: assimilationism and, 81;
  cultural capital in, 79; cultural
  wealth in, 77; deficit thinking in, 79–
  80; immigrant compared to, 80–81;
  reparation in, 77; transnationalism
  of, 81, 165n2
Dickinson, Emily, 143, 167n4
#DignidadLiteraria, 13, 14
Dreby, Joanna, 107, 108, 126
Dyrness, Andrea, 69, 71

education, 24, 26, 40, 64. See also
  specific topics
Efrén Divided (Cisneros, E.), 3, 6, 19;
  activism in, 127–28, 132–33; agency
  in, 131–32; cage-free chickens
  in, 127; conocimiento in, 133;
  deportability in, 126, 128; exclusion
  in, 126–27; fear and anxiety in,
  125–26; food in, 125; future path
  in, 130; ICE in, 127; iron wall in,
  130–31; Jennifer in, 127–28, 132–33;
  left alone or left behind in, 129–30,
  166n7; limbo in, 129–30; nepantla
  in, 131–32; pain in, 104; resilience
  in, 130–31; Rhodes on, 131–32;
  rumors in, 126; sacrifice in, 129;
  seeds in, 127–28; taxicab driver in,
  128–30; Tijuana journey in, 129–32;
  transformation in, 128, 133; truth of,
  132; united while separated in, 128–
  31; victimizing narratives and, 132
empathy, 28–29, 30–31, 147
Enciso, Patricia, 152
English language, 37, 38, 59–60, 165n5.
  See also specific topics
"En Los Estados Unidos," 165n2
En mi familia. See *In My Family / En
  mi familia*
ensueño (illusion), 49–50, 135, 160
Espinoza, Dionne, 11
Estrella (fictional character), 25, 164n3,
  164n11–12. See also *Under the Feet
  of Jesus*
Excitable Speech (Butler), 48
Eysturoy, Annie, 43

Faist, Thomas, 165n2
family detention, 108–9, 120–21, 123,
  124, 132
Faris, Wendy, 97, 100, 101, 102
farmworkers, 16–17, 24–25
Fish, Stanley, 37
food, 110–11, 122, 125
From North to South / Del norte al sur
  (Colato Laínez), 6, 19; conocimiento
  in, 113–15; creativity in, 111, 113;

From North to South (continued)
embrace in, 110, *112*; empowerment in, 114; fear in, 109–11; food in, 110–11; gardening in, *112*, 113–15; hopes in, 111, 114–15; inspiration for, 110; racism and, 109; resilience in, 111; seed game in, 113–15; transformation in, 114; trauma in, 110

Gabi, a Girl in Pieces (Quintero), 6, 15, 167n6; adaptations in, 154; autohistoria in, 137, 160; beating in, 148; challenges in, 149–50, 152–53; conocimiento in, 153, 154, 155, 157, 158–60; contradictions in, 149; desconocimiento in, 153; gender and ethnicity in, 148–49; identity in, 152; images in, 155, *156*, 157; interconnectivity in, 155, *156*, 157–59; intersectionality in, 148–50, 153, 160; name in, 148; nepantla in, 150, 153, 160; poetry in, 150–51, 153; pregnancies in, 153–54; questions in, 149, 152, 159; rape in, 157–58; responsibility in, 155; revenge in, 158; Serros in, 151; sex in, 150, 154; shame in, 153–55, 157; social justice related to, 151–52, 158–59; strength in, 155; transformation in, 155, 159, 160, 167n6; translanguage in, 150–52; translation in, 150, 159; whiteness in, 149, 167n5; writing for change in, 152–55; zines, 155–59, *156*
Gaiman, Neil, 92
García McCall, Guadalupe, 2, 11, 18. See also *Summer of the Mariposas*
Garza, Carmen Lomas, 20
Garza, Xavier, 18. See also *Maximilian and the Mystery of the Guardian Angel*
Gavrilos, Dina, 165n5
Genova, Nicholas De, 107
God and Savior, 164n12. See also *Under the Feet of Jesus*

Greek myths and stories, 92–93
Guidotti-Hernández, Nicole, 22
Gulbas, Lauren, 111
Guzmán Huerta, Rodolfo, 165n1

Hanney, Lesley, 111, 113
"Harm's Way" (Pratt), 48
healing, 6–7, 104; in *Land of the Cranes*, 121, 124–25; in *Mexican Daughter*, 144, 147–48; in *Summer of the Mariposas*, 98–102
Herrera, Cristina, 95, 153
Herrera, Juan Felipe, 116
Heyman, Josiah, 126
histerimonia, 42–43
history, 24, 50, 116–17, 163n2, 166–68. See also autohistorias
Homer, 11
hopes, 8–15, *10*, 163n3; in *Land of the Cranes*, 107–9; in *From North to South / Del norte al sur*, 111, 114–15
The House on Mango Street (Cisneros, S.), 62–63
Huerta, Dolores, 24, 32, 34, 163n2. See also *Side by Side / Lado a lado*

I Am Not Your Perfect Mexican Daughter (Mexican Daughter) (Sánchez), 6, 19–20; Americanization in, 138–40, 141; autohistoria in, 147–48, 159–60; border related to, 139, 145–46; cockroaches in, 141; conocimiento in, 143–44, 146, 147; Coyolxauhqui in, 144, 146, 147; cultural mix in, 136; details in, 135–36; dissonance in, 140; dreams in, 139–40; healing in, 144, 147–48; immigration in, 145–46; intersectionality related to, 138–39, 147–48; journals' destruction in, 142–43; Mexican-ness in, 140–41; nepantla/nepantlera in, 136, 143, 160; nonconformism in, 138; Olga in, 138, 140, 141, 142,

146–47, 159–60; questions in, 138; quinceañera in, 140–41, 167nn3–4; reconstruction in, 136–37; sadness in, 145; sainthood in, 138; Salinger in, 136; social identities in, 138–39, 147; stereotypes in, 144, 145, 147; suicide attempt in, 142, 143, 145; television in, 136, 167n1; transformation in, 144, 160; whiteness in, 167n5
ICE. *See* Immigration and Customs Enforcement
identities, 138–39, 147, 152, 165n5; in *Maximilian*, 86, 88; in *Summer of the Mariposas*, 95–96; in *They Call Me Güero*, 68–69, 74; in *Under the Mesquite*, 61–62
illusion (ensueño), 49–50
immigrants, 80–81, 126, 145–46; involuntary separation of, 107, 166n1; segregation related to, 107–8
Immigration and Customs Enforcement (ICE), 8, 109, 127; in *Land of the Cranes*, 116, 118, 120, 123, 124, 125
In My Family / En mi familia (Lomas Garza), 20
interconnectivity, 22
intersectionality, 148–50, 160; of belonging, 136, 137, 138, 143, 153, 161–62

Jennifer (fictional character), 127–28, 132–33
Jiménez, Francisco, 62–63, 165n4
Jiménez García, Marilisa, 3–4
José. *See From North to South / Del norte al sur*
Judith Slaying Holofernes, 138
Julia. *See I Am Not Your Perfect Mexican Daughter*
justice, 24. *See also* social justice

Keating, AnaLouise, 4, 28–29
Keen, Suzanne, 30

Kozlowska, Kasia, 111, 113
künstlerroman, 25, 43, 53, 56, 62, 76, 165n4

Lado a lado. *See Side by Side / Lado a lado*
Lalo. *See Efrén Divided*
Land of the Cranes (Salazar), 6, 11, 19, 21, 166n4; abuse and, 121; agency in, 118, 120, 124; ancestrality and, 116–17, 121, 123; artists/activists in, 123–25; Aztlán in, 115–16, 118, 166n3; on beating, 122–23; cages in, 120, 122; conocimiento of, 120, 123–24; deportation and, 118, 120; family detention of, 120; on food, 122; healing in, 121, 124–25; hope and home in, 107–9; ICE in, 116, 118, 120, 123, 124, 125; intimacy related to, 105–6; mythohistorical intervention in, 116–17; nepantlera in, 123–24; origin story in, 115–16; poetry in, 118–20, *119*, 121, 123–25; prophecy in, 115–16; Quetzalcoatl related to, 118; spells from, 121–22; understanding and, 123; witnesses in, 106, 121
languages, 1, 11–12, 40, 63, 71; in *Tomás and the Library Lady*, 37, *38*, 40–41; translanguage, 1, 2, 11–12, 150–52; in *Under the Mesquite*, 59–60, 165n5
LatCrit, 19, 105
Latimer, Dan, 43, 47
Latino/a Children's and Young Adult Writers on the Art of Storytelling (Aldama), 9
Latinx: social justice related to, 22; term use of, 21–22
#LatinxPitch, 13–14
Latorre, Guisela, 43
left alone/behind, 129–30, 166n7
León, Edizon, 65–66, 67
León-Portillo, Miguel, 71
Levi, Heather, 165n3

Levins Morales, Aurora, 3, 4, 8, 19, 24, 42–43; on healing, 104, 121; on history, 50; on listening, 127
"Library Magic" (Mora), 41–42
Light in the Dark / Luz en lo oscuro (Anzaldúa), 23, 52, 77
linguistic assimilation, 57, 59
literary mirrors and windows, 81, 147, 162
La Llorona, 93–96, 97, 98, 100, 102
Lo, Malindo, 13
Lomas Garza, Carmen, 20
love, 74–75
lucha libre, 21, 82, 165n1, 165n3, 166n4; Guardian Angel as, 77–78, 83–91
Lupita (fictional character), 2, 55, 164n1. See also *Under the Mesquite*

magical realism, 92–93, 96–97, 100, 102
male heroes, mythological, 92
Martín, Desirée, 86
Martínez, Antonio, 82
Massey, Corbin James (Cyclone Mackey, el Ciclón McKey), 82
Maximilian and the Mystery of the Guardian Angel (Maximilian) (Garza), 18; Back Breaker Haven in, 90; bilingualism in, 78, 85; as bilingual thriller, 85; cheating in, 90; contradictions in, 82; cosmic battle in, 87; cultural geography in, 85, 86; cultural wealth in, 78, 86, 91–92, 102–3; death in, 88, 89; deficit thinking and, 91–92; desconocimiento in, 86; family dysfunction in, 83–84; identity in, 86, 88; immigrants related to, 80; inheritance in, 91; jealousy in, 89; luchador masks in, 82, 83–84; masked wrestlers and, 82; names in, 85, 88, 89; redemptions in, 89–92; secular saints in, 85–88; shame in, 91; stigmata in, 87, 88; training in, 88–89, 90–91; transnationalism in, 82–83; El Vampiro in, 87. See also lucha libre
McCall, Leslie, 139
McCracken, Ellen, 48–49
Medicine Stories (Levins Morales), 42
Medina, Carmen L., 81, 91
"Memoir—My Calling" (Anzaldúa), 72
memory, 65, 66, 130, 131, 164n11
memory retrofit. See *Land of the Cranes*
Mersault, 167n3
Mexican Daughter. See *I Am Not Your Perfect Mexican Daughter*
Mexican Whiteboy (Peña), 12
Mickenberg, Julia, 3
migration, 5–6
Miller, Madeline, 92, 95
Mora, Pat, 24–25, 26; for Rivera, 41–42
Moraga, Cherríe, 42–43
Morales, Yuyi, 82–83
movidas, 11–12, 163n3
Movidas of Hope, 163n3
My Papi Has a Motorcycle (Quintero): blending in, 1–2; foregrounding in, 8–9; Latinx culture in, 1; mobility and freedom in, 2; reading in, 8; translanguage in, 1, 11–12; working class in, 8–9, 11
mythohistorical intervention, 116–17
mythological realism, 92–93, 96, 98, 102

names, 85, 88, 89, 148
National Council for La Raza, 163n2
National Farm Workers Association (NFWA), 27, 163n2
nationalism, 4. See also transnationalism
Nel, Philip, 3
nepantla/nepantlera, 2, 4–5, 17–18, 52; in *Efrén Divided*, 131–32; in *Gabi, a*

Girl in Pieces, 150, 153, 160; as home, 20; in *Land of the Cranes*, 123–24; in *Mexican Daughter*, 136, 143, 160; *Summer of the Mariposas* related to, 101–2
nepantlera-roman, 56–61, 62, 75–76
NFWA. *See* National Farm Workers Association
Nikolajeva, Maria, 30
9/11, 5–6
Núñez-Mchiri, Guillermina Gina, 126

Obama, Barack, 28
Odyssey (Homer), 11, 78
Oh, Ellen, 13
Olga (fictional character), 138, 140, 141; affair of, 142, 146–47; autohistoria related to, 159–60
Ong, Walter, 39
oral history, 39, 163n2
orality and literacy, 35, 37, 39
Orality and Literacy (Ong), 39
"Oranges" (Soto), 71–72
Ordinary Enchantments (Faris), 97

Pacheco, Mark, 151
Papá Grande (fictional character), 35, 36, *36*, 37, *38*, 41, 42
Papi (fictional character), 1–2
Peña, Ezequiel (Zeke), 10, *10*
Peña, Matt de la, 12
Pérez, Ashley Hope, 152
Pérez, Emma, 80–81
Pérez, Roy, 21–22
Pew Research Center, 107, 108
picture books, 16–17. *See also My Papi Has a Motorcycle*
Plumita (fictional character), 116, 117–18. *See also Land of the Cranes*
"The Poet at Fifteen" (Sánchez), 167n4
poetry, 150–51, 153; in *Land of the Cranes*, 118–20, *119*, 121, 123–25; in *They Call Me Güero*, 63, 66–68, 71–72, 73–75; in *Under the Mesquite*, 54–55, 164n1
"The Politics of Childhood" (Levins Morales), 108
Portes, Alejandro, 140
Pratt, Mary Louise, 48
Prieta (fictional character), 72–73, 75
problem-solving, 25, 164n4

Quetzalcoatl, 118
quinceañera, 140–41, 167nn3–4
Quintero, Isabel, 1–2, 6, 19–20; on oppression by omission, 15

racism, 37–38, 39, 105, 109, 134, 149
raíces / roots, 23, 34, 63, 77, 80, 96, 147, 165n5
Ramona, Daisy (fictional character), 1–2
Rangel, Dolores E., 164n12
rape, 107, 121, 157–58
reading, 8, 12, 21, 72. *See also Tomás and the Library Lady*
resilience, 111, 130–31
resistance, 7–8, 11–12, 15, 79–80; in *Land of the Cranes*, 122; in *Mexican Daughter*, 136, 150–51; nepantla as, 17; Regan and, 20; in *Side by Side / Lado a lado*, 24, 34; in *Summer of the Mariposas*, 95; in *They Call Me Güero*, 67; in *Tomás and the Library Lady*, 39; in *Under the Feet of Jesus*, 43; in *Under the Mesquite*, 55–56
restorying, 118
retrofitted memory. *See Land of the Cranes*
Rhodes, Cristina, 7, 12, 109; on childhood agency, 131–32; on transformation, 62
Riordan, Rick, 92
Ritivoi, Andreea Deciu, 31
Rivera, Tomás, 24–25, 164n12, 165n4; Mora for, 41–42; tribute to, 50

Rodolfo, 165n1
Rodríguez, Sonia, 25–26, 113, 114–15
role of elders. *See* ancestrality
Romano, U. Roberto, 23
Rumbaut, Rubén, 140

Salazar, Aida, 6, 11, 19, 21, 132. See also *Land of the Cranes*
Salinger, J. D., 136
Sánchez, Erika L., 6, 19–20, 167n4
Sandoval, Chela, 43
El Santo, 21, 83, 165n1
secular saints, 85–86. See also *Side by Side / Lado a lado*
seed game, 113–15
segregation, 107–8
Sepúlveda, Enrique, 69, 71
Serrato, Phillip, 164n4
Serros, Michele, 151
sexuality, 22, 137; rape, 107, 121, 157–58. See also *I Am Not Your Perfect Mexican Daughter*; Olga
Shea, Anne, 164n11
Shuldiner, David, 39
Side by Side / Lado a lado (Brown), 16–17, 24, 26; La Causa in, 27–28, 29, 29, 31–32; collaboration and communal support in, 31–32; conocimiento in, 27, 50, 51; as conocimiento mirror, 28, 31, 34; current injustices and, 34; empathy related to, 28, 30–31; grape boycott in, 28; interconnectivity in, 30–31; male-dominated narratives and, 32, 34; as model, 28; social justice activism in, 27–28, 32; solidarity and, 28, 31–32; UFW in, 28; visual images in, 30
social identities, 138–39, 147
social justice, 22, 26–27
social justice activism: by conocimiento children, 7–8; deportation related to, 134; in *Side by Side / Lado a lado*, 27–28, 32

solidarity, 28, 31–32
Soto, Gary, 71–72
Soto-Santiago, Sandra, 22
Step Up mentoring program, 20
Stone-Mediatore, Shari, 39
storytelling, 9, 65; counter-, 19, 43, 53, 64, 105, 160; in *Tomás and the Library Lady*, 34–35, 35, 36–40, 38, 42
The Stranger (Camus), 167n3
Summer of the Mariposas (García McCall), 11, 18; as adaptation, 78; ancestrality in, 78–79, 94, 97–98; birth certificates in, 99–100; butterflies in, 96–97, 98; Cihuacóatl in, 98; cultural wealth in, 78–79, 96, 102–3; divine in, 93–94; drought in, 96, 97; drowning in, 94–95; ear pendant in, 98, 99; father's loss in, 97; feminism in, 95–96; guardians of life in, 100–101; healing in, 98–102; identity in, 95–96; magical realism in, 96–100, 102; male heroes and, 93; mythological realism related to, 78, 92–93, 100–101, 102; nepantleras related to, 101–2; *Odyssey* related to, 78, 93–94, 100; patriarchy in, 95; penance in, 95; redemption in, 94; shaman's cure in, 100–102; social crises in, 100–101; space in, 97; time in, 99–100; transformation in, 97–98; transnationalism in, 94, 98; Virgen in, 93–96, 97, 98, 100, 102

Talavera, Victor, 126
testimonio/testimony, 5, 18, 19, 67; on deportation, 104–6; oral history compared to, 163n2; word origin of, 42
They Call Me Güero (Bowles), 2, 13, 17–18, 52; ancestrality in, 65–68; assimilation in, 69, 71; belonging in, 65–68; border checkpoint in, 63–64; border educators in,

69, 71–72; bully in, 73–74; casa adentro in, 68; community in, 71; conocimiento and desconocimiento in, 53; conocimiento in, 68–72, 70; contradictions in, 63, 75–76; education in, 64; ethnography and, 69; fun in, 63; identities in, 68–69, 74; illustrations in, 68–70, 70; künstlerroman in, 76; languages in, 63, 71; love in, 74–75; macro- and microaggressions in, 67; mandate in, 67–68; nature in, 75; poetry in, 63, 66–68, 71–72, 73–75; skin tones in, 73–74; stolen cookies in, 65, 66; storytelling in, 65; superheroes in, 72–73; transformation in, 64, 72; truth in, 64; whitewashing in, 67

This Bridge Called My Back (Levins Morales, Anzaldúa, Moraga), 42–43

This Bridge We Call Home (Anzaldúa), 2

Tomás and the Library Lady (Mora), 24–25, 26, 51; Anzaldúa and, 35, 37; basis of, 34–35, 50; community building in, 41; conocimiento of, 34, 35, 36–42, 38; continuum of, 39; in English, 37, 38; family in, 35, 38, 41, 42; inclusion of, 39, 40; interconnectedness in, 39–40; interpretive community and, 37; language in, 37, 38, 40–41; linear model of progress and, 35, 37; orality and literacy of, 36, 38, 39; Papá Grande in, 35, 36, 36, 37, 38, 41, 42; role reversal in, 40–41; self-representation in, 39; storytelling in, 34–35, 35, 36–40, 38, 42

Tonantzin, 99

transformations, 7–8, 15, 62, 114; in *Efrén Divided*, 128, 133; in *Gabi, a Girl in Pieces*, 155, 159, 160, 167n6; in *Mexican Daughter*, 144, 160; in *They Call Me Güero*, 64, 72; in *Under the Mesquite*, 55–56, 62

translanguage, 1, 2, 11–12, 150–52

transmutation, 2–3

transnationalism, 18, 20, 22, 94, 98; of diasporic, 81, 165n2; in *Maximilian*, 82–83

trauma, 110. *See also* deportation

Trump, Donald, 23, 107

"The Truth Our Bodies Tell" (Levins Morales), 42

UFW. *See* United Farm Workers of America

"Uncle Joe's History Lesson" (Bowles), 66–68

Under the Feet of Jesus (Viramontes), 17, 24, 25, 26; artist-activist in, 42–44, 47–49; community building in, 45–46; conocimiento in, 43–44, 46, 50, 51; correlation in, 46–47; gratitude in, 45; histerimonia related to, 42–43; illusion in, 49–50; power of words in, 44–46, 50; summoning all who strayed in, 48–51; survival in, 46–47, 164n11; symbolic beheading in, 48; symbolism in, 48–49; tools in, 44–45; violence in, 47–48; voice in, 47–48; words to comfort and fight, 44–48

Under the Mesquite (García McCall), 2, 17–18, 52; assimilation and, 55, 57, 59–60; border fence in, 54; church in, 54–55; conocimiento and desconocimiento in, 53; dual allegiances in, 54–55; English language in, 59–60, 165n5; ethnic identity negotiation in, 61–62; international bridge in, 54; künstlerroman in, 53, 56, 62, 165n4; nepantlera-roman in, 56–61, 62, 75–76; plantings in, 54; as resistance novel, 55–56; self-agency in, 62; space transformation in, 55–56; system inequality in, 62; transformation in, 55–56, 62; two mesquites

Under the Mesquite (continued)
in, 56; two worlds poetry in, 54–55, 164n1, 165n2; writing in, 62–63
United Farm Workers of America (UFW), 23–24, 27, 28, 163n2

Viramontes, Helena Maria, 17, 24, 25, 26, 164n3
La Virgen de Guadalupe/Tonantzin, 93–94, 99

Walsh, Catherine, 65–66, 67
Warren Dunes, 167n3
We Need Diverse Books, 13
whiteness, 14, 67, 149, 161–62, 165n5, 167n5
"Whose Culture Has Capital?" (Yosso), 79
wrestlers. *See* lucha libre
writing, 7. *See also specific topics*

YA. *See* young adult literature
Ybarra-Frausto, Tomás, 12, 163n3
Yosso, Tara, 79
young adult literature (YA), 4

Zayas, Luis, 111
zines, 155–59, *156*

www.ingramcontent.com/pod-product-compliance
Lightning Source LLC
Chambersburg PA
CBHW030654230426
43665CB00011B/1087